The Author

FIFTY YEARS
of
SONG

Peter Dawson

With 16 Illustrations

HUTCHINSON & CO. (Publishers) LTD
London   New York   Melbourne
Sydney   Cape Town

First published October 1951
Reprinted . January 1952

Printed in Great Britain
by The Anchor Press, Ltd.,
Tiptree, Essex

TO MY DEAR WIFE

NAN

MY COMPANION

THROUGH IT ALL

My sincere thanks to

TOM NOBLE

who urged me into starting it and
insisted with great patience till it
was—with his help—completed.

CONTENTS

PART ONE

LIST OF ILLUSTRATIONS

9

*The author wishes to thank the H.M.V. Company and
the Graphic Photo Union for use of the photographs*

Part One

CHAPTER I

CHILDHOOD AND TRAINING

THE boy lay tossing and turning in bed as the sound of music rose to his ears from the drawing-room beneath. Why couldn't he be there also, listening to his sisters and friends? Presently the beauty of the music proved too much for the youngster to resist and he slipped out of bed, made his way to the top of the stairs with great care, and after a few moments ventured down step by step. Soon he was at the door of the music-room, listening to the playing and singing. Then quite suddenly the door opened and he was discovered.

Surprise and laughter greeted this small figure in the doorway, together with a certain consternation on the part of his mother, but finally he was allowed to stay. A little later he was persuaded to sing a song.

It was the first he had ever really sung in his life and he was greatly abashed. It was called "The poor little Sailor Boy".

> *'Neath the wild waves they laid him,*
> *Far, far away from the shore,*
> *In a coral cot you'll find him*
> *Never to rise any more . . .*

etc., etc.

Yes, I was the little boy of six, and that was the first time I ever performed. I was given threepence. My mother considered this too much and allowed me one penny per week.

But as this is my life story I must go back to the beginning. I was born of Scottish parents in Adelaide, South Australia, on 31 January, 1882. Incredible! I don't feel a day older than forty. I have just passed a strict medical examination by an insurance doctor, and have been classed 'A.1. First Class'. I am in fine voice, and very happy that the musical critics agree on this.

I had four brothers and four sisters. I was the youngest son.

My father and mother were both strict disciplinarians, and woe betide the recalcitrant boy! The girls could do no wrong. Dad was a big, powerful man who had sailed the seven seas nigh

on a hundred years ago and he possessed a heavy hand. It required
the great patience of my dear mother the live-long day to keep
'the boys in order' and listen to the outpourings of their troubles.
It might be anything from tummy to toothache, barked shins
and knees, splinters in the feet and, of course, torn clothing. "I'll
tell your father," was her oft-repeated threat. But she never did,
the sweet darling.

In a pocket of her dress she always carried a stout piece of
leather, an old breeching-strap, and when she brought this to
light it was a case of 'scatter' and run for your life! If Mother was
lucky enough to score a hit it kept me as docile as a fawn for
days. When I think back, what a prodigious worker she was!
She made all the boys' clothes, knitted our stockings, did all the
cooking, cleaning, washing, with, of course, the assistance of
my elder sisters, who in turn became proficient in all things
domestic. Mother also made hundredweights of jam and mar-
malade, butter and cheese. During the winter months there was
always something going in the way of soups and hot scones—
not forgetting the inevitable brimstone and treacle!

It was indeed a happy household. Every night my father
did the grand round in order to make sure that all outside doors
were bolted or barred, and that everybody was really and truly
'tucked up' and comfortable.

Getting us all off to school must have been a real business, as
none of us kids could judge the time, and as every clock in the
house showed a different time it was a marvel that our punctuality
was exemplary. I never had to tender the old saw, "Please excuse
my son for being late"—which reminds me of the boy who
telephoned his schoolmaster to the effect that "George could not
attend the school that day". "Who is that speaking?" asked the
master. "My father," replied the boy.

After school I usually brought Bessie the cow home from
the paddock a mile away to be milked. Bessie knew my whistle.
She would raise her head from grazing and deliberately walk to
the slip panel to await her release and accompany me home.

My father, after many years at sea, had settled in Adelaide
and established in Weymouth Street an ironworking business,
which also included plumbing, gas-fitting, deep drainage and
'water laid on'. In those early days the local population had to
rely on rain-water tanks, catchments and wells for household
requirements, so my dad did a fine trade in the making of cor-
rugated circular galvanized tanks, double-riveted at all joints
and soldered inside and out—guaranteed sound for five years.

These tanks were made in all sizes from 200- to 5,000-gallon capacity. The business grew, and today is in the capable hands of my brother Will; it is one of the largest canister works in Australia. The factories, however, are now in Sydney.

I received my first education at the East Adelaide public school. Singing played an important part in the school curriculum, and for at least one hour daily we indulged in community singing. Once a month a 'Penny Concert' was given in the largest room of the school. The programme was made up entirely by scholars, and the headmaster acted as chairman.

There was some very good piano playing, dancing, recitation and singing. I always remember one little fellow being especially adept on the cornet. The latter was almost as big as the boy. I usually sang, but at one concert I decided to 'show off' my versatility, and sneaked my sister Violet's violin. I spirited it out of the house by some miraculous ruse and duly arrived at the concert.

And so my name was written in the programme against a 'Violin solo: "The Bluebells of Scotland", by Peter Dawson'. It was the only tune I could play, and that by ear! The solo over —and it was unaccompanied—I received terrific applause and much stamping of feet, which raised the fine dust from the cracks and joints in the wooden floor up to the ceiling. An encore was demanded. And so "The Bluebells of Scotland" it had to be again, for I knew no other piece.

To get the violin back into the house without being observed by any member of my family was most difficult. It had been easy enough to get it out of the house. I decided to leave it outside our front gate while I went round to the back fence to reconnoitre. And that was my fatal mistake. It was also the end of my sister's violin. Someone had stolen it during my brief visit to the back of the house!

Having somewhat recovered from the effects of my father's heavy hand, which he had used following the loss of the fiddle, I was almost immediately involved in another escapade, with even more serious consequences.

My brother Will and I were playing with matches near a ten-ton haystack, daring each other how far the stack would light before putting it out with our caps. This went on and on, until eventually the flames got the better of us, and we were unable to stop their rapid spreading. There was nothing for us to do but run home, a short distance down the road. We sat on the front verandah, looking the picture of innocence. Suddenly a man

came rushing down the road towards the house, and as he was
about to pass gave us a withering glance, at which I immediately
piped out, "WE DIDN'T DO IT."

The game was up. It cost my father £10. I won't tell you what
it cost my brother and me. Anyhow, when I see folks standing
at a snack-counter, it takes me back to that ten-ton haystack
blaze.

I certainly had lots of fun as a kid. One of my favourite games
was football. But it was not the football as played today. The ball
was not the usual or regulation high-pressure one, but rather
flabby. We used a pig's bladder, having to resort to nature, for
none of us had any money to spare to buy a real rubber-and-
leather ball. There was a slaughter-house in the neighbourhood,
and the owner, a good sportsman, used to save all the pigs'
bladders for us.

Tough things they were when properly dried and treated.
One of them easily lasted a couple of games.

This game was played in such a way that the winners were
those who finished the fittest! Having no coin to toss with, we
used a flat stone, one side of which was marked with chalk or
spittle to distinguish 'heads from tails'. The captains would then
begin to pick their respective teams. "I'll have 'Dodger',"
chirped captain No. 1. "I'll have 'Hookie'," said captain No.
2, and so on alternatively until the teams were complete.

All the boys had nicknames, and many were far from compli-
mentary! I recall 'Wonkie', 'Chops', 'Loppy', 'Lugs', 'Stinker',
'Snorkie', 'Spuds', 'Trickie', 'Walloper', 'Bully', 'Beadie',
'Scrapper', 'Champ', 'Chump', and I myself was 'Brandie'.

The boys were not always chosen for their ability to play
football, but rather for their 'rough-house' prowess when the
fight started. And the odds that a fight would take place was
roughly 25 to 1 on.

We had no set rules for the game, and if any boy escaped
without a torn pair of trousers, shirt or worse, he was very,
very lucky.

One Saturday afternoon the usual fight occurred after a
dispute over a goal. The game was automatically stopped and
the players formed a ring round the two contestants—the boy
who kicked the goal, and the goalkeeper who denied it. It was a
ding-dong affair, as both boys were good fighters. After about
five minutes a young man approached with the intention of stopping the row, but then another young man took exception to this
interference, and a second fight started. There was no more

football that day because the father of one of the boys kicked the backside of the lad who was fighting his son, and that started yet another fight. And so it spread until the whole crowd of us were at it. Fortunately, a policeman put in an appearance, and at a warning the whole crowd of contestants fled—to fight it out during or after the next game. It was a rough school, but it taught me to look after myself confidently as I grew older.

*   *   *

I have often been asked the question, "What prompted you to become a public singer?"

Well, as a child, music of almost any kind attracted me. My mother possessed a sweetly modulated voice, and she sang the old Scottish songs most charmingly; everybody who knew her was immediately fascinated by the soft, velvet-like quality of her speech. My father was highly appreciative of good music and singing. Both he and my mother gave all us children encouragement and facilities for the development of our musical education. All my sisters played remarkably well, either the piano, the organ, or the violin, and sang effectively. My brothers possessed voices similar to my own in quality, but none of them had the flair for singing apart from their own amusement at home. So you see our home in Adelaide was never a dull one as far as music-making was concerned.

You can well imagine the vast use that our piano was put to —it was hardly ever idle.

I made my first public appearance at the age of eight, at a social in connection with the College Park Congregational Church in St. Peter's, Adelaide. My sister Agnes played my accompaniment, but I forgot the words and faded out!

At the age of seventeen I joined the choir of St. Andrew's Church, and took lessons in singing under the late C. J. Stevens. When I was nineteen I competed for and won the first prize for bass solo at the South Street competitions in the city of Ballarat. This was to prove the turning point of my career. On leaving school I had entered my father's business. My working hours were 7.30 a.m. to 5 p.m. It was hard work too. I was apprenticed to learn the various operations in connection with the business, and these included plumbing. Despite the exertions of the work I was determined not to lose any opportunity for practising my singing and studying singing exercises.

My routine practice had to be done between 6.30 a.m. and

7 a.m. each morning, and for an hour every evening because Father was firm believer in the rule of 'early to bed'. In order to get more practice I used to carry a piece of chalk in my pocket, and when I was working anywhere that gave me an opportunity of chalking up a scale or two I would do so, and practice that way. On one occasion I was on a slate roof. This was a heaven-sent opportunity. I pencilled out my exercises and let myself go, practicing for a considerable time. My father could not understand why the job took so long. He little thought that I was putting in more time on my music than on my plumbing.

After I had won my prize at Ballarat, concert engagements —local affairs—came my way, and these naturally interfered with my manual labours.

At that time my father was anxious that I should continue in the business, but he usually gave me the afternoon off from work to rest and compose myself prior to an evening concert. Eventually both he and my mother came to realize that I must either be a tradesman or a professional singer.

It was here that my old singing master, Mr. C. J. Stevens, came into the picture. It was he who first suggested to my father that I ought to be sent to England to have my voice properly trained by Charles Santley. But that was a heavy expense. My father, whose business was growing successfully, battled with himself whether he ought to let me take the risk of making a living by singing in preference to a certain living and a future in the works. By this time it had become obvious to him (my mother already knew) that my heart was set on singing. When Mr. Stevens again approached him about the advisability of sending me to Charles Santley, my father finally consented. It was a very serious decision, and my present position in the world of musical entertainment is due to my parents' great self-sacrifice and unstinted financial assistance.

My mother was particularly anxious that I should not travel to England alone, and it was arranged that my elder brother Jim should accompany me to London. Once I had met Charles Santley, started my lessons, and been safely installed in a boarding-house, Jim could return home. When I knew that I was going to London to be taught singing by that famous man Charles Santley, I walked about on air for days.

In less than no time I was making my own cabin-trunk for the voyage. And I've still got that trunk! It has travelled all over the Empire with me and is none the worse for wear—I made it in 1900.

Now whether it was caused by the excitement of my coming voyage or not, I caught typhoid fever and my departure for England was delayed for a whole year. I began to wonder whether I should ever really go. However, the great day arrived, and, accompanied by my brother James, I left on the S.S. *Afric* for London.

We arrived in London on Derby Day, and in a moment I was as happy as a schoolboy. What a wonderful experience on my first day!

The huge crowds returning from Epsom! I had never seen such a variety of vehicles in all my life. What tickled my fancy most of all was the sight of the costers. The 'Arrys and the 'Arriets in their donkey-carts! The picturesque costumes with those thousands of pearlies! And I thought we would die of laughing when we saw a donkey dressed up in a woman's long pair of pantaloons with pointed lace and all on its front legs!

Everyone singing, everyone happy, all carefree. It was a glorious sight and immediately put us in really good humour. We had lodgings in Kennington, which is on the main road to Epsom. I have kept a soft corner in my heart for Kennington, not because of the chance it gave me to see my first Derby Day crowd, but because it was there I spent my first six months in London.

I paid seven shillings and sixpence a week for a bed-sitting-room and breakfast and use of the piano! It's hard to believe in these days, but it's true. Let me say at once that the place was well furnished, very comfortable and spotlessly clean.

One of the first things I did was to carry out my father's advice and buy a complete outfit. So I went along to the Elephant and Castle and bought a tail coat, striped trousers and a waistcoat. The coat was braided. With this I wore a shining silk top hat with a pair of tan shoes. In that fashion I called on Mr. Charles Santley for my first interview! I often wonder what the old gentleman must have thought when he saw me in his studio.

Whatever he thought, he never made the slightest suggestion that I was dressed other than in a normal manner.

The first song I sang for Santley was "O ruddier than the Cherry", from Handel's *Acis and Galatea*. I still sing that grand old air. I regard it as my luckiest one.

My brother Jim insisted upon being present at my first audition, and it was here he made his remark, "Will he be famous

B

like you, sir?" He followed it up by the request, "Will you sing that song Peter has just sung, so that I can compare your voice with his?"

Santley, the acme of politeness, replied, "All I can tell you, Mr. Dawson, is that your brother has a very good voice." Santley explained that he could not take me as a pupil for some while, and recommended that I should go to F. L. Bamford, in Glasgow, then return to him later on. This fitted in well, for I had relatives in Scotland.

My uncle, Captain James Dawson, owned the Rock Line of sailing vessels. Each of his ships was named after a well-known Scottish rock: Bass Rock, Ted Rock, Beacon, Inchcape, etc. He held the blue riband for the fastest service between London and Calcutta with his tea-clippers.

My arrival at my uncle's house in Rutherglen, Glasgow, caused a sensation. Not because I had arrived from Australia, but because I arrived dressed in my striped trousers, black-braided tail coat, tan boots and top hat.

My cousins were very, very polite, but the next day I was taken to a Glasgow tailor's and measured for a lounge suit, full evening dress; taken to a boot shop and bought black boots, and to a hatter's for a sensible hat. Yes, I wore a top hat in those days. It was the custom not only among the gentry but among the middle classes.

I remember that a few months later, after a very heavy fall of snow, I was walking along a main street, when suddenly a huge lump of snow from a roof fell right on to my top hat. It knocked me to the ground and flattened the hat. Ever after that—in winter time—I walked in the middle of the road!

I enjoyed my stay in Scotland, and between lessons with Mr. Bamford I did a lot of sailing on the Clyde. In the winter I played hockey.

Mr. F. L. Bamford lived at Kelvin. In the evenings I practiced vocalizing in the open air in Stonelaw Woods, Rutherglen. But the Scots were not appreciative: they thought I was 'daft', and said so.

Mr. Bamford was a fine teacher. He took me through a labyrinth of vocal exercises, taught me *arias*, opera, oratorio and the classic songs. After six months' hard study I was ready to visit Charles Santley in London once more.

On my return to London I was a very different person. Gone was my quaint sartorial outfit, and in its place the correct wear for any occasion. When I called on Charles Santley at 67 Carlton Hill,

St. John's Wood, he smiled and remarked that I was looking much better.

I knew exactly what he meant!

It was arranged that I should receive one lesson every week, for which I paid one guinea.

What a grand teacher he was! What encouragement he gave me! He taught me all there was to know about voice production, and the correct rendering of the standard oratorios.

I was taken meticulously through works such as "The Messiah", "Elijah" and "The Creation", until I knew all those wonderful works from the first to the last note. When I took my last lesson I was confident that I knew everything I had been taught both by Bamford and Santley. The day I said farewell to Santley, in his London studio, a momentous and sad occasion, he was kind enough to say: "Well, Peter, there is nothing more that I can teach you. You have the ball at your feet. It's entirely up to you now to make your career. But don't neglect your practice; don't, whatever you do, neglect that. If I can help, promise that you will not hesitate to call on me."

A grand English gentleman, of the same calibre as Sir Charles Villiers Stanford, Sir Walford Davies, Sir Edward Elgar and Sir Alexander Mackenzie.

As an example of Charles Santley's kindness, soon after my tuition period had expired, and when I should have been receiving professional engagements, my father wrote asking me to return to Australia as it did not seem to him that I was likely to make my living by my voice. I explained the situation to Santley and he would not hear of my foregoing my few final lessons, and refused to accept any further fees. He also arranged my first real engagement, a tour of the West of England with Mme Albani, in which he also appeared.

About a year later, when I met him with my wife, I told him that it would give me great pleasure to pay his fees which he had so kindly waived when I could not afford to pay. With a smile he said: "My dear Peter. It was nice of you to offer. Please accept it as a small wedding present from me."

There are certain incidents in one's life that will always remain fresh and ineffaceable. Some of my most treasured memories are my visits to the Royal Opera House, Covent Garden, to hear the operas and the finest singers. In order to get a seat in the gallery for the performance that began at eight o'clock, I had to get into the queue about three o'clock in the afternoon. Fortunately I had met a friend who was as keen as myself, and the time passed quickly. Leonard Young was a very good friend. He steered me away from many of the temptations that beset a young fellow who is a stranger in London, or for that matter any big city.

When we finally reached our seats on my very first visit to the Opera House, we found ourselves—through Young's foresight—in the front row.

What a sight greeted my eyes! Young told me afterwards that he thought I would never close my mouth again, that I sat open-mouthed looking round the house, and then at the audience for what seemed to him hours before I turned to him and said: "Isn't it marvellous? Look at those people in the boxes. Did you ever see so many diamonds? . . . Look at those chaps in uniform. . . . Look at the flowers . . . millions of them. . . . What a size the place is! . . . And look at the orchestra pit, it's big enough to hold a ship!"

Leonard was most helpful, and later pointed out many of the great celebrities of society in the boxes. He also told me that the flowers, although they looked very beautiful, were in fact imitation. Real flowers affect singers, and cause sneezing. Some singers are allergic to pollen, but are unable to tell from which particular flower. Sufferers from hay fever will understand how disastrous it would be for a great singer to suddenly have an attack during a performance! Hay fever and its more serious companion rhinitis are more prevalent in the United States, and it was over there that the deleterious effect of real flowers on singers was first discovered.

To return to Covent Garden. The gallery cost me half a crown, but it was a wonderful investment.

The first opera I saw was *Carmen*, with Caruso and Mme Emma Calvé. To say that I was enthralled is to put it too mildly. Remember, I had set out to make my living as a singer. Here I was hearing and seeing the greatest singers in the world. I was listening, not as the average opera enthusiast listens, but watching the rendering from every musical angle. By studying the various tenors, baritones and basses I was fortunate enough to hear, I learnt that each artiste possessed his own interpretation of the part, and that they all put their own idea over as to what was the best rendering.

During the first act I was astonished again by the terrific shouting of the galleryites. I had been far too interested in the audience and the glittering jewels and lovely dresses to notice the men and women who were sharing the gallery with me. But in the interval I had a good look at the people who had been creating such a din with their applause, and, to me, in such a strange manner and in a strange language. Young explained that the place was filled with Italians. "It looks as though all the Italian colony in London is here," I remember him saying. During the interval I was thoroughly happy watching the Italians at work on the refreshments they had brought. What a variety of food! What a galaxy of smells! Leonard and I amused ourselves by naming the different aromas we could identify: onions, garlic, salami, cheese, oranges, sardines, other fish. And these foods were being washed down with bottles of Chianti!

What a cheery, happy crowd they were! It was difficult to believe that this noisy, gesticulating crowd of Italians could remain absolutely dead quiet during the singing. And their applause was always spontaneous and sincere.

In the second act, however, their shouting of "*Viva! Viva!*" compelled me to join in the fun, and as they yelled, so I yelled: "Ice cream! Ice cream! Ice cream!" But it made no impression, they were all too excited to take any notice.

I did not miss one opera. I heard *Carmen, Rigoletto, Pagliacci, Tosca, Faust, Otello, La Bohème, Il Trovatore, Cavalleria Rusticana,* the first performance of *Madame Butterfly, Don Giovanni, La Traviata, Lucia di Lammermoor* and *Aïda.*

Among the Italian singers I had the great pleasure of hearing I remember Caruso, Titta Ruffo, Scotti, Boninsegna, Amato, Battistini, Galvany and Sammarco.

I did not hear Tetrazzini for some years or, for that matter, any other really outstanding Italian soprano, and for a very good reason. I heard that our own Dame Nellie Melba had signed a contract with Covent Garden which precluded the appearance of any other soprano without her consent! I understand that this embargo was held by Melba for over twenty years. Another clause in her contract stipulated that no other artistes were to receive as much payment as herself. When Caruso was at the zenith of his career an arrangement had to be made whereby he received £1 less than Melba for each appearance he made. Melba's fee was £400, Caruso's £399. I was told that Caruso received additional fees in the way of 'expenses'.

Among the famous French artistes I heard were Plançon, Journet, Gilibert and the de Rezske brothers.

At that time, too, there was a certain controversy going on in the Press about the Wagnerian operas. Many voiced the opinion that his music was blatant noise. Nevertheless many

of the Wagner operas were produced, and I grew to admire
them.

I heard *Tannhäuser*, *Lohengrin*, *Die Meistersinger* and *The Ring*.

A few years after I had heard these grand German operas I had
the immense satisfaction of singing in *Die Meistersinger* with an
English cast and Hans Richter conducting. I remember that
Walter Hyde sang the part of David. In the cast was Claude
Fleming, that versatile artiste who acted with Beerbohm Tree,
and sang the part of Nachtigall in this German opera.

Let me say at once that I was not very impressed with operatic
work. It struck me as too much work for too little pay. And this
reminds me that during the performance a most embarrassing
incident occurred.

While waiting for our cue to 'go on' we used to play poker.
A particularly large 'kitty' was on the table when only Claude
Fleming and myself were left in the game. After raising our bids,
Claude suddenly said: "Well, it's not worth taking any more of
your good money, Peter. I've four kings!" But to his surprise I
put down four aces! Almost immediately there was an urgent
call for my appearance on the stage. I swept up my winnings and
put them into the small bag I carried in my costume. And then
the worst happened. Moving about the stage, I was bumped
by another character, the bag was knocked off, and my poker
winnings were scattered all over the stage.

Such a thing to happen on the stage of Covent Garden was
unheard of. I, however, although temporarily worried by the
accident, was far more disturbed that my hard-earned winnings
had been lost. When the curtain fell I tried to recover some of
the money, but it was hopeless. I managed to find two shillings
out of about thirty! The stage manager gave me a quiet but
grim talk about my carelessness. That incident taught me a lesson:
not to play cards during a performance!

This reminds me of a joke played on Madame Melba. When
singing at Covent Garden she was in the habit of chewing a little
Australian 'Wattle' gum. It was very soothing for the throat.
In the wings was a small piece of plate glass, on which she would
deposit the piece of gum while she was singing. When she had
finished her *aria* she would put the gum back into her mouth.
Unfortunately, she had made herself very unpopular with the
stage hands, particularly because she insisted that they must wear
plimsolls during their work because the noise of their shuffling
upset her.

One night she took up her piece of gum as usual, but screeched and spat it out; she flew into a furious temper and stormed and raved about the stage. Someone had replaced the gum with a quid of tobacco made up to look exactly like the gum.

To make matters worse, Caruso went into peals of laughter when he heard about it. Melba demanded the dismissal of all the stage hands. They were dismissed; but the next day they turned up as usual, the manager making the excuse that he was unable to engage any others.

After this the gum was guarded by a dresser, a woman who afterwards said, "I'd like to have put something stronger than tobacco in its place, but she'd 'a known 'oo it was."

Caruso once blew into the ear of Mme Kirkby Lunn just before a solo in *Rigoletto*, and to his astonishment received a terrific slap in the face that nearly knocked him over. The audience thought it was part of the show and shrieked with laughter.

Caruso never tried any of his jokes on her again. But he was always up to a 'lark'.

Before leaving Covent Garden, I must mention the art gallery. This display of art is enjoyed only by the 'galleryites', but anyone interested (I do hope that it still exists) should pay it a visit. Just walk up the stairs leading from the gallery entrance and look at the array of clever, weird and artistic sketches that decorate the walls on both sides.

I was told by a fine-art dealer in St. James's Street that a few were magnificent works of art and what a tragedy it was that they could not be removed from the wall.

Yes, the galleryites were the people who understood the beauty of the music and singing in those days. On the other hand, I must comment on the amazing advance in the appreciation of music since then. Opera was patronized by society, but they knew little or nothing about operas and cared less! To the majority it was just another 'social occasion' and they just had to be present. The display of dresses and jewellery was the attraction; music took a bad second place.

Today, thanks to the success of the gramophone and wireless, a vast public has become interested: good music and singing is heard regularly over the air. And make no mistake, the operas and symphonies are really enjoyed by those people who were then referred to as 'the masses'.

I have often been asked what is my favourite opera.

I find this a difficult question to answer; but the opera I

enjoyed most, and one that I have recommended to a great many students, is *Louise* (Charpentier).

*   *   *

By this time I had moved from Kennington to Ealing Common, and it was in Ealing that I first met Nan. She was the daughter of T. J. Noble, box-office manager of the Alhambra Theatre, Leicester Square, for twenty-five years. Later he went into management on his own and ran the Ealing Theatre. It was here I met his daughter.

Eighteen months later we were married.

I have been married over forty years, and consider myself a lucky man, blessed as I am with a good wife, good health and a good voice. Nannie has been my constant companion, my shrewdest critic and faithful adviser.

I was delighted, when I found that my wife possessed a fine soprano voice, and had sung professionally in London and the larger provincial towns. Her professional name was Annette George. Later she joined me in many of my tours all over the Empire.

We both took a big risk in marrying, but I knew that if I failed as a singer I could always return to my father's business, which was growing year by year.

During the early years of my struggle for recognition in the concert world there were times when, but for Nan's encouragement and faith, I might have been tempted to abandon my effort to make a living by singing. When I failed to find engagements after I had been studying for two years, my father strongly advised me to return home and rejoin the firm. Later he cut my allowance, solely in the hope that this would force me to return.

At last engagements began to arrive and, even more important, I began making phonograph records.

But with the dead-summer seasons for vocalists in those early days, it was primarily Nan's strong belief in my future and her unflagging encouragement that helped me put my two feet on to the ladder of success.

It was only a very serious car accident in 1925 from which she escaped death by a miracle that has prevented her from making any further public appearances. Today her fine voice is heard only by relatives and friends.

Before the accident, 'Annette George' had made a big success touring with me in Australia, New Zealand, South Africa, India, and of course throughout the British Isles.

You will hear more about Nan as this story proceeds, for she is my inseparable companion.

Yes, as Burns puts it, "I hae a wife o' my ain."

And now to my first professional engagements.

*   *   *

My first appearance as a professional singer in England was at a church in the East End of London, in Burdett Road, Stepney. I sang a number of songs which included "I fear no Foe in shining Armour", "Rocked in the Cradle of the Deep", "The Bandolero" and "Long ago in Alcala".

The fee was SEVEN SHILLINGS AND SIXPENCE!

I must confess that I did not get any particular thrill from this *début*. I had sung so often in churches in Australia that I could not regard this engagement as the real start of my professional career.

Charles Santley was not only my musical mentor, but a very good friend. It was through his influence I secured my first big chance to make a name for myself. It remains as fresh in my memory today as when he told me he had arranged an engagement for me to join the company that Madame Albani was taking on a tour of the West of England. I was twenty-two.

At that time the name of Albani was on everybody's lips. After a tremendous success in London she had started a series of tours all over Great Britain. The tour of the West was the last of the season and but for Santley I might have missed the opportunity.

The first concert of the tour was held in the famous Guildhall at Plymouth. Naturally from that moment I have always cherished a strong regard and affection for Plymouth. When I visited the town after the War (1948) and saw the ghastly devastation that had obliterated the Guildhall and many other familiar landmarks, I was much overcome. It was gratifying to be shown the wonderful new plan for the reconstruction of the city.

Now back to 1904. In the company supporting Madame Albani were Santley himself, Johannes Wolf (violinist), Ravogli (contralto), Adele Verne (pianist), William Green (tenor), Theodore Flint (accompanist) and myself.

Sandwiched in amongst such a galaxy of world-renowned artistes I can be forgiven the nervousness I suffered before my first concert. I remember waiting at the side of the stage listening to the other artistes sing or play; listening to the applause, and noting the smiles of satisfaction as the artistes came off, obviously

pleased with what they had done. Just before I was to make my
appearance a hand was placed on my shoulder and Santley was
saying: "Now, Peter, you're singing in front of a very friendly
audience. They are going to like your voice. Go on with a smile,
and enjoy yourself!" It was perfect timing. I did go on with a smile,
thanks to the intuition of the great master. My first song was
"Hybrias the Cretan". Thanks to Santley's advice, I had gone on
assured of the friendliness of the audience, and I was at ease and
sang this fine old song with satisfaction. The applause that
greeted me when it was over was a great comfort, and I felt
extraordinarily happy and strangely confident, as though I had
been singing for years. That first appearance at Plymouth stood
me in good stead for the rest of my life.

For an encore I sang "The Bedouin Love Song".

When I came off I was greeted by Mme Albani, who could
not restrain her kindly enthusiasm, and almost came out of the
wings to embrace me. There were tears in her eyes as she
congratulated me.

I was smiling through tears in my own eyes, for her spontaneous felicitations was all that was needed to release my
pent-up emotions.

In the second part of the programme I sang "Blow, blow, thou
Winter Wind" and received another very warm reception, and
for an encore "The Bandolero". Such was the success I made
that Mme Albani decided I should sing a duet with Mme
Ravogli at the end of the second half. After that I didn't care if
it snowed! I would have sung with anyone. Nevertheless, it was
as well that the duet came *after* my success; for I have never
experienced a more embarrassing five minutes in all my concert
life. The duet from *Don Giovanni* is a very lovely number, but
unfortunately I had to read my part from the score, while Madame
Ravogli was 'doing her stuff', moving around and gesticulating
in true Italian operatic style. It must have looked ridiculous, but
the audience liked the singing, and that was that.

But I made a silent resolution never to sing another duet
without knowing it sufficiently well to avoid holding a copy in
my hand.

It was after this concert that I read my first Press notices.
Here again I received great encouragement. The critics praised
my voice and the clearness of my diction. One critic wrote:

"The refreshing clearness of his diction, after so much
incoherence from so many of today's singers, was most

pleasing. This young man has a good future before him. His phrasing in the difficult 'Hybrias the Cretan' was a revelation in its perfection."

That, of course, was really a compliment to Santley's tuition.

The tour lasted eight weeks, and gave me invaluable experience. There was not much money attached to the engagement, for I received only two guineas for each concert, but the publicity, even in those days, was of inestimable value. Just before the Albani tour I had been paid the phenomenal sum of *seven* guineas to sing at a concert in Glasgow.

Soon after the tour I received much help from engagements given to me by the various musical societies in London. What a fine training-ground those concerts were! The musical societies had a really sincere love of good songs and they expected a good performance. There was nothing quite like these societies in any part of the world, made up as they were by a collection of musical enthusiasts, mostly City men, each society being roughly 400 strong. Those to whom I owe my thanks include the Chough, Kentish Town and Chingford Musical Societies. I had been accepting a number of engagements for smoking concerts, and the smoke-laden atmosphere with the 'give-us-a-rollicking-song' angle, was not the most conducive for a young bass-baritone.

I nearly 'blotted my copybook' on one occasion, and the incident might have cost me my good name with the various societies.

During the singing of a light-comedy number, "Everything in the Country is alien", by one of the artistes, I was at the side of the stage swapping jokes with another artiste. From jokes we went on to demonstrations of ju-jutsu, which was the vogue at that time. I was being shown a particular fall or hold, and suffered intense pain. In order to get out of my opponent's grip I made a strong effort, and it resulted in the man being thrown completely on to the stage.

This naturally caused trouble. The singer was not dismayed. He paused, looked round, and then said to the audience, "Another alien." The house roared their approval of this witty remark, and the programme went on without further incident. But not so back stage!

The secretary of the concert came round and, with a very grim expression on his face, made some inquiries. He then approached me with the words: "You needn't worry about waiting for the rest of the programme, Mr. Dawson. We are not used to these rough antics in this country, and what is more, we don't intend to have them."

Fortunately, the secretary of the Kentish Town Musical Society, Mr. W. O. Robbins, who had started me with my first musical-society engagement at Stanley Hall, Kentish Town, was not so 'put out' by the incident as the local secretary, and through his kindness the real explanation of the incident was given to the various societies.

As a sequel, one year later I was singing at the hall, where I had precipitated an artiste on to the stage, at a fee of seven guineas, instead of the two guineas of the previous occasion.

Mr. Robbins had helped very considerably. It was through him that I received many of my first most welcome engagements. I had pleased him and he recommended me to the secretaries of all the other musical-society secretaries. It was as a result of these recommendations that I also received dates for Lodge dinners, and those smoking concerts I have already mentioned. In this world chance plays an important part in all our lives. The kindness of Mr. Robbins, and his introduction to his friend Mr. Teddy Bowen, of the Chingford Musical Society, gave me valuable guineas when they were sorely needed. It only required their "By the way, Peter Dawson is a darned good singer, you should engage him" to mutual friends, and I was 'in'.

But I cannot emphasize too strongly what grand work these musical societies did for lovers of music. Remember, this was in the days before wireless, and the phonograph was in its infancy.

When I spoke to Santley about the work I was doing and sought his advice whether or not I should accept engagements for smoking concerts, he said: "Peter, you are on the threshold of your career. All the experience you can gain today will stand you in good stead later. Go ahead, but for heaven's sake take care not to participate in the frivolities of the occasion. In short, Peter, don't be persuaded to 'stay on and enjoy the rest of the evening'. That means smoking and drinking of the kind a professional vocalist just cannot and must not indulge in.

"The time will come," he added, "when you will not need to accept smoking-concert engagements. Use them as a means to an end, and not as a habit. The musical-society engagements, on the other hand, are invaluable. They will want to hear your best work. I cannot recommend them too highly."

*   *   *

After Santley the next man I have to thank is Professor Kantorez, a Russian singing specialist. He made himself a nuisance to me for several months by seeking an interview with the suggestion that he 'wanted to show me how to extend my voice'. Finally Nan said: "Oh, why not see the man? He seems very convinced that he can help you. He cannot do you any harm." I did see Kantorez, and I have been grateful ever since!

He changed my voice from a bass into a baritone. He made me sing four notes higher than I had ever sung in my life. I could sing top A♭ with the greatest of ease, and to the amazement of all singers. Having succeeded in turning me into a baritone, he had a serious talk with me one morning, and said, "Now, Mr. Dawson, I wish to speak to you most seriously." I wondered what was coming. But he continued: "You know that I have made you into a fine baritone. Now, if you will help, I can make you into the finest *tenor* of the age."

But I refused to co-operate. I was immensely satisfied with his truly remarkable achievement of increasing my range, and without in the slightest degree interfering or affecting my low notes. In fact, in fairness to that great teacher, I must confess that he enhanced them. But I had no desire to be a tenor. I was afraid that I might lose my middle register. So I stayed a bass-baritone. When there was nothing more the professor could do, he said, "Well, Mr. Dawson, you will sing until you are ninety!" A comforting thought—or is it?

For those interested, my range is E♭ to top A. Before the Kantorez episode it was E♭ to D.

CHAPTER II

MY FIRST RECORDINGS

BEFORE I relate the story of how I made my first phonograph record, I want to confess that my reputation as a gramophone artiste was the dominating success of my career as a singer.

Despite the many tours I made throughout the British Isles and the Empire, during the first twenty years of my carrer, there is no doubt that many more people knew me through my gramophone records than my concerts.

During the last few years it is only fair to say that broadcasting is taking the lead. This is not surprising when one considers the vastness of the audience 'over the air'. But to return to the making of my first test as a talking-machine singer. I must tell you how I very nearly failed in my first efforts!

After one of my early concerts, a charming, bearded gentleman introduced himself to me as Mr. James Hough, managing director of the Edison Bell Phonograph Company.

He asked me whether I would care to visit his recording-studio and have my voice tested with a view to making records. I was absolutely dumbfounded, and, of course, I could not rush from the place fast enough to tell the news to—yes, of course—Nan.

This chance had arrived at a time when, as the result of the stopping of my allowance from Australia plus the scarcity of concerts, I was without funds. But I did not realize until the following morning that we could hardly muster enough ready cash to pay my fare to the recording-studio. It was too late to start worrying. I had to get to the recording-studio in Euston Buildings, London, N.W., and I did not have the time to get money from relatives in the form of a temporary loan.

Fortunately, Nan came to the rescue. She always does!

She suddenly remembered that when she played the Fairy Queen in a London pantomime the previous year or so she used to use pennies to keep the long silk stockings attached to the bottom of the corsage. She rushed to her trunk, and sure enough found six pennies twisted in the top of the stockings to form buttons! With these fortuitous coppers I was able to arrive at the studio in time for the test.

But I had to walk home again from the Euston Road to

Ealing! Only eight miles, but what a wonderful walk it was. I was able to ruminate on the possibilities of my future as a recorder. But before I go into that I must relate what happened at the test.

I shall never forget my first sight of the little funnel which I had to stand in front of, and sing into, and the shock of feeling a hand on my shoulder during the singing of my song, which pushed me closer or farther away from the funnel as the song proceeded.

The song they chose for my test was called "Long ago in Alcala".

After I had finished I was taken into another room, where the wax cylinder that contained my effort was played over on what looked like an ordinary phonograph.

That first experience of hearing my own voice is as vivid in my memory as if it had occurred yesterday.

It was a very strange feeling, and Edward Hesse, the musical director of the Edison Bell Company, told me afterwards that my face was a study. Apparently I sat open-mouthed with a look of astonishment when the record started, but that my expression changed as the record played on, and that when it finished my features indicated quite clearly that I was very pleased with the result.

I confess I was pleased. There were a few blasts, but for my first attempt I was quite satisfied. But whatever I thought, the recording chief, an American named Russell Hunting, thought otherwise. His verdict to Mr. Hough was, "His voice is too powerful, and that makes it very difficult to record."

Fortunately his word was not the final one, or my voice may not have been heard on a record until many years later. Mr. Hough, who had watched the test and listened quietly to the reproduction, said: "Yes. His voice is powerful. But the diaphragm you used is too ruddy sensitive. I'm sure you can make adjustments to overcome that trouble." And turning to me with a friendly smile he asked, "When can you come again for another trial?" He must have seen the look of disappointment on my face at Hunting's remark, and went out of his way to put things right. As I left the office I heard Mr. Hough say to Hesse, "I think his voice is a winner."

It was not until I had reached the street that I realized that I had to walk home. I felt too happy to worry about that and by the time I had covered two miles I had made a fortune—in my thoughts.

I pipe-dreamed, in the fashion of excitable youth, that my

success as a recorder would be followed by a great success as a
concert artiste. Then it started to rain. With the rain my optimism
changed to pessimism.

Supposing the American could not record my voice? This
thought was followed by annoyance that I had to walk home.
But after a while I began to count my blessings. That made me
much happier. What right had I to feel depressed? I possessed a
voice, I was young, and had my future before me, and at the end
of the walk I should find Nan waiting anxiously to hear the result
of my audition. I had heard Mr. Hough say, "His voice is a
winner." Something about the set of his jaw, and his North
Country accent, assured me that he would see that I did make
records.

I covered the remaining mile or so of my walk full of content-
ment, and probably singing over in my mind a score of songs.

Naturally on my next visit to the recording-studio I was not
too well received by Russell Hunting. But he knew that Hough
had put the onus on him to make a record of my voice, and he
had certainly made preparations. He used an entirely different
funnel and made me sing the song over before I recorded, so
as to know where the full tones occurred. While the song was
being recorded he stood by my side and pushed me carefully to
and fro in front of the funnel for the low and the open notes.

The result? I shall never forget that walk from the recording-
studio to the listening-room; that wait for the cylinder to be put
on the phonograph; listening to the result and realizing the
almost complete absence of blast, but holding my breath until I
heard Russell Hunting's verdict. After a pause he gave his
opinion: "Yeah. That's it." Turning to me, he said, "You've
got a darned good voice."

As in a dream I heard them discussing the kind of song I
should sing for the first record I was to make for sale. It was
only then that I knew I had made a success and that I was actually
going to start making records.

The song finally decided on by Edward Hesse, the musical
director, was "Navaho", which was being sung with success
on the music-halls at that time. But before the recording date
was fixed, Hunting commenced another fractious argument.
"We gotta do one thing. That's change the name. Every Negro
in the States is called 'Pete'." Sure enough my Christian name
was changed from Peter to Leonard. My first phonograph
records were issued as by Leonard Dawson. But after a few weeks
Mr. Hough changed it back. "This young man is making a name

As a member of the Adelaide
Choral Society—Christmas 1901

Hector Grant, alias Peter
Dawson, as a Scottish
comedian in 1906

Mr. and Mrs. Peter Dawson
with Niedzielsky during South
African Tour 1935

1914–1918 War. Peter Dawson and Captain Ramkina (*centre*),
with the Mayor of Brisbane's son, at 'cigarette inspection'

Peter Dawson recording in a special studio erected at the Ideal Home
Exhibition in 1926

for himself in the concert world, and it's bad business on our part not to use his real name." So Peter Dawson's name came into the catalogues; and Harry Bluff, who used to make those famous announcements on each record which will be remembered by the older generation, gave me my first thrill when he said, "'The Bandolero', sung by Peter Dawson. Edison Bell record"!

Little did I realize then that in a few years I should be singing for record purposes under several fictitious names because of the demand for a wide variety of songs by different companies. But that is another story with which I will deal later.

Once I had been informed that I was to make my first record I was anxious to know what terms I was to be given. "We'll pay you five shillings a round," said Mr. Hough. A round meant that each time I sang on the record (after rehearsing) I would receive that sum. It usually took four attempts before what was called a 'master' record was obtained. A little error here or there: a fault in the texture of the wax cylinder, a musical fault, or the song being too long or too short. I sang four rounds! I shall always remember the delight with which I accepted a golden sovereign. And more so when I was given other songs to take home and learn for another recording session.

Although I was not told of the success of my early records, I finally learned of it when I was chosen to sing a Scottish comic song called "John, John, John, go and put your Troosers on". It was a number being sung by the comedian Billy Williams, the 'man in the velvet suit' on the halls, and was a terrific success. Billy was recording it for another record company. I made this song for the Edison Bell Company.

In those early days the master records (the original wax cylinders from which the black ones were manufactured and sold to the public) did not last very long. In other words, it was not possible to make very many copies from each master before the sound waves on the master record failed. This meant that a record which sold in thousands would have to be sung many times by the artiste to make enough master records to satisfy the demand.

In order to cope with the unprecedented demand for this song I had to sing it over and over again. I used to begin at 10 a.m. and go on till 1 p.m., when I had lunch; start again at 2.15 and work through until 5 p.m.

I kept that up for *five consecutive days*! But I made £75. I received it in gold. Yes, seventy-five golden sovereigns!

I shall always remember my concern and anxiety in having so

much money in my trousers pocket. I held up the pocket with my hand, and held on to it with a grip of iron, and walked warily for fear that it might burst. When I did reach home I called out to Nan, "Come and see a budding Rockefeller unload a gold mine." I proceeded to empty the sovereigns in a cascade on to a table. It was a very happy moment in our lives. We had only recently been married. I have always regarded that strangely named song, "John, John, John, go and put your Troosers on", as a wedding present.

The next day we went to an auction sale and bought our first furniture—a bedroom suite. It was a bargain: £10 for a bed, wardrobe, washstand and dressing-table!

It was about then that I was making records for other phonograph companies. At the Edison Company I met a young Irish singer with whom I became very friendly. He, like myself, was just starting a career as a professional singer. Like me, too, he was on his first sojourn in London. He suggested that I should ask a higher price for my services.

Soon afterwards he left for Italy to finish his training, and I did not see him again for two years. By this time he was a fully trained opera singer and had made his *début* at the Royal Opera House, Covent Garden. It was John McCormack.

The Edison record sold at a higher price than the others, and they were worth the extra. They did not alter their price when, about this time, another company started making a record which they put on the market for sale at ninepence! That was threepence cheaper than the Edison Bell, and sixpence less than the Edison.

The Sterling Record was the name of the new company.

Mr. Sterling, who persuaded me to sing for his records, was a short, dark, rather small man with an American accent, who at first sight did not impress me as a man capable of fighting companies like the two I have mentioned. But as I got to know him better I began to appreciate the drive, determination and the strong personality behind the somewhat frail physique of the man. Despite his cleverness, however, he was not able to make a success of his records; not because they were inferior in any way or that they did not sell as well as those of the other companies; but the disc record had been launched and the 'writing on the wall' for the future of the cylinder record was there for all to read. Sterling was wise enough to get into the disc side of the business soon after cutting his losses on the cylinders.

That was typical of Louis Sterling. He was the first to realize that the phonograph record would be killed by a successful disc record and acted accordingly. Yet even this shrewd man could not have hazarded a prophecy that he would some day become the head of the great E.M.I.: Electrical and Musical Industries, Ltd.

Yes, the man who threw out a challenge to the great phonograph companies in 1905—and, as he has since told me, did it with practically no money whatever—is now Sir Louis Sterling.

To return to the work I was doing. As a result of my success, the Edison Company (in view of the Sterling record) asked me to sing for them exclusively, and put my fee up to three guineas minimum. The Thomas Edison Company was far more advanced technically in their recording, and took infinitely more pains in securing the best combination of recording diaphragm and funnel for the different voices.

Only when the best result was found in various tests did they start to make the master records.

In those days one of the most important secrets of making a good evenly balanced record was the weaving in and out from the mouth of the funnel. You had to think ahead of your tone emission to know when to move forward and when to move away.

I have always concentrated throughout my career on diction or enunciation. I am not going to pull my punches, and shall not apologize for claiming that the clarity of my diction was one of the fundamental reasons for my success. I can state without any qualification that gramophone recording taught me more about correcting my enunciation than any teacher could possibly have done!

It was also of incalculable advantage in finding and demonstrating all faults in rendition. In front of my teacher I knew only that I was giving a correct rendition of a lesson; in a record I could 'hear' my rendering and 'see' my faults. It was, in short, the teaching of Charles Santley and, later, Professor Kantorez, plus being able to listen to the recording tests, that put me on the road to what has been a successful career.

But the phonograph companies had many difficulties to contend with. In order to get popular songs recorded by artistes who possessed 'recording voices' it was necessary to carry out a fair amount of pirate tactics. Songs had to be taken down in some way or other as they were being sung either at a music-hall or theatre. A miniature recording phonograph was taken into the theatre or hall to record the melody. A stenographer took down the words verbatim.

It was sometimes necessary to make three and four visits before a satisfactory result was obtained. From these records, and the stenographers' notes, an orchestration was made and an artiste selected to make the record.

In a couple of weeks or less it would be on the market and selling in thousands. The owner of the song had no claim, and the original singer could take no legal action. Were any action contemplated it was usually quashed by the theatre or music-hall manager, who found that the records helped business, just as today a broadcast helps the sale of a song and the popularity of an artiste, because the public, having heard an artiste they like, want to 'see' him.

The practice of 'lifting' songs in this fashion was finally put a stop to by the Copyright Act. The recording companies were pleased, because by this time the successful future of the industry was assured, and the pernicious system of pirate copying was distasteful to them.

Today the copyright fees and the mechanical-reproduction rights bring in large sums to successful composers—and rightly so. The fees help young composers and encourage others. I know, because I have written a number of songs, and the ripples of fees come in with welcome regularity—like sweet music.

The life of the cylinder record was fading fast. The disc record was giving better and more natural results, and it was obvious that it would oust the cylinder.

So I made my next step forward in my recording life. I was introduced to the brothers Will and Fred Gaisberg of His Master's Voice Company. They were here from the States to make disc records.

I had heard of these famous brothers during my recording life, and how they were revolutionizing the industry of the talking machine.

In the meantime I had made records for a few 'budding' disc concerns, including the Nicole Company. The recorder was Arthur Brooks, who shortly afterwards became the chief recording manager for the powerful Columbia Company. He has now retired and for many years has been the cheery and popular secretary of the Savage Club in London. The manager of the Columbia was the little American who had tried to revivify the cylinder record by selling them at ninepence each—Louis Sterling.

The Gaisbergs apparently liked my voice, because on my first meeting with them they persuaded me to sign a contract to sing for H.M.V. exclusively.

That was in 1906. The contract was for one year. A minimum guarantee of £25 for the year!

Fortunately, that word 'minimum' was just a word. The Gaisbergs had promised that I should earn more than the minimum, and they kept their word. In the first year I received £72. Believe me, to a young singer in those days it represented a whole lot of money. To me it meant more. It was money earned apart from what I called my legitimate work—that is, as a concert singer.

That contract was the first of many. I have not sung for any other company since that date in 1906 when I signed 'on the dotted line' for Will and Fred Gaisberg. Will died some years ago, but Fred is still keeping a 'kindly' eye on the recording department.

By 1908 the H.M.V. Company was beginning to advertise my records in a fairly big way. I found them in the national papers—Sunday and daily issues, the provincial press, and the magazines. By 1909 I was receiving letters from Australia telling me of the success of my records out there. That was a big surprise to me. I did not realize that my records had been 'hailed' in the Australian press, and that I was being acclaimed a star in my own country, until I arrived there for my first return visit with Amy Castle's company.

It was not until then that I really understood what my success as a gramophone artiste had brought me.

And now about my fees. The contract I made with H.M.V. was for £1 1s. for each solo, 10s. 6d. for each duet or quartette.

I am sure that Santley did not approve of the songs I was singing for the phonograph companies, but he was wise enough to realize that I had to live and that concerts at this time were few and far between.

Immediately a song became a success on the music-halls I was asked to learn and record it. I was always a quick reader, and this helped my success in those days of rapid recording of song successes. The various competitive companies were fighting to get their record on sale before their rivals.

One of my most popular records at that time was recorded 'on the spur of the moment'. It was immediately after the successful first night of *Chu Chin Chow*, with my friend Oscar Asche in the lead. I was recording a series of songs at the H.M.V. studios when Fred Gaisberg, the recording manager, handed me a song and said, "You might have a look at that, Peter." I looked at the song, it was "The Cobbler's Song" from *Chu Chin Chow*. After glancing through it I said I thought it was a good number and asked, "Do you want me to make it?" "Yes," replied Fred, "right away, Peter." As I shall explain later in this book, I prefer to know and study a song thoroughly before I sing it. But in this case I was recording the song in ten minutes.

What a success! It sold in scores of thousands.

But enough of recording for a while, I will return to it later. The music-hall boom was interfering very much with concerts at this period, and in the next chapter I shall tell you of a sensational decision I made in my career.

CHAPTER III

PETER DAWSON *ALIAS* HECTOR GRANT

THE next step on the ladder of my career occurred when I was put in touch with Mr. William Boosey, who in those days was the uncrowned king of the musical world of London. Through him I was given my first engagement at the Promenade Concerts, then held at the Queen's Hall.

And it was here I had my first meeting with the bearded Henry Wood.

I cannot praise William Boosey too much. In my estimation he did more for young talent than any of his rivals. He was scrupulously fair and just in his dealings, and his judgment was impeccable. But woe betide anyone who dared to cross words with him.

He bore the title of 'Emperor of Bond Street', given to him by all members of the musical profession. Boosey not only looked the part, but carried it off with much dignity. He was dictatorial, as an emperor must be, but he tempered his severity with justice.

I had a pretty serious experience of his power and his implacable rule of the concert world. And it compelled me to get out of Britain for a spell!

It all started so innocently. After I had made a few successful appearances, he asked me to 'pencil in' every date in the next Ballad session at the Queen's Hall. But also, at this time, I was receiving a number of requests for my appearance in the provinces. Now 'pencilling in' does not guarantee that the date will be positively confirmed. In fact, 'pencilling in' can be a bugbear to young artistes. It can result in refusing the offer of an engagement because of a pencilled date which later is not confirmed. This was often my experience. Several dates were offered to me by agents, and I had to say that I had those dates pencilled in for the Queen's Hall. But after a few weeks, having received no confirmation from William Boosey about the Ballad dates, I decided to write and ask whether the 'pencillings' for the Queen's Hall were certainties. And did I stick my chin out!

Back came the reply, devastating in its brevity and proscription: "I do not require your services at all for the coming season, nor at any time. And you can cut your cloth accordingly."

But that was not all. The Emperor issued other commands

and other ukases. The commands were sent to those in close association with him; the ukases were sent to anyone who might want to do business with him or with me. The former included his brother Arthur Boosey, and a number of provincial agents. The latter included Mr. Henry Mills, secretary of the National Sunday League Concerts.

The letter to Mr. Mills was a 'request' not to give Mr. Peter Dawson any engagements, or else . . . !

This action was the Emperor at his dictatorial worst.

Fortunately, my good friend Mills was not to be drawn by Boosey or by any other dictator. He advised me to avoid any contentious correspondence with Boosey over the matter for a season. "The Emperor is very angry with you. You have questioned his word. Unlike most impresarios, Boosey does not ask an artiste to pencil in a date or dates unless he wants him. Should something turn up to change his plans, he is the first to let the artiste know. In that way a singer can rest assured that an engagement with Boosey will mature after he receives the instruction, 'Pencil these dates in'.

"Take my advice, Peter, and try for a tour abroad," he concluded.

Mills, however, had no intention of boycotting me, and said so. He also gave me a good insight into the extraordinary make-up of William Boosey. I had rather stupidly aroused his ire through daring to question his integrity. I ought to have known that not hearing or receiving any confirmation I had no need to worry about the engagement. Don't forget, he had asked me to pencil in all the dates for the Queen's Hall, and he was not likely to forget such a proposition.

Well, I decided to write him a letter a few weeks after, just before I sailed for Australia in 1910. I apologized for my error in questioning his promise, and informed him that I was soon to leave for a tour of Australia. I received no reply!

But on my return to London from that Australian tour one of the first letters I received was from the Emperor. In it he wrote that he wanted to 'bury the hatchet' and I was to go to his office. No man could have been kinder, and no man could have buried the hatchet so charmingly. When I left his office he had appointed me principal baritone for all his concerts at the Queen's Hall.

Another artiste who had failed to respect the authority and the power of the Emperor suffered very seriously. It was that fine baritone Stewart Gardiner. He was fortunate enough to be told by Boosey to 'pencil in' a date for one of the Chappell Ballad Concerts.

To a young artiste that was the opportunity of opportunities. Unfortunately, Stewart, who was perhaps a little spoilt by some very flattering Press notices he was receiving at the time, wrote in a somewhat bumptious manner:

"I have your letter asking me to pencil in Chappell Ballad Concert on so and so, but before I do this I must know how much the fee is. Please let me know by return as I have other offers for my services at that time."

The Emperor never forgave him, and Stewart Gardiner's promising career was definitely jeopardized. But for this feud I have no doubt that he would have become our best and most sought-after baritone. The Boosey embargo was his sword of Damocles.

In fairness to the Emperor, the young singer's attitude was provocatively patronizing, and to make matters worse, instead of trying to appease Boosey, he blatantly defied him. That was fatal. Boosey had friends everywhere in the profession, and any 'unseemly' reflections on the integrity of the Emperor were duly reported.

Mr. Van Leer, the head of the music-publishing side of the firm of Keith Prowse, and incidentally one of the finest judges of a song in the world, told me that one of the sights of London was to watch Boosey arrive at his office each morning. He was contemptuous of the motor-car.

"Driving a magnificent four-in-hand, he would swing into Bond Street from Piccadilly and drive through the street to the admiration of not only all his Bond Street business colleagues, but of the shopping crowds of society folk who frequented that very fashionable centre. He looked the part," Van Leer went on. "He handled the horses superbly, as well as he handled his business. I cannot pay him a better compliment than that. And although the other shopkeepers and owners in that very exclusive shopping and business centre were envious and perhaps a trifle jealous, they all agreed that Boosey did a great deal to keep up the dignity of the street."

Van Leer, too, is a remarkable man. He has bought songs that have been rejected by rivals and seen them soar to immense popularity.

*   *   *

It was in 1906 that I was confronted with the fact that unless I became a member of a seaside concert party or troupe I could starve, as far as concert engagements were concerned, during the summer.

In those days the concert world just did not function during the months of June–August inclusive. There was no B.B.C.

At that time Harry Lauder was making a phenomenal success as a Scottish comedian, with a fine repertoire of catchy, easy-on-the-ear songs.

At the gramophone company one day I gave an imitation of Lauder singing "I love a Lassie". I was astonished at the reaction among the recording staff. Fred Gaisberg, the chief, came up to me excitedly and said: "Peter, can you do any more like that? I mean, can you sing Scottish?" I was amused at the way the little American put it, and answered: "Yes, of course. I can sing all his songs, including 'Stop your tickling, Jock' and 'We parted on the Shore'. Don't forget I am a Scot by birth."

A little later he asked me what I thought of the idea of singing Lauder's songs for the Zonophone Company (a subsidiary of the H.M.V.) under another name. In response to my argument that it might ruin my future if it became known, I was assured that no one would suspect that a singer of Lauder's rollicking Scottish songs could be Peter Dawson. I promised them a decision in twenty-four hours. At home, chatting it over with my wife, we both agreed that with a lean summer ahead it would help our finances. And so I recorded Lauder's songs. They were a great success. The next worry came from the H.M.V. Company. "What about some more songs? The sales are terrific. But we want some more Scottish songs." To my astonishment I found myself saying, "Don't worry, I'll write some." By this time, of course, I had assumed a name for the purpose of these Scottish songs: it was HECTOR GRANT.

It was while I was writing these songs that the idea came to me: why not take up the identity of Hector Grant and fill in a few weeks on the music-halls as a Scottish comedian? I could wear a wig, false side-whiskers, bushy eyebrows, and keep up my Scottish accent, and no one would recognize me as Peter Dawson.

I put the idea to my father-in-law, and when he heard me sing the Lauder songs he promised to get in touch immediately with his friend Frank Allen of the Oxford Music-Hall and arrange an audition for me as Hector Grant. In the meantime, I had been busy writing a number of songs. One of them, "Lassie, dinna sigh for Me", sold more records than any of those I made of Lauder's!

My father-in-law, T. J. Noble, was a fast worker, and as soon as he knew that I had a repertoire of songs ready he made an appointment for me to see Frank Allen. He also informed me that I was to call myself Hector Grant, and that I was to say that I had come down from Scotland for the audition.

When I kept the appointment I was really scared for the first time in my life. I was so afraid that the duplicity might become known, and was worried what effect the news would have on my dear old father.

Eventually I was ushered into the presence of Mr. Frank Allen.

After a few perfunctory questions he took me on to the stage and introduced me to an accompanist. I sang "Lassie, dinna sigh for Me" with appropriate gestures, walking up and down the stage. He then asked me to sing another number, which I did. Then, to my utter astonishment, he said, "Mr. Noble tells me you are ready for an immediate trial." And he went on: "I will put you on as an extra turn this afternoon at this hall. Leave your music with the accompanist." But he wasn't finished. "Be here ready to go on at four o'clock, and made-up."

It was then 11.15 a.m. I had no costume, no wig, no make-up; in fact I was totally unprepared, but I didn't let Allen know. I reasoned it out. The fact that he had decided to hear two songs and was putting me on for an immediate trial meant that so far I had not failed.

I thought the best plan was for me to rush home and get Nan's advice.

It was decided that I could hire a kilt from Morris Angel's in Shaftesbury Avenue, some whiskers and a wig from Clarkson's. I bought a coat in Hammersmith. I arrived at the Oxford at three-thirty. Suddenly I remembered that I had no make-up, but a friendly dresser came to my rescue. "That's all right, Jock. I'll get you some from next door."

That 'Jock' pleased me. I hadn't forgotten to speak with a fairly broad Scottish accent!

Once I was on the stage I was full of confidence. I knew my songs—I had written them! And judging by the reaction of the audience, I sensed that I had not failed in my audition. After the show Mr. Allen said he would like me to give another extra turn, at the Canterbury Music-Hall this time, before he made up his mind.

I duly appeared, but before going on for my turn I had a most embarrassing moment. Harry Lauder at the time was a howling success, and some resentment was being manifested by other comedians because of the show of impatience on the part of the audience to all turns preceding the great comedian. One of the turns that had suffered from this treatment was 'The Poluski Brothers'.

While I was dressing at the Canterbury, the dressing-room door opened and a couple of men walked in. They hesitated for a moment, but when they saw me wearing a kilt they merely grunted in disgust, turned on their heels and left the room with a "Jees! Here's another of that bloody tribe." It was 'The Poluskis'.

On the same bill was Florrie Forde. What a great-hearted woman she was! She stood on the side while I was singing, and as I walked off from my 'extra turn' she came up to me and said, "Young fellah, you got a grand voice; but you'll just have to put a bit more laughter in your songs, and then you can't go wrong," and with a smile, as she walked on to the stage, she said: "Good luck to you, lad." That was a most encouraging remark, particularly after the Poluski incident.

Some years later when I was singing in the Isle of Man we met in the hotel, and I reminded her of the incident. She wouldn't believe at first that I was Hector Grant. When she did: "Lumme! I wouldn't have believed it if you hadn't told me yerself. But one thing, Peter, I did say you had a fine voice. You must gimme credit for that."

As a result of the extra turns at the Oxford and Canterbury music-halls I was engaged for twelve weeks, opening at the Coliseum, Glasgow! (I did not tell my relatives there about my *début* as a Scottish comedian.) The salary was £15 per week.

The novelty of the idea interested me for a week or two and the experience I gained of music-hall audiences proved invaluable, but I was determined not to go on with the deception.

I had made a success—I knew from the 'curtains' I was taking after each performance. And the local managers were good enough to tell me that they had asked for a return date. I had taken Florrie Forde's advice and put more laughter into the act. After about four weeks I felt as confident as an old 'pro'.

When the tour was finally over—I had stipulated for twelve weeks only—Mr. Allen asked me to come and see him. He told me that he had received satisfactory reports from the local managers and that he would like me to do another tour of forty-eight weeks. The salary was to be raised to £25 per week, and that at the end of the tour he would star me at the Tivoli, in London. I told him that I could not accept the offer. To my surprise he said: "Look here, Hector! I like your turn. I'll tell you what, I'll give you a contract for a year at £40 per week, and star you at the Tivoli during that year."

It was a staggering offer at that time, and I must confess that for a moment or two I hesitated, but ultimately I knew that I could not possibly consider it seriously any longer. So I decided to be frank with Mr. Allen and confess my real identity. I said:

"Mr. Allen, I am afraid I have deceived you. I am not really Hector Grant; that is an assumed name for the purpose of making records of songs of the type sung by Harry Lauder. My real name is Peter Dawson. I am a baritone, and hope to make a success of my career as a singer. I did this Scottish comedian act because of the lack of concert engagements. My concert agent has already booked me for appearance this autumn at the London Promenade Concerts in the Queen's Hall."

Allen was, and looked, astonished. "Absolutely incredible. No wonder my managers sent me reports that you sing a fine song, and that they wanted return dates. But what a pity. You know, I believe you would make a fortune on the halls quicker than you would on the concert platform. But see here, Mr. Dawson, if ever you change your mind, and want to return to the music-hall, will you give me your promise to give me the first option on your services? If you do that, I will promise to keep your secret. Is that a fair proposition?"

I was happy to promise, and with that and a very cordial handshake I said good-bye to my life as a Scottish comedian— but I was wrong! My success as Hector Grant had intrigued the Gramophone Company, and because of my appearance on the halls they put a proposition to me that I did a short tour with one or two other H.M.V. artistes. The programme was to be divided into two parts. In the first I was to sing as Peter Dawson. In the latter end of the second half of the programme I was to appear, made-up, as Hector Grant.

The Gramophone was a great part in my life, and I decided to accept the proposal.

The tour was a great success, and to my knowledge no one knew that Peter Dawson and Hector Grant were one and the same man.

Some time later I met Harry Lauder at the recording-studio. I was making a Peter Dawson record. He was always an admirer of mine, and I have always had a soft corner in my heart for him. He was a supreme artiste. I shall never forget the wonderful work he did on Britain's behalf in America during the First World War.

On this particular day he approached me with that embracing smile of his and said: "Hello, Peter. D'ye ken Ah'm half roads th' day? Aye, Ah'm fifty."

After congratulating him, we chatted about old times, and he suddenly said, turning to Fred Gaisberg and myself: "Did ye no ken a chap by the name of Hector Grant? He had a grrrand voice. He must have been killed in the war."

I said to Fred, "Tell Harry who Hector Grant is."

Fred grinned, and in his quiet American way asked, "Didn't you know, Harry, that Hector Grant was Peter?"

But with obvious disbelief he replied: "Nah, nah, ye canna tell me that. I saw him in Glasgie. Yon was a much older man. And besides, I've come doon to mak' records an' no tae argue nonsense." And away he stalked, firm in his conviction that we had been trying to pull his leg!

I met him on several other occasions since that day, but I was never able to convince him that I was, in fact, Hector Grant, and now dear Sir Harry has passed over.

CHAPTER IV

FIRST AUSTRALIAN TOUR

AS a result of the Boosey incident I took the advice of Henry Mills and settled on a tour of Australia. And then I was faced with a distressing problem. I could not take my wife because of the expense, but we were both convinced that the opportunity of making a tour of my own country must not be missed. Nan, as usual, solved the difficulty by telling Miss Castles personally that Peter Dawson would gladly accept the offer to join her company in the tour.

Amy Castles' company included Anderson Nichol, the Scottish tenor; Victor Buesst, Australian pianist (brother of the celebrated conductor); and Adrian Amato, flautist; with, of course, Amy Castles.

I went through a wretched time before sailing. The realization that I could not take my wife made me very unhappy, especially as I knew my family would ask awkward questions. But Nan eventually succeeded in convincing me that I must think of the future. "When you sing in Australia you'll be a big success. Then you can make arrangements to take your own company out next time, and I shall be with you." And that is exactly what I did. She told me of her intention to study with Professor Kantorez while I was away, and promised that on my return she would have a repertoire which would surprise me.

I travelled out on the Orient liner *Otway*. The voyage was uneventful. As we approached Adelaide, my home town, I was boiling over with excitement. On the quayside I saw my mother and father and a huge crowd of relatives—the Dawson clan. For in addition to all my brothers and sisters, uncles, aunts, nephews, nieces, cousins, relatives by marriage of the first to the umpteenth degree turned up in force. And suddenly I was overcome with emotion. I think it was the sight of my darling mother smiling up at me with tears in her eyes. I remember feeling somewhat embarrassed and turning away. But fortunately at that moment a young man, one of those privileged to come aboard early, called out to me, "Mr. Dawson." I recognized him immediately. "Hullo, Brewer!" I yelled, and grabbed his hand in relief and in delight. "What are you doing aboard?" There was real astonishment on his face as he replied: "Good heavens! Fancy you

47

remembering me!" To which I was happy to answer: "Why shouldn't I remember my old school mate? And how's your finger now, Brewy?" Again his look of amazement made me laugh. "Cripes, fancy you remembering that too!" and he held up a broken finger. Naturally I was now completely at ease. Brewer explained that he was a reporter on a newspaper and wanted an interview. We had a short chat then but arranged for another meeting later, for I was about to get off the ship and meet my family. But at the bottom of the gangway I had another big and pleasant surprise waiting me. A crowd of newspaper reporters and photographers immediately surrounded me. However, they were no match for the Dawson clan. In a couple of moments the family had overrun the journalists. I was holding my mother in my arms and shaking my father's hand at the same time. The newspaper boys were quick to grasp the situation and signified their intention of contacting me later—at the station at Adelaide.

To say that I was surprised by the reception, the crowd and the enthusiasm is an understatement. Remember, I was only twenty-seven. I was knocked off my balance. It was all a complete and very wonderful surprise. And when in the train my dear father quietly warned me that a bigger welcome was waiting me at Adelaide station. "You had better have a few words ready, Peter. All sorts of folk are going to speak about you." Thanks to his insistence I was left alone for a few minutes to turn over in my mind some words of thanks I should have ready in answer to what might be said on my arrival.

When I alighted from the train a remarkable sight met my gaze. I was greeted almost immediately by the Mayor of Adelaide, who made a speech welcoming me home to my birth town. I remember returning thanks to the Mayor (and how grateful I was to my father for his wise advice), and then being greeted by hundreds of others. The next great moment was seeing my old music master, Mr. C. J. Stevens, again. We had an affectionate handshake, for he was the man who first discovered the potentialities of my voice. He had taught and encouraged me, and had finally won over my father to the idea of sending me to Britain to be trained by Sir Charles Santley.

From the station I was taken to the rehearsal hall of the Adelaide Choral Society, where the Society was assembled, and gave me a truly remarkable reception. Sir Josiah Simon made a most flattering speech of welcome, and then the Choral Society sang with gusto, "For He's a jolly good Fellow". I was presented with an enlarged framed photograph of the Society. It was in this hall that it was revealed to me why I was being welcomed so rapturously and, let me add with sincere gratitude, affectionately. From the speeches I learnt that my concert appearances in London had been the interest of Australian journalists in that city. They had noted my success and advised Australia accordingly, adding, I am proud to say, their own very kind encomiums. My more or less sensational success as a gramophone artiste, too, had been most generously hailed, not only in my own town, but throughout Australia. To say I was absolutely astonished is the only way to express my feelings. And what was particularly comforting to me as I listened to the kindly remarks of my fellow countrymen was the realization that I had not failed my father, and the man who had believed in me all through, Mr. Stevens.

My only regret was that Nannie was not with me. I could not tell my people or those who asked after my wife the real reason she did not accompany me. It would have been an incredible revelation to most of them had they been told that my big success in Britain had not been a correspondingly big financial one. Nevertheless, it was obvious to me that if I could make good in Australia it would mean the beginning of a brighter financial future. And how I looked forward to my first concert! It would mean so much to those who had been so kind, and it would be of the most vital importance for me to make a success after such generous acclamation.

After the reception by the Choral Society I was finally carried home in a sort of triumphant cavalcade. And here were my Press friends and photographers to welcome me on to my doorstep, as it were.

We had a very happy party that night. The effect my first song made will always be an ineffaceable memory. I chose "Sincerity". It seemed the most appropriate song to sing to such an affectionate gathering of relatives and friends. Let me confess I was very, very nervous. I suddenly realized what this song meant to my parents. They had not heard me sing since I left Australia as a raw youngster to have my voice trained. It would mean so much to them. They were to hear their boy sing as a professional vocalist for the first time.

I suppose it was to be expected that there would be tears of happiness. But my sister Agnes cried so healthily that the tension was relieved by the laughter that followed.

Naturally my first concert in Australia would be of special importance to me—and of course my parents and my old master.

D

It was to be in Melbourne. My mother and father accompanied me on the train to that city. But we were doomed to a disappointment. Outside the town of Murtoa a big wash-away had occurred following very heavy floods that had devastated and inundated vast areas of the land and washed away the railway line ahead of us for a considerable distance. The damage was beyond immediate repair, and we were held up at Murtoa for seven days!

Messages were sent through to Melbourne, but nothing could be done to get me to that city in time for my first concert.

My second concert at Melbourne had been scheduled for a week later. My contract was therefore postponed by Tait for a week, and this meant, for some strange reason, that I had to pay my own fare from Adelaide to Melbourne, or some other expense which I did not expect to pay, amounting to £3. This amount of money meant nothing to Tait but for reasons I have already explained it meant a lot to me, particularly after my unexpected stay at Murtoa. This rankled in my mind. But before telling you about my Melbourne concert I will tell you how I recovered the money. A week or so after the Melbourne concert we were travelling between Melbourne and Newcastle, and a game of poker started. The party consisted of John Tait, myself and three others. When the game ended and the score was added up, I had won £3. John Tait had lost just £3, and the other three had finished about as they started. Turning to John Tait I said, "Well, John, I had to fight like hell to get it, but I'll take this three pounds from you with particular pleasure, because it just compensates me nicely for the fare you refused to pay when the floods stopped me appearing at my first concert in Melbourne."

John merely grunted, and reached for his hat. We met many times after that on railway trains, but we never had another game of poker. However, he could not and did not resist the old challenge, "John, I'll toss you for two shaves." And we would toss and John would win. I never did win a toss against John for two shaves, and we tossed many times. When I think back, he must have used a coin given to him by Don Bradman's father.

To return to my tour.

On my arrival at Melbourne I had another agreeable surprise in the reception that awaited me at the station. There was another Press reception, and they were particularly kind in their references to me. But when I walked on to the platform for my first song I was 'hit' back by the loud, absolutely spontaneous, outburst of applause. It was a truly wonderful moment in my life, and

I was genuinely overcome. I bowed again and again, but instead of the applause ending, it went on and on. And I was grateful when my accompanist decided that enough was as good as a feast, and played the introductory notes for my first song. This was that fine song, popular wherever I go, "O ruddier than the Cherry". And the success that greeted the song was truly gratifying. For remember, this was my first song given to an Australian audience, and in my heart I had dreaded the possibility of failing to live up to the reputation that had reached my country ahead of me. But the applause soon set my troubled mind at rest. An artiste can always 'sense' the reaction of an audience, and I was in no doubt that I had achieved what I was so anxious to—success before my own people and my parents. I was tremendously happy, and remarked to my accompanist, "I feel like the Cock o' the North." I forget the full number of songs, but I remember that I sang "Little grey Home in the West", "The Sergeant of the Line", "Phil the Fluter's Ball" and "The Mountains o' Mourne". I know I gave about a dozen songs. Normally the other artistes would have objected to me taking up so much of the programme, but they were good enough to realize that this was a special occasion and were as delighted as myself at the success I had so obviously made on my home ground, and on my first appearance.

The Press the following day were most kind and, in fact, very generous in their praise. But the happiest people in the whole wide world were my mother and father.

I have been grateful to one critic all my life, for it was he who, having given me a splendid notice, regretted that I had not sung better material. He mentioned "O ruddier than the Cherry", writing that I had sung this with fine effect, clearly demonstrating my ability to sing songs other than those that might be called the smoking-concert type of song. And he went on to say about my rendering of "O ruddier than the Cherry": "This was given with fine effect; the *aria* was of exceeding volubility and meaning, the singer phrasing the theme delightfully with an evenly sustained flow of tone, and perfect breathing control."

Despite the full and hearty praise of all the other critics and my personal triumph, I took this critic's advice with gratitude. And from that moment I determined to better my musical outlook.

I decided that on my return to London I would make that my first task. And in due course I did. I studied and acquired a repertoire of German *Lieder*. Later, at the Wigmore Hall in London, I gave a recital which included German *Lieder*, French and Russian songs. That I had succeeded in my efforts to take the

Melbourne critic's advice can be gathered from the fine reception I earned and the unanimous praise of the critics the next day. And forgive me if I give you the words of the most feared musical critic in London in those days. He wrote: "Hitherto I had known Peter Dawson to be a singer of note of gramophone records, but in the Wigmore Hall last night I maintain that if he cared he would become one of the world's greatest *Lieder* singers."

My success in Melbourne was most gratifying and it increased at each concert. I was very conscious that I was in good voice. At first I put this down to not smoking or taking any strong alcoholic drink whatever, but I became convinced later that it was the climate. To this day I find that in Australia my voice is clearer and easier and just a little more resonant than it is in Britain, and yet for some inexplicable reason my records are very much better in Britain than in Australia.

On several occasions I have been compelled to remake a number of my Australian records in London because they were not satisfactory.

It is probably 'atmosphere'. I remember my brother-in-law Tommy Noble telling me that when he first joined the Edison Bell Company as recording manager, although a recording-studio was designed with the same material, the same size, the same recording diaphragm, the wax cylinder at the same heat, and the funnels of the same size, shape and metal as that used by the Edison Company in New Jersey, U.S.A., the 'tone' was entirely different.

I suppose there is an explanation somewhere, but I don't know what it is. It's rather like drinking tea in France or Belgium. They use Indian tea, pour boiling water on to it, but it still does not taste like tea. And it's beyond me to tell you what it does taste like. Certainly something unearthly. But that I sing better in Australia than anywhere else is an axiom.

On 7 August, 1909, the concert that I had been looking forward to since my arrival in Australia was reached. This was my first appearance before my own townspeople at Adelaide.

Never before or since have I looked forward to singing at a concert with so much relish as I did at this one. I had established the fact in my own mind that I had been blessed with success in my Australian tour, and that gave me enormous confidence to face the critical audience of Adelaide. Nan has kept the letter I wrote after the concert, and an extract from this will give my feelings of the occasion better than my memory could recall:

"No sooner had I set foot on the platform than a regular storm of applause and 'bravos' rent the air. And it was fully three minutes before silence was restored. And then the silence was eerie. Like myself, everybody seemed pent up with excitement, waiting for my first notes. I sang 'She alone'. I sang well, although you can imagine I was very tired after an eighteen hours' journey from Melbourne. And when I finished with my low 'E' there was a wonderful burst of applause which went on and on, and in the midst of it I was handed up a wreath of laurel tied with tartan ribbons, with a card inscribed 'Welcome to your native heath'. The excitement was great, and of course there were further demands for songs, to which I complied with real pleasure. I must say that I was as excited as those in the audience, and I ran up and down the platform stairs on thin air—holding my wreath like some big fool.

All the Dawson clan was there, shivering like jellies with excitement. Dear old Mum had a silent weep, and so did all my sisters. I sang seven times during the night, including a double encore. And to make matters even more pleasant my dear old master, Mr. Stevens, played my accompaniments, and, barring a little fumbling owing to excitement, did them remarkably well. Mrs. Stevens was also present, prouder of her husband for this accomplishment than for whatever he had done before.

When the concert was over and I came down the steps outside the hall I came in for a very rough time. The crowd scrambled for pieces of my laurel wreath as a souvenir. Fortunately, my big brother Bill was next to me and he saved the wreath from disintegration—I hope I have spelt that right—and I was able to reach the cab without losing any clothes. It was all very thrilling, and I enjoyed it thoroughly.

I finally got home at 11 p.m., and was happy to take a running jump into some nice clean sheets and enjoy a good sleep."

In the letters I wrote to my wife during my tour I have come across some remarks I have made about places I visited or something I have experienced, and I shall finish this chapter with a few extracts from these letters.

"Sydney.
30 Sept., '09.

This morning brother Bill and I ran down in the car to Cogee. This is a lovely seaside resort. The day is beautiful with a clear blue sky, and not a breath of wind. This place knocks anything I've met for years. Cogee is a celebrated place for surf-bathing. The tremendous breakers from Southern Ocean simply roar in, and the bathers are uncannily clever in the manner they shoot or ride them. Sharks swarm there, but are too afraid to come within reach of the bathers. At least, that's what I was told. But don't send me a cable 'not to attempt a bathe, or else . . .'. It may be quite true that the sharks are too scared, but not half as scared as I should be. Sydneyites are great people for entertainment. All the shows here are packed out. And I am told it's always the same."

> "Brisbane.
> 3.10.09.

Here I am safe and sound after a wretched train journey from Sydney. Am installed in this nice hotel at 30s. per week, including food and everything! How does that strike your eye, Nan? George Castles, brother Bill, Nichol and myself are allotted the second floor. The rooms are excellent—everything being spotlessly clean. The food is really great, with plenty of variety, and as much as you care to eat. As for fruit, it's in abundance—pineapples, bananas, oranges, pears, plums, figs, grapes, apples, in fact anything you can mention. Just think of it. And all for thirty bob a week! Add to this the fact that my appetite is absolutely shameful. I seem to be developing into a man with a gluttonous relish for food. I can only attribute this to the glorious air of this wonderful country."

> "*En route* to Gympie from Bundaberg.
> October 7th.

Well, this is a most marvellous country, and continues to surpass anything I ever dreamt of. The country we are passing through is filled with forests of palms, tree ferns, wattle, gum, cedar, banana and in fact all the tropical growths. There is an observation-car on the train and we are able to enjoy the glory of the country under the most favourable conditions. We have seen large teams of bullocks hauling timber down the mountain side at one place, and the team must have numbered fifty; hitched up two abreast. Can you imagine how thrilled I am at all these sights? We have passed hundreds of acres of sugar cane and pineapple fields, orange and lemon groves. You must see all this. The beauty is beyond description."

"Narribri.

20.10.09.

We travelled by coach from Warwick to this place. *A two-day journey*. The most uncomfortable ride I have ever suffered. I had a seat at the back and had a wonderful view of more of this great country. I saw thousands of rabbits, parrots and cockatoos, and a large-sized snake. The driver whirled his whip round and cut it across the back, and the snake tied itself into indescribable knots and then flew for its life.

At one point we passed a great waggonload of bales of wool drawn by twenty-eight oxen, an astonishing sight. The driver had a whip with a handle about ten feet in length and a lash as long again. He would whirl this enormous whip and cut whatever beast he wanted into line. He guides the oxen with the whip and yells frightful language at them. The loads of wool usually consist of about fifty bales, each worth about £15.

Wool growing is the chief industry in these parts of Australia, and the people are very prosperous. An ordinary working man gets 12s. per day, and the sheep shearers can earn as much as £5 per day. It's a common sight to see a rough-whiskered bushman stalk into a hotel bar, order a drink and toss down a ten- or twenty-pound note. Unfortunately, some of them get 'shickered' and look for a fight with anyone who might accommodate them. On my way to the concert one of a couple of rough bushmen said as I approached: 'Cripes, Bill! Look at that "pea" in his ruddy tea-gown. He's like a ruddy "Boshter" whisky advertisement in front, and a ruddy claw hammer behind.' I hurried on."

"West Maitland.

22.10.09.

This hotel is very comfortable (Page's Grand Central). The proprietor is an old musical-comedy comedian and a cousin of the popular Gaiety Theatre comedian, Edmund Payne. Of course, we had many a yarn and it made my stay very enjoyable.

A great admirer of mine, Dr. Barton of this town, gave me a fine day out. He took us (Nichol and myself) to see the largest sheep station in this country. The drive was simply glorious. But I roared with laughter at Nichol's face with his eyes almost falling out of their sockets as he watched hundreds of rabbits running like fury in front of our vehicle along the beaten track. I had seen this sort of thing before, but Nichol was positively dumbfounded.

When we arrived at Woollengabba (nice name) station we were met by the manager, a Mr. Scott, and he conducted us to the enormous shearing-sheds in which scores of men were hard at work shearing the sheep by machinery. It was a remarkable sight to watch these men at work. They could shear a sheep as quickly as you could peel a potato. But on the whole it is not a pleasant operation to watch. The men in their speed are unwittingly cruel —or appear so to the uninitiated—and the sheep who does not 'help' the shearer is very roughly handled. One man accidentally cut a large gash in one of the poor beasts—ripping its stomach for about six inches. And when he had taken off the wool he proceeded to sew the wound up with a needle and string.

Later we had lunch, and afterwards horses were saddled and away we went. My 'bronco' was a beauty and I had a grand gallop—the first for eight years. Later we chased a couple of dingos for miles, but they eluded our guns. Suddenly we came upon a scene which I will carry with me all my life. It was a flock of 20,000 shorn sheep.

The manager told me that one sheep yields six shillings' worth of wool a year, and after two years is sold to the butcher. The turnover from this station was £12,000 a year.

Mr. Page took us about fifteen miles out of Maitland to witness a prizefight. I've never seen a rougher-looking bunch of 'fans' in all my experience. They kept yelling at the referee: 'Hi, Ref! D'you want to be done in? Yer askin' fer it,' and so on. The last referee for a fight in Weston barely escaped with his life. He was badly beaten up. The referee tonight carried a revolver— conspicuously for all to see.

Most of the 'supporters' are miners, and it is not surprising with so few amenities the men find an outlet for their energy in fierce fighting. A few weeks earlier a man had been kicked to death after a straight fight. The custom is the old Welsh one, 'all-in'. If one of the brawlers falls to the ground the other fellow has the privilege of kicking him. After a few drinks the men can get very awkward walking along the streets. Mr. Page took the precaution of having us escorted by four of the boxers: O'Brien, Daphney, Miles and Williams."

"Shepparton.

17.11.09.

What a terrible journey from Wangaratta to this place! The joys of touring are beginning to pall when it includes painful travelling in almost unbearable heat. We caught the 9.15 a.m.

train, which took us as far as Benalla. From that little place we had to journey forty-two miles by brake. The roads were the worst I've ever experienced or *seen*. Chock full of pot-holes, and in many cases we had to crash over big protruding roots of gum-trees. And we were rattled, bumped, flung and jolted about quite helplessly. Amy Castles is quite ill as a result. I am all aches and pains.

At one place where we stopped for some refreshment and a little respite from our travail, all we had was polony sausage, bread and butter and tea. And wow! what tea. We were all very depressed and oh! so sore. A few miles further on we came upon a school of Gohanna lizards. Very large indeed. Some were the size of a sheep's body. They scuttled in all directions—a strange sight. But the male members of the party welcomed a little diversion and we got down from the brake, armed ourselves with sticks and tried to catch one. But, alas, no luck. They were too nimble, and in a few minutes they were safely away or hiding in the trees. But some of them looked down on us and opened their mouths in anger.

These lizards are a terrible pest to the farmers as they devour chickens, fowls or any live birds they can. Although they are most evil-looking and repulsive creatures they are not dangerous to humans.

On our arrival at Shepparton, after five and a half hours' brake ride, we looked like a set of dirty tramps; we were completely covered with a dirty white dust, as the roads are devoid of metal, and darned nearly a foot deep in dust. The drag was drawn by five fine horses, and you can therefore imagine the clouds of dust that enveloped us the whole way. I cannot conceive any worse conditions for anyone to travel under, but the effect it might have had on throats was giving us a lot of worry. Amy Castles was the most distressed, which was only natural, and she suffered great discomfort. We have all decided that there is to be no more of this kind of travelling.

Anyhow, a few hours later we were at the concert hall, and a more washed-out-looking lot of mortals you never did see. Poor Amy Castles was in tears. Nichol could hardly sing a note, and for the first time in my life it was an absolute task for me to sing. But after about twenty minutes' rehearsing my voice broke through the barrage of dust in my lungs. We all agreed that the Taits were hard taskmasters, but that they would not catch us again like that."

"Maryborough.

25.11.09.

The heat is overwhelming. A hundred and ten in the shade! I am at present perspiring like a bull, and panting like a pup."

"St. Arnaud.

28.11.09.

A beautiful bouquet had been sent to the stage door for 'Mme Amy Castles'. The doorman, quite unaccustomed to this sort of thing, decided that it must be given to the *diva* immediately. She was in the middle of one of her fine *arias*, when on to the platform thumped the doorman, oblivious to her singing, and handed her the bouquet. Naturally the whole house roared with laughter; but Amy was rightly embarrassed, annoyed and confused. And she decided it was best to leave the platform for a few minutes. She did not really recover from this incident, so that, when she arrived at the hotel and found her bedroom topsy-turvy, we can forgive her failure to enter into the spirit of the joke."

"Ballarat.

Dec. 3rd, '09.

This is the town in which I won the championship for bass singing nine years ago. I can only recognize the hotel near the station, and a couple of streets. The old hall is pulled down, and a new one, the Coliseum, capable of seating 7,000, erected in its place. We had a little upset in the train just before we arrived. We had been playing bridge, George Castles and myself as partners against Anderson Nichol and Victor Buesst. Towards the end of the journey George and I had some appalling cards. The game was brought to an abrupt and dramatic end when, after Victor Buesst had called 'Four no trumps', and George led a card, Dummy (Nichol) laid his cards on the table and showed four aces. This proved too much for George and he turned and threw his remaining hand of twelve cards out of the window. Poor Nichol was white with anger. Buesst merely shrugged his shoulders and said quietly, 'That's ten shillings you owe for the rubber; and a shilling for another pack of cards.' I laughed loudly not only at Victor's reaction, but the transfixed expression on Andy's face. It was quite a minute before he was able to find his voice, and anything he contemplated saying was lost—which was fortunate. George quickly apologized, saying: 'It was the last hand, and I have never played with such a rotten pack in my life.

Think of it, old man. One partner calls "Four no trumps" and his dummy lays down four aces.' "

"Geelong.
4.12.09.

When we arrived here a brass band was waiting to greet us, and the station was swarming with cheery people. The band was Australia's Champion Boys' Band. And they played the Mascagni 'Intermezzo' splendidly, and I was sincerely surprised at their fine tone and balance.

I arrived at the hotel about 6 p.m., and feeling very tired I threw myself on the bed for a short rest. I awoke quite suddenly at 8.30. The concert started at 8 o'clock! I leapt to the wash-basin, shaved and washed, and as I was dressing I heard the sound of hurried footsteps approaching my door. The door was thrown open and in rushed our manager Campbell, saying, 'For God's sake, Peter, are you all right?' I explained what had happened, and with his help I finished dressing and was out of the hotel, into the cab, and at the side of the platform at 8.55. Campbell had already announced that I had been delayed but would sing after Madame Castles.

This goes to prove how wrong it is to be overtired before a concert. It is not fair on the artiste or on the public."

An appendix at the end of the book gives the list of the tour to illustrate the hard labour such an itinerary meant. Amy Castles found the work particularly grim.

"Mount Gambier.
13.12.09.

Well, I am happy that we are back in South Australia, nearer to Adelaide. And what is more cheering, I am returning for special three concerts there before returning to Britain. These concerts are apart from my contract, and means additional fees.

In many places along the Victorian border we encountered swamps that reached the axles of the coach, and the four horses made the water fly in all directions, and of course over all we travellers. The forty-eight miles' run took seven hours. We had left at 10.30 a.m. and arrived at Mount Gambier at 5.30 p.m. There was no concert that night and I went to bed about 8 o'clock. I was tired and wanted to see Gambier in the morning. At 7.30 a.m., after a welcome shower and breakfast, Campbell and I set out to climb Mount Gambier, about a mile away. The morning was beautiful and cool, and we soon arrived at the crater. And what an impressive sight it is.

At some time unknown to history, this mountain was in eruption. After the eruption the crater became inexplicably filled with perfect fresh water from underground rivers. The depth of the water is unknown; and as I gazed down with the sun shining on its surface I saw it was a glorious deep blue. At times it changes to a milky white, due to disturbances below.

All the water used in the town comes from this blue lake. And it never rises or falls above a certain level."

"Adelaide.
16.12.09.

With my mother and father again. A wonderful reunion. I have been busy relating all my experiences.

The concert here was another big success. The second part of the programme was composed of excerpts from oratorios and operas. I sang 'Honour and Arms'. I had to sing it twice; they yelled for it. Then 'O Star of Eve'. At the second concert I sang 'O ruddier than the Cherry'. I took the top 'C', and it brought the audience to its feet! But something happened to the orchestra: I don't know who won, but it was a race between the piccolo and myself."

"Adelaide.
Christmas Day 1909 and Boxing Day.

I was glad to be here for Christmas. A great reunion of the Dawson clan. But the H E A T ! On Xmas Day it hovered between 110 and 115. It was almost unbearable at the concert Xmas night. Everything and everywhere was red hot. It's the furnace heat of the North wind. The wind comes down from Central Australia, and across its sandy deserts, and of course gathers up heat all the way. Nichol's collar capsized under the weight of perspiration."

"December 27th.

It's hot enough to burn the thatch off my head. Shall be glad to get to Tasmania, where it is sure to be cooler."

"Hobart.
January 1st, 1910.

I don't think I have sung better than I did last night, on my first appearance in Tasmania. The Press notices are grand. All the same, I missed the fun and gaiety of our New Year's Eve in old London. Nichol and I went out at midnight, but apart from a lot of noise there was little to compensate my memory.

The company took a trip out to Point William today, eleven miles out. Through some magnificent scenery. I don't think I have seen anything more beautiful than the Bay. When you and I make our tour in two years' time we must include Tasmania. You will love it."

"Euroa.
12.1.10.

Lord Kitchener is here and is stirring things up. He is at present visiting the encampment at Seymour, where the crack Australian regiments are quartered. I have not seen him yet, but I hope to before he leaves."

"Seymour.
Jan. 17.10.

This place is crowded with soldiers, they are camped here in honour of Kitchener. You should see them. They are fine specimens of men, and the majority are magnificent horsemen. The town is decorated with bunting and flags of all kinds. A very cheery sight. The man who is running the concert here is a Chinaman, Lee Yet. He speaks the English of the English, and is very popular. It's quite surprising the polished style of his conversation, and his 'really "exquisite" manners', as Amy Castles puts it. I decided to ask him where he learnt to speak such good English. 'Well, you see, Mr. Dawson, I was educated at Harrow and later Oxford.' "

"Nhill.
Feb. 2.10.

This is the last of the small concert towns. And now for the return journey home."

And so my first memorable tour of Australia came to an end, and I sailed from Perth after a wonderful send-off. Almost all the town bade me farewell, and I can be pardoned for feeling the most important man in the world at that particular time.

What were my reactions to the tour?

First of all the realization that I had made a success. That was not egoism, I had my Press notices. I intended to study these on the boat, and 'take notice' where advice was given to accept it.

And let me say at once that the advice of the Australian critics has proved a very great help in my career.

My second reaction was concerned with the necessity of studying very carefully any future contract I might sign. True, I was a comparatively young man, but the tour was more or less hard labour for half the time. When I signed the contract it was for three months. I had overlooked the clause that Tait Brothers had the option of extending it for another three months *on the same terms*.

I had agreed to accept a fee of £22 per week, but it never entered my head that I might be called upon to sing as many as *six concerts in a week at various places*.

I endeavoured to cancel the extra three months, or have my fee raised, but the Taits were adamant. And let me say that I can appreciate their point of view. I had, as they reminded me, signed the contract 'of my own free will'. It was a salutary lesson, and part and parcel of the experience I had to gain in my career. But nevertheless I had appeared at 81 concerts in 20 weeks!

My last reaction was the vital necessity of extending my repertoire. And on my return to London that was to be my first concern.

Here is the list of the songs I used during the tour:

1. "O Ruddier than the Cherry"
2. "Sincerity"
3. "Young Tom o' Devon"
4. "Mountains o' Mourne"
5. "Arrow and the Song"
6. "O Star of Eve"
7. "Honour and Arms"
8. "Why do the Nations"
9. "It is Enough"
10. "Arm, Arm, ye Brave"
11. "She alone charmeth my sadness"
12. "Rocked in the Cradle of the Deep"
13. "Little Grey Home in the West"
14. "Sergeant of the Line"
15. "Phil the Fluter's Ball"
16. "Mad Dog"
17. "I am a Roamer"
18. Solos in *Garden of Allah*
19. "Off to Philadelphia"
20. "My old Shako"
21. "Droop not, young Lover"
22. "What might have been"
23. "Haste to the Fair"
24. "Rip Van Winkle"
25. "Bonnie Banks of Loch Lomond"
26. "Kangaroo and Dingo"
27. "Rolling down to Rio"
28. "A Corner in your Heart"
29. "The Drummer Boy"
30. " 'Tis I"

Looking through this today I find that less than half of them survive, or perhaps it would be better to say that I do not continue to sing them. And these are primarily the classics—oratorio and operatic. Some of the popular numbers, and they were very good songs (and many of them sung still) that I rarely sing today, include "Sincerity", "Rocked in the cradle of the Deep", "The mad Dog", "Little grey Home in the West", "I'm a Roamer", "Off to Philadelphia", "My old Shako", "What might have been", "Rip Van Winkle", "Rolling down to Rio", "A Corner in your Heart", "The Drummer Boy" and " 'Tis I".

The song that met with the greatest success on the tour throughout Australia was Handel's "O ruddier than the Cherry", from his *Acis and Galatea*. And this was followed by "Sincerity". "Sincerity" was a favourite of mine. It was the song, too, that my parents, and Nan's parents, always wanted to hear me sing.

My one regret on the tour was that we only gave "The Messiah" once. I enjoy singing oratorio, and "The Messiah" is my favourite.

CHAPTER V

THE 'PROMS'

I WAS so anxious to reach London after my successful Australian tour that I took only a cursory interest in the sea trip. I do remember that I felt I was now a man of experience! I had been hailed as a successful singer in Australia, and had been interviewed by the Press in every town I appeared. It gave me a sense of confidence that I had lacked on the outward journey. That feeling of 'being somebody' is indescribable. It is sometimes the curse of success, that thankfulness can turn to conceit. I am satisfied that I have never let success get to my head. There is nothing I abhor more than conceit in an artiste.

On the boat I had time to ruminate on my tour, and to study the various aspects governing my future. I had returned to my home and made my parents happy. The people who had believed in my future as a singer had been vindicated. And as for myself, I was the happiest young man alive!

A few days after my arrival at my London home I had a most agreeable surprise. I knew that my wife Nan had a really good voice, and had sung with success all over Britain. But while I was away she was determined to be ready with a repertoire of songs that would satisfy the most discriminating of the critics. To this end she had been studying with Professor Kantorez. Imagine my surprise when I discovered that Nan had not only improved her very beautiful soprano voice, but had studied a really fine collection of songs. She had taken serious cognizance of the remarks the Melbourne critic had made about my repertoire, and she was not going to make my mistake.

My next agreeable surprise was a communication from William Boosey, who had barred me from any concerts under his jurisdiction and had practically forced me to make a tour abroad. His letter was extremely kind. He suggested that we 'bury the hatchet' and 'let bygones be bygones', and ended his letter, "and I want you to be the principal baritone in the Chappell's Ballad Concerts this season"!

That was in 1910. And I can borrow a phrase of that great man Winston Churchill and say that this was the beginning of the beginning of my career. I had made a successful tour of Australia, and on my return had been appointed to the coveted position of principal baritone with the 'Emperor' of Bond Street, William Boosey. And I did not ask 'How much?'

Boosey was responsible for the success of the Promenade Concerts, in which he not only found and encouraged young artistes but gave encouragement and opportunities to budding conductors.

Some of the younger generation of budding composers who were contemporaries with me included Montague Phillips, Haydn Wood and Eric Coates.

All these composers owed their early success to the influence of William Boosey. Boosey never made a mistake in diagnosing musical ability in an artiste. His way of helping young composers was most revolutionary. He did not merely accept their work for presentation, but allowed the young fellows to conduct their own compositions. In this way he gave the composer the opportunity of presenting his creation in the manner he wrote it. It is true that some of them were literally terrified when called upon to conduct a famous orchestra, and they walked on to the rehearsal platform as nervous wrecks. But musicians are kind-hearted souls, quick to recognize genius or unusual musical accomplishment, and the young men were immediately put at ease by their kindly and spontaneous co-operation.

Dr. Richter, the famous German conductor, was in London around this time. Another brilliant conductor, Nikisch, was also appearing, and he was acclaimed by the Press as a young man with the ball at his feet. Richter, of course, was already an established artiste. He was a musical genius.

Nikisch was extraordinarly strict in his teaching of senior students. Unless they were capable of playing from a full orchestral score he would not 'waste time' in instruction. Frankly, I have only seen one man do this on the piano, Albert Coates, although Sir Malcolm Sargent did with the orchestral score of *Hiawatha*. But on the other hand Richter could play all the Wagnerian operas by memory! He knew all the interlacing parts of the orchestra, the voices and the harmonies. He would play the piano from the full score at rehearsals. And he noted miraculously the rendition of every member of the ensemble. He would say, "You did not come in just here," and correct a passage by a singer, and so on. His mind was unique. He seemed to possess a quintuple brain.

He did inestimable good to young British conductors and instrumentalists with his advice and instruction, a tyrant for work, but a genius in his understanding and knowledge of music.

Yes, he was somewhat arrogant in his approach to British

E

musical accomplishment, and a little contemptuous of our instrumentalists. Later he was the first to admit that British composers, instrumentalists and conductors would take their place in the world of music, and might ultimately lead the world, but he never changed his opinion about British music audiences. He considered them the worst in Europe. He once told me that he 'almost despaired' of making even a London audience music-conscious! That was many years ago. He would realize what a great change has taken place were he able to pay us a visit today—nearly forty years later.

Other famous men like the late Landon Ronald, Adrian Boult and Malcolm Sargent were making slow but sure progress in the musical world at that time. Landon Ronald, who originally started as an accompanist, made a sensational success with his beautiful song "Down in the Forest". From that moment he made rapid headway as a composer, conductor, and finally as head of the famous Guildhall School of Music.

Montague Phillips made his first great success with his beautiful work *The Rebel Maid*. Unfortunately, almost immediately after it was produced there was a coal strike, and the receipts dropped—as they did in every theatre at that time. But in the contract for *The Rebel Maid* production there was a clause which stated that if the receipts fell below a certain amount for two weeks the show would be taken off. And that was the fate of this magnificent musical.

Of course it has been revived many times with success. Haydn Wood's most popular successes were "Roses of Picardy" and "A Brown Bird singing". Both these composers have added a valuable chapter to British music over the past thirty years.

Apropos of "A Brown Bird singing", I came to loathe the song a year or two later. But only for a while. I was a judge at a musical festival in Douglas, Isle of Man, and had to adjudicate solo voices. One of the songs chosen by the committee for a test was "A Brown Bird singing". I had to listen to that lovely song sung fifty different times! By the end of the session I felt that if I didn't escape from it I should go scatty!

Fortunately I was born with a sense of humour and it helped me in my task. Luckily, too, the judges were screened from the singers, or otherwise they might have been very severely jolted by the sight of some of the very respectable judges almost rolling off their seats with smothered laughter at some of the renderings of "The Bird". It was lucky that Haydn Wood did not have to suffer as we did. I believe he would have run completely off the island!

At the end of the contest I had to listen again to the finalists, and give my verdict for the first, second and third winners. The singers were judged on 1, Voice; 2, Diction; 3, Appearance; 4, Deportment.

Incidentally Haydn Wood's other winner, "Roses of Picardy", I often sing today. And I am always receiving requests to sing it from all parts of the country. A great tribute to a fine song and a brilliant composer.

All the composers I have mentioned in this chapter were good pianists. Fritz Kreisler once told me that if he had not made the fairly rapid success he did with the violin he would have switched to the piano. He was passionately fond of it. But, like the wise man he was, he resisted the temptation to play it too often. "It is a mistake to have two loves—both in life and in music," he told me. And he very rarely played the piano—that is, seriously—in the later days of his brilliant career.

Landon Ronald, on the other hand, lived for the piano. In a recording-studio when chatting with other artistes he would suddenly move away, and in a moment or two he would be playing the piano, which up till then nobody but Landon had noticed in the room.

And now to my first engagement to appear at a Promenade Concert at the Queen's Hall.

Here I met for the first time that mercurial man, Henry Wood. By this time he had established his reputation, and he was, as the war communications used to say, consolidating his position.

I remember that the other artistes appearing on the programme were most circumspect in the presence of the maestro at the rehearsals. Whether it was my Australian upbringing or my ignorance of the position he held in the musical world I do not know, but I must confess that I could not enthuse over Henry Wood's great musical accomplishments. I admired his zest; his determination to succeed; and his sincere love of music, but I could never appreciate his work as a conductor, particularly when conducting an orchestra accompanying a singer, and especially myself.

He had a strangely brusque way of quashing artistes, and in those days few dared to protest. "Don't take him too seriously," was the advice given me by a well-known tenor; "he does not mean to be hard, and he is very competent." This remark was made to me after I had an exchange of opinion with Henry over a certain pause I wanted made in a number I was to sing. After

I had very respectfully indicated what I desired, Wood shouted: "What nonsense. Whoever heard of such abuse?" To his surprise (and my own) I said, "Nevertheless, Mr. Wood, that is how I should like to sing it, please." When we tried the phrase over with the orchestra I noticed Wood was nodding his head in agreement at the improvement. A grand gesture indeed. Afterwards he asked me who had made the annotations in the score. When I informed him that it was Santley, he smiled and said: "Oh. He's right. It's a big improvement." We got on better after that!

Later I was surprised to learn that he had originally been trained to become a painter, and had spent some time in Paris under one of the great masters. I have not discovered why he gave up the brush for the baton, but it did explain some of his emotional idiosyncrasies.

Throughout his musical career he was a man who always 'sat in the driver's seat'. That is not a fault, as his remarkably successful life proved. We became good friends over the years, and I was able to understand his adamantine front, but we had one severe duel over a song I put on at the last Promenade Concert before the B.B.C. took over the Proms. The song I sung was "Boots". It met with spontaneous success. I was about to take a bow because of the tumultuous applause, when he stood in my way in a towering rage, and shouted: "Don't ever sing rubbish like that here again. Boots, Boots . . . sing them songs that uplift 'em. Brahms or Schubert." Before I could answer I had to take a few more calls. Then I went up to him and said, "Do you seriously call 'Boots' rubbish?" And then I added, "If you do, you are insulting Rudyard Kipling."

And with that I walked proudly away. The audience were still applauding "Boots".

Henry was too surprised to answer. But later, in the dressing-room, he came to me, and we laughed it off. The song had been the success of the concert, and he was the first to admit it. Sir Henry had a sense of humour, too, and he proceeded to pull my leg about some new records issued by the Columbia Company of a one-thousand voice choir. He was working exclusively for Columbia, and I for H.M.V. Incidentally, these records were creating a sensation, but only for the proverbial nine days. The director of recording (in America) of the Columbia Company had decided to install a recording machine in one of the concert halls, and make a record of a huge choir. It was a success, and the record caused a world-wide sensation. I had just been given a bonus cheque by the Gramophone Company, and some nice remarks had been published about my sales. Henry was humorously kidding me to look to my laurels. It was all in good fun.

But suddenly this jolly occasion was marred by another incident involving poor Henry. A young man was smoking a pipe near him, and Henry turned to this chap and yelled: "For heaven's sake put that pipe out, please. It smells!"

To the astonishment of everyone, including myself, the young man yelled back in a cultured voice: "You can go to hell. I'm not putting this perfectly clean pipe out for you, or any other temperamental stick waggler."

Henry just shrugged his shoulders, and whispered to me: "I'll see that these stars' dressing-rooms are not used by any Tom, Dick or Harry in future. I don't suppose he has the slightest right to be here." And he left the room hurriedly, but not before I had noticed how the incident had affected his bad eye. The lids of one of his eyes, I am not sure which, had a habit of perpetually blinking. This blinking or winking became more pronounced under nervous stress. And it was most disconcerting until you became accustomed to it.

Talking of Henry's bad eye reminds me of an incident that occurred when the late Malcolm McEachern (Jetsam, of Flotsam and Jetsam) made his first appearance at a Promenade Concert with Henry Wood.

There is no doubt that this flickering eyelid of Henry Wood's worried Mac very much. The conductor always insisted that the vocalist should watch him during the song—not to sing to him; but to 'keep the baton in his vision'.

After Mac had finished his two numbers he walked off the platform in a towering rage. "When that —— comes off, I'm going to crack him as sure as I'm an Aussie." Robert Newman finally got a chance to fathom the reason for Mac's anger. "Do you think I'm going to allow that fellah to wink at the orchestra while I'm singing, as though I was a complete bloody dud?" Mac thundered.

It didn't take the tactful Newman a few moments to relieve Mac's mind.

Which reminds me of another incident in which Mac gave a more demonstrative display of his anger. It occurred at the Savoy Hotel, London, at the inaugural lunch of the Australians in London, to launch "The Society of Australians in London".

Winston Churchill was the guest of honour. The High Commissioner, Sir Stanley Bruce (later Lord Bruce), was in the chair.

At my table, in addition to Mac, were fellow Australians. Suddenly the cheery atmosphere round the table was disturbed by Mac, with raised voice shouting: "Well, I'm damned! Would you believe it? Not a ruddy Australian wine mentioned on the list!"—followed by a stentorian "Waiter!" When the waiter arrived, Mac asked, "Have you any Australian wine?" To which the waiter replied: "No, sir. We have no Australian wine, but we have some very good South African wines." That did it. Mac's fury rose to boiling point. He demanded the presence of the manager. The manager committed the same *faux pas* as the waiter; "We have no Australian wine, but we have some good South African wines."

Mac then demanded a messenger who could go to Australia House at once. The messenger arrived immediately. (Mac could look most formidable in a temper.) He despatched the messenger to Australia House, about a quarter of a mile away, and fifteen minutes later a number of bottles of Australian wines were placed on the table.

The wine, however, did not appease Mac, and it was now obvious to all at the table that Mac was hell bent for making trouble. It came in a few moments. Getting to his feet, he asked the permission of the chairman to make a toast. This was granted, and Mac called out, "The Australians at this table would like to take wine with those who, like ourselves, are drinking Australian wine, at this Australian lunch."

There was an ominous pause, the buzz of whispering, but not one man stood up. "Well," shouted Mac, "all I can say is that you're a lousy lot of cows!" and sat down, his face showing genuine disgust.

'Cows' by the way, as used by Mac in the above expression, is a commonplace word in Australia, meaning 'a mean fellow'.

I don't know what reaction came from Churchill, but I do know that Winnie seemed to thoroughly enjoy the incident, for he turned to his immediate neighbour with a beaming face, and the other fellow laughed uproariously.

Dear old Mac! His early death was a great shock to his many pals.

Returning to Henry Wood, I was always intrigued by the system he used to ensure that his orchestra was in tune. As the players came on to the platform to take their places for rehearsal they had to pass by Henry, who was seated next to a huge tuning fork. He would strike the tuning fork, and the musician would sound his 'A'. Henry then gave out his order: A little up or a little down. When he was satisfied, he passed the musician on and the next would sound his 'A', and so on.

Perhaps the most amusing story concerning this tuning ceremony was a joke played by five 'cellists, including Cedric Sharpe and Lauri Kennedy. Cedric Sharpe played his 'A', was told by Henry a little up and then a little down, and finally passed. Cedric walked away and passed his 'cello to the second player, who approached the maestro, sounded the 'A' and was told to put it up a trifle and then down a trifle. The 'cellist then passed the 'cello to the third player, who again was told to put it down a trifle, and then up a little. The five 'cellists used the same 'cello! Henry was never told of this trick.

Perhaps the strangest incident in this tuning affair was the joke played by that brilliant trombonist, Tom Gutteridge. Tom walked to the side of Henry, pulled out his trombone slide, but did not blow the 'A'. Wood nodded his head and said, "That's quite all right!"

I was never able to discover whether Henry Wood carried through this tuning ceremony to impress upon his orchestra the vital necessity of being in tune, or to ascertain that every member of the orchestra was present! Whatever the reason, the members of the orchestra immediately commenced to tune up *after* Henry had listened to their 'A's'.

*   *   *

As a result of my experience at the Proms our association with Kantorez was renewed, for I decided to study grand opera, with Nan, under this clever teacher. And by hard work we succeeded in mastering a fairly representative repertoire.

In addition I decided to arrange a *pot-pourri* of *arias* from the operas for Nan to sing. This was revolutionary, and Kantorez, although most appreciative of my construction, was most apprehensive as to what would happen to me when the publishers heard what I was doing. Nevertheless I finished a *pot-pourri* of the soprano *arias* of *Cavalleria Rusticana*.

To avoid any trouble with the publishers I thought it wiser not to launch them in England, for by this time I had made up my mind to return to Australia with Nan as promised, and on the way back pay a visit to South Africa. And it was in South Africa that Nan first sang the *pot-pourri* from *Cavalleria*. It was acclaimed by the critics. But instead of pleasing, it worried me, for I knew that I had no right to write these *pot-pourris*, and the publicity might reach the ears of the publishers. However, realizing that the critics took no exception to the idea, we went ahead and during the tour Nan also sang *pot-pourris* I arranged of *La Tosca* and *Madame Butterfly*.

But at least we did manage to introduce a new idea in the first tour we did together of the West of England. Singing under the name of Annette George, Nan gave *arias* from several of the operas. The first was "One Fine Day" from Puccini's *Madame Butterfly*.

That West Country tour convinced me that we were ready to undertake an overseas tour. We were working extremely hard in our studies: Nan on the operatic and choral side, myself on operatic, choral and *lieder*.

Before a couple of years had passed I had corrected the error revealed by the Melbourne critic, and now possessed a repertoire that Charles Tree said was "not only remarkable, but the most extensive that he had ever encountered in his experience, including as it did the full range of operatic, choral, *lieder* and art songs". And then Charles added: "But, Peter, you are exceptionally lucky. You have the full repertoire of the bass, bass-baritone and baritone. It must be unique. I know of no other artiste—living or dead—blessed with such a range." This latter remark was made after he heard me give top A♭.

Apropos of my exceptional range, I recall the compliment paid to me by that great Italian baritone Sammanco, who listened while I made a record at the H.M.V. studio. After the session was over he patted me on the shoulder and said: "Bravo. Very good, very good. But how you get the range? You sing two songs—one bass, the other baritone." And after hesitating to find the appropriate words in English he added, "You sing the low E from underneath the stool, and the A♭ above it."

It was Battistini who gave me the advice to take off my collar and loosen my shirt when singing for record purposes. "You come and watch me." And I did. He took off his tunic, waistcoat, collar, shirt and braces! "That is how I should like to sing on the stage. And this is why I like so much, singing for the records." He was a lovable character, always cheery, full of jokes, and ready to have a word with any of the staff. He acquired an almost legendary fame for his vocal mastery.

I studied his rendering of the Prologue of *Pagliacci* on the advice of Kantorez, who declared that Battistini was a genius in the art of perfect vocalizing.

But there was one critic who resented my range. He wrote (in Australia) that "If Peter Dawson persists in singing 'out of his collar-stud' he will have no voice left in a year." Twelve years later he was kind enough to show me the cutting, and apologized for his, as he put it, "pretty poor prognostication".

CHAPTER VI

AUSTRALIAN AND NEW ZEALAND TOURS
WITH MY OWN COMPANY

BUT to return to the next step in my career; the tour of Australia and New Zealand with my own company.

The first big shock I received in making the necessary preparations for the tour was one that I expect many men have encountered in one form or another.

It was the realization of the responsibilities of a married man!

In making arrangements for the tour, the fact that my wife would require a considerable wardrobe had not entered my head.

When I did realize it, and the full extent of the number of different dresses required for a six months' tour, with sometimes six concerts a week, I remarked to Nan: "Well, I have just been working it out. I believe that if we are careful, and nothing interferes with our programme, we ought to pay off the dress bill with the first *sixty* concerts."

But that it was imperative to have a good number of dresses to fit all occasions was common sense. And so I explained the situation to the Gramophone Company, and I was given a good deal of extra work which removed that worry.

The day came when, fully equipped, sartorially and musically, we left for our Australasian tour.

At the station, representatives of the Gramophone Company, the music publishers and the Press came along to wish us godspeed. And I felt very proud and grateful for their kindness.

On the ship the cabin had been filled with glorious bouquets from friends and relatives. What a contrast to my previous voyage, when I had travelled alone, and had had to watch every penny I spent!

On the ship we enjoyed a good rest, and with a small portable piano in our cabin we were able to practice in comfort.

The journey passed off without incident, and we duly arrived in Australia ready for our own tour.

Now, although I had made progress in my career in Britain, I can be forgiven a little anxiety as to how Australia would receive me as the principal of a programme, when two years before I had been merely a supporter in Miss Amy Castles' programme. I have always been sensitive about 'trying to ride before you can walk', and therefore I was keen to see what kind of welcome we should receive.

On the quayside our reception was wonderful. Apart from friends and relatives, the Press came along for photographs and interviews, and the local dignitaries were kind enough to give me an official welcome.

It was up to me now to show whether I was good enough to lead my own company in a tour of Australia and New Zealand. I was confident that I had improved my repertoire; that I was in good voice; and I had studied and worked very, very hard.

Here is a copy of the first notice I read the morning after the opening concert:

"An audience which filled the Jubilee Exhibition Hall in every seat welcomed Mr. Peter Dawson, the South Australian basso, who has won world-wide fame as a concert artiste, last night on the occasion of his first public appearance since his return to his native country.

Nothing more enthusiastic than the greeting accorded Mr. Dawson could have been desired by any artiste. His appearance on the platform was the signal for hearty and prolonged applause, and he had repeatedly to bow his acknowledgements before he could open his programme. Similar scenes followed each of his songs, and the fine quality of his singing and the perfect control of his magnificent voice fully justified the ample appreciation of the vast audience."

And here the critic showed me that I had not worked hard in vain, for he continued:

"The programme had apparently been arranged with a view of affording the basso an opportunity of displaying his mastery of different styles of vocalization demanded by a variety of schools of composition, and nothing was lacking to stamp each individual effort with the mark of complete success."

I felt very happy about that criticism. The others were just as laudatory. For those interested in versatility, here is the list of songs I sang at that first concert:

1. "Prologue" from *Pagliacci* (Leoncavallo)
2. "The Arrow and the Song" (Balfe)
3. "Why do the Nations" from "The Messiah" (Handel)
4. "Sincerity" (Clarke)
5. "Drink to me only with Thine Eyes" (Calcott)
6. "Little Grey Home in the West" (Lohr)
7. "Thy Remembrance" (A. Williamson)
8. "It was a Song you sang me" (Lohr)
9. "The Song of the Flea" (Moussorgsky)
10. "Still as the Night" (Goetz), as a duet with Nan (Annette George)
11. "Sweet and Low" (Barnby), as a duet with Nan (Annette George)
12 "The Admiral's Yarn" (P. Rubens)
13. "The Blue Dragoons" (Kennedy Russell)
14. "The Floral Dance" (Katie Moss)
15. "Hybrias the Cretan"

Fifteen songs! But the audience wanted songs, and I wanted to sing them. It is a grand and glorious feeling to know that you are a success, and that you are making the people happy. I respond to that mood. I always have, and I always shall!

Which reminds me that soon after this a letter appeared in an Australian paper referring to a concert I had given, and at which I sang many encores:

"To the Editor
RE PETER DAWSON'S CONCERT.

Sir,
        I awaited your report on this concert, and was disappointed that no notice was taken of the insistent demands for encores by certain portions of the audience.

        To compel a performer to sing four or five songs running is bad taste on the part of the public, and is certainly not a compliment to the singer."

(The matter is entirely in the hands of the singer; we were under the impression that in graciously acceding to recalls Mr. Dawson was as pleased as the audience.—EDITOR.)

My comment is that I was as pleased as the audience. I agree with the Editor that it is entirely in the hands of the artiste. If he is unappreciative of his popularity, he is not compelled to sing more than he cares to. *But* he ought to be grateful and show his gratitude.

The next concern was whether Nan (Annette George) would

appeal to the Australian audiences. And here again we were 'on top of the world'. This was a typical notice the morning after the first concert:

"Miss Annette George, a soprano with a most pleasing voice of great flexibility, was also accorded a very hearty welcome. Her first song, 'Santuzza's Song' from *Cavalleria Rusticana*, won for her the appreciation and the confidence of the audience. It was not surprising that Miss George was called on for three encores . . . an infallible sign of success in an audience unaccustomed to demonstrative applause."

The tour was a triumph. In the first month I had decided to accept an offer for a return tour in 1914!

I have already told you about my first tour of Australia, and shall go straight ahead and tell you of my first visit to that paradise of scenery and climate—New Zealand. And my meeting with the Maoris.

The tour included towns in the North and the South Islands, and a visit to the Maoris, including a Maori reception at Bay of Plenty. Much of the travelling was done in the great coaches drawn by five horses.

It was on this tour that we had an accident on the mountain road between Gisborne and Wairoa. The Cadillac in which we were travelling skidded on the wet clay road which skirted the mountain-side. Fortunately it skidded the right way, and finished up with a crash against the wall of the mountain. Had it skidded the other way, this story would not have been written. The wheel of the car was smashed off, and we were stranded. Fortunately some Maoris came along and we were able to despatch a note to the manager of the theatre in Wairoa, who after a few hours picked us up in two relief cars. The concert was scheduled to commence at seven o'clock; we arrived at eight. We all went on in the clothes we had travelled in!

However, the rain and heavy gales played merry hell with our other arrangements. The roads were impassable, and the harbour bar was blocked by shingle thrown up by the great gales. No ship was able to enter or leave the harbour. Extensive floods around Wairoa held us up there for many days.

But this hold-up proved a blessing in disguise. When the Maoris in the area heard that I was held up, they approached me and asked if I would take part in a concert they proposed to organize for funds to build an English church in Wairoa. The man who interviewed me was Patu Te Ritu, son of the chief of the Maoris.

I gladly consented, and a few days later the concert was held. It began at eleven o'clock in the morning, and finished twelve hours later. In the morning the Maoris gave a display of their national dancing. A wondrous sight. The Maoris are, or were, a warlike race, and also great hunters. In their dances, for which they wear regalia of picturesque designs and in all colours of the rainbow, they demonstrate these traits. The men carry and wield in alarming fashion war weapons of many varieties. But to my mind their finest performance was in what is called the "Canoe Song". The men take up their position one behind the other in single file, and look for all the world as though they are sitting in a racing eight. And then they sing, and move their arms and bodies in astonishing rhythmical motions, which convey the most realistic impression that their craft is actually moving. I remember saying to my wife, "What a tremendous success that number would be at the London Palladium." I echoed that remark again when the Maori girls gave a demonstration of their graceful dances. The swish, swish, of their grass skirts as they twist and turn, the natural grace as they twirl the *pois* (tiny ball on end of string) and the strange yet haunting melodies of the songs they sing to accompany their dancing.

After the concert at night, which was a great success and pleased the Maoris immensely, I was asked to stay 'for a few minutes' because they wished to make a small presentation.

Imagine my surprise when I returned to the stage ten minutes later to find it filled with Maoris. In a few moments I was thanked for my kindness in supporting the concert, and for my 'very nice' singing. Then the presentation was made! Presentation was the wrong word, it should have been presentations. First I received greenstone 'Tiki' charms, then a Maori hand-woven mat, and then one of the biggest men I have ever met—he must have been six feet six inches and weighed sixteen stone, without a morsel of fat, tattooed all over, clear-eyed and with perfect teeth—came forward and presented me with a real Maori battle-axe.

Next was a present of several multi-coloured *pois* from the leader of the Maori dancing girls, followed by bead belts, and cleverly carved wooden ornaments. I was overwhelmed, but the big thrill was to come.

The son of the chief called for silence. With a few words addressed to me in Maori, he turned to one of the dancing girls and made a gesture. The girl stepped forward, and in a moment he had untied her grass skirt, took it off and handed it to me, leaving the girl in her natal state, and me in an embarrassed one.

I must have looked foolish, for in a few moments all the Maoris were laughing at me, and of course I quickly joined in.

Fortunately I had learned a few words of Maori to express my thanks and they literally went crazy. Apparently I had acquired a good accent. One of the artistes came to me and said with a smile: "Where you know Maori, eh? Nice Maori girl teach you, yes?" and before I could reply he had gone away laughing his head off.

Later I visited the Bay of Plenty and met the Hon. E. Gnata, Maori Member of Parliament in the New Zealand Legislature, and at his invitation attended a meeting of a 'Land Court'. Here I really got to know more about the Maoris, for this part of New Zealand is the Maori area. This was at picturesque Tiki Tiki. When we arrived at the Court, the whole proceedings stopped to give me a Maori welcome. They did *hakas*, those wonderfully fascinating rhythmic chants and acclamations; and sang songs in which the Hon. Gnata took the lead, after which the proceedings continued.

In those days there was a good deal of unscrupulous dealing going on over the purchase of land owned by Maoris. These courts were designed to hear all sales or contemplated sales of property owned by Maoris. It was the old story of the perfidious white man persuading a Maori to take whisky, after which he gets the man to sign away his land for a pittance.

The Land Court put a stop to this sort of infamy. If a Maori wished to sell his property he had to state the reason why he wanted to sell, who was the prospective buyer, and give details of the offer.

Special precautions were made, too, that a Maori addicted to a little surreptitious drinking was not 'persuaded' by the promise of a bottle of whisky to exaggerate his reasons for desiring to sell a part of his land. The Court showed me how a Maori can keep his word. On two occasions the Court discovered that the purchaser had supplied whisky, but in both cases the Maori could not be 'persuaded' to name the man who supplied him. "I find bottle", or "I don't remember", were the monotonously repeated answers.

Later in the day the Hon. Gnata took me along to a large gathering of Maoris, quite a thousand strong, and I was greeted with the traditional *hakas*, but in the open and by so many it was awe-inspiring.

I was so astonished and happy that I decided to sing a Maori song I had learnt. When I told Gnata this, and hummed a little of it to him, he was tickled to death, and excitedly made the announcement to the large assembly. And here it was I sung in Maori *"Waiata Poi"* ("Tiny ball on end of string"). They went crazy. My pronunciation was apparently all that could be desired. I held up my hands to quieten them and said: "I will now try to sing another song in Maori. This song is sung by all British soldiers fighting the Germans." I sung them "It's a long Way to Tipperary" *in their own Maori*.

Pandemonium broke loose. They rushed to me and began wonderful *hakas*, repeating their entertainment until Gnata had to stop them. I promised to sing them another very short song in Maori before I left. And the singing went on, accompanied by their spirited dancing, rhythmic chanting and twirling of the *pois*.

At the end I made a short announcement that I wanted them to sing a song with me. I should sing it through once, and then they must join with me when I put my hands up. I then sang in Maori "For he's a jolly good Fellow", indicating the Hon. Gnata. They listened in silence at the beginning, and I began to wonder whether they understood what it was all about. But as the song progressed I could tell by their faces that they understood. When I raised my hands to tell them to sing with me there was a wonderful response. For the first time the Maoris sang "For he's a jolly good Fellow". To say that I had made a success with the Maoris would be an understatement. But I have a soft corner in my heart for them, and I am proud to know that they reciprocate that expression of goodwill.

Later, with Gnata, I heard a haunting little song sung by a Maori, and was so intrigued with it that I copied it out. It was called in Maori, *"Mai Pahi Aipo"*. Thirty-four years later I revived it. I tell the story of the song under the chapter 'Songs' later in this book.

But I must return to Waiora, where owing to floods we were held up, and where I had received such a fine array of presents for my part in the concert held to raise funds for the Maori English Church.

Here is a list of the fascinatingly named towns I visited between Napier and Waiora: Fort Awanui, Te Ara Hoha, Tokomaru, Tiki Tiki, Tolago Bay. Other names of similar quality: Waikato, Taranaki, Wanganui, Manawatu, Whangarei, Otago, Oamaru.

Yes. They are puzzling in the pronunciation, but when you know how they are attractive and roll off the tongue easily.

I have visited New Zealand many times since, and the more I see of it the greater its appeal to my often expressed desire to settle down there.

I cannot praise too highly the conditions of life in New Zealand. I found a remarkable spirit of *camaraderie*, and its people exhibit a spontaneous friendliness that is lacking in so many other countries today. It reminds me, too, of England, in that the grass is amazingly green and fresh. And I recall how well fed the stock are, and how the people live in the lap of the gods as far as climate, soil and other natural blessings are concerned. It was with regret I left New Zealand, but I have kept my faith, and have paid many return visits.

F

CHAPTER VII

THE FIRST WORLD WAR

ON 4 August, 1914, I was in Goulburn, N.S.W. The concert had just commenced when a message was brought to me that Britain had declared war on Germany. There had been talk of war, but most people believed that Germany would change her mind when she realized that Britain was not bluffing. However, when I received the news it was a shock. Without hesitation I decided to announce the news to the audience.

Their reaction was remarkable. Everyone started to cheer, and someone started to sing "God save the King", which the accompanist soon led with the piano. More cheering, and then "Rule Britannia" was sung. More excitement and cheering and again we all sang "God save the King". While I was turning over in my mind what was the best thing to do about the concert I found that that problem was already being solved.

The audience slowly melted away. They were far too excited to stay in a concert hall, but wanted to be in the town, where there would be some fun and games. Not one person asked for their money back. One hour after the concert was due to commence the hall was empty.

Before the audience left I had made an announcement which I have no doubt was responsible for much of the excitement. A runner from the town came round to me about a quarter of an hour after the war declaration, and gave me the news that there had been a naval battle in the North Sea, and that *seventeen* German warships had been sunk.

Pandemonium broke out, and the singing and shouting and dancing were carried on into the street. Fortunately the news had also been circulated in the town, so that I was not responsible for spreading a rumour which turned out to be, like Mark Twain's death, 'much exaggerated'.

The following morning we were away early for our next concert at Wagga. Excitement was running high there, and during the concert I made a number of announcements by arrangement with the local newspaper office. But I would not make any announcement that was not from an official source.

At Albury, N.S.W., on the border of Victoria, we met the first incident of the smashing up of shops owned by Germans.

All very sad, because these people were so obviously harmless, and were settling down to become decent Australian citizens. But feeling began to run high when some of the propaganda stories reached Australia. You know the sort of thing. Atrocities to Belgian women and children.

But after a while the war excitement quietened down, and business and life proceeded on its normal way. We were too far away from the scene of war to be really affected. Our tour continued, and we played to good houses.

The war was brought home to the people of Australia and New Zealand when the first casualty lists from Gallipoli appeared. I was touring New Zealand. I shall never forget the shock of those first lists of casualties. And when I was informed by a Government official that the lists were so many that they daren't issue them all at once, for fear of what the reaction of the people might be, my heart was heavy.

Of course, it ruined my concert tour. We had no alternative but to continue, although in some places we took as little as £15, not enough to pay for the hire of the hall and the billing.

The losses I suffered were crippling. I was on a percentage basis, which meant that I took the risk of whatever happened—success or failure. I remember that in one town we had come to the end of our resources. The concert had been a flop. The papers were filled with the tragic stories of glory and death at Gallipoli, and the people were numb with the tragic starkness of the losses. On my return to Australia I found similar conditions. The bottom had dropped out of the concert world. At Brisbane, where my concert clashed with Harry Lauder, and Daisy Jerome, who was a big attraction at that time, I had not enough money to pay the hotel bill. It was only by pawning some of Nan's jewellery that we were able to pay our bill at Ruddle's Hotel and get to the next town.

The appalling casualties of the war made me anxious to do my bit, and I made up my mind that at the end of the tour I would return to England, for Nan, by this time, was terribly anxious to get home, and I would then join up. But the tour did not improve my financial condition, and I found myself quite unable to find the money to pay for our fares. But just then I found a good Samaritan. It was that remarkable man, Hugh D. MacKintosh. 'Hugh D.', as he was popularly known in Australia, will be remembered as the man who promoted the first world heavyweight championship to be held in Australia. That was between Tommy Burns and the American black, Jack Johnson.

This fight put Hugh D. on the road to a fortune. He had joined a few other men to promote the fight, but the others had dropped out one by one, leaving Hugh to 'hold the baby'. The costs were so high very few believed it was possible to make a financial success of the fight. But Hugh went ahead. The result is well known. It was a great success. Later Hugh bought interests in music-halls and in newspapers in Sydney, and he ultimately made a fortune. It was Hugh D. who started the first 'Black and White' milk bars in London.

Well, just as I was beginning to despair at the failure of the concerts because of the war, Hugh D. offered me a music-hall tour of the Australian States. It was indeed a godsend. I was starred, and had no further money worries. I was receiving a good salary, and had no worry about percentages! The music-halls were doing big business, and I am glad to say that I played to capacity houses everywhere I appeared. I soon had enough money to enable me to arrange for our return to England. Hearing of my intention, Hugh D. again came forward with his helping hand, and one morning he 'phoned and asked whether I would care to play a six weeks' music-hall engagement in South Africa on my way home to England. Fares would be paid in the contract!

And that was how I made my first visit to South Africa.

The voyage to South Africa was not without a certain amount of risk. But Nan was anxious to get back to England, and as she didn't mind 'taking a chance' with German submarines, who was I to gainsay her?

And we had plenty of excitement. We were in convoy. The S.S. *Osterley* was carrying troops and stores, and only a very few passengers.

At the time the adventures we encountered appeared thrilling, but time, and the experiences of the British people in the Second World War, make them trivial in comparison now.

We saw one of the vessels in our convoy sunk by a torpedo from a German submarine, and the *Osterley* caught fire in one of her holds, and was on fire for many days. In fact the fire was not put out until we reached Durban. That was a nerve-racking experience, but the assurance of the captain and the cheeriness of the crew soon put the rest of us more or less at ease.

Owing to censorship on the movements of ships, my arrival time was unknown in South Africa. The South African Press put it this way:

"Mr. Peter Dawson arrived here from Australia by the S.S. *Osterley* this week, and opens a six weeks' tour at the Criterion on Monday night. Mr. Dawson has been touring Australia and New Zealand during the past eighteen months, and owing to the 'erratic' sailings of late, his arrival here on Monday was quite unexpected. It was soon learned that the African Theatres Trust had made it possible to induce Mr. Dawson to jump off here on the way to England, and his presence at the Bayside next week marks one of the big vocal events of the Durban Gala or any other season that comes along."

I took a liking to South Africa. I was particularly impressed by the hospitality of the people, the grandeur of the scenery, which often reminded me of Australia, and the wonderful atmospheric visibility. The crossing of the Calbury Mountains was an unforgettable experience. We seemed to be thousands of feet up before we realized it, and in no time at all. And looking down was a revelation, for in all my travels I have never encountered such clear visibility. It was as though someone had been cleaning the fields below for our special benefit. The cattle and the vehicles on the roads below stood out in stereoscopic clearness.

I found the audiences as appreciative of a good song as any in the world. They are discriminating, and are not prone to the 'habit complex' of applauding anything out of politeness.

After the South African tour we reached England following a nerve-racking trip from Durban, for the submarine war was at its height. There could not have been two more contented people in this world than Nan and myself when we finally felt the good dear earth of England under our feet. We were living in Ealing, West London, at the time, and it was a grand and glorious feeling to be 'home' again, despite the war.

I quickly obtained recording dates and concert engagements, but did a great deal of work for various war charities all over the country. This pleased me very much. I had been to the High Commissioner for Australia in London immediately after my arrival and sought his advice about joining up. He said that as an Australian I ought to join the Australian Army, but that there was plenty of good war work for me to do in England without joining the army here. He sent my name forward to various war organizations, and in no time I was busy helping in all sorts of ways to raise funds for War Loan and War Comforts Funds.

It was during this period that I made my first concert tour of Ireland, which I shall describe later.

But what a change I found in England! I had left it when war was but a remote possibility. I was now overawed. The change wrought in every sphere of life was inconceivable. The interesting human tide that flowed along the thoroughfares of the great metropolis by day and by night had now changed its colour to khaki and gold. I found myself jostled by a totally different set of humans in 'civvies'—men and women who had come from all parts of the Empire to work for the big victory, and who were either on holiday or 'off shift'. Many's the time I stood and wondered if ever London would see the old times back again. How on earth would the existing military machine eventually dispose of its millions of workers? How was the great settling up, as well as the great settling down, to be accomplished? Would London ever be again as I knew it in pre-war times—the dazzling splendour, the opera, theatres, concerts, music-halls, banquets, and the thousand-and-one rounds of festivities during the golden Season? It was indeed good to be alive then.

I found Covent Garden Opera House, where I had performed and witnessed many a brilliant gala night, transformed, alas! into a furniture repository, storing the goods and chattels of many of London's greatest and most famous hotels that had been commandeered by the Government for military purposes. Concerts and banquets were practically *non est*. I found, however, that the music-halls, theatres, revues and cinemas were enjoying a prosperity hitherto unknown. The reason was obvious. The multitude of munition workers and war workers were earning splendid wages—quite double or treble those of pre-war days—and accordingly they had to have their recreation. Extravagance and waste were rife. And little sign of thrift. It was quite a common thing for a family of the ordinary working class to be earning £20 a week. I was in Nottingham soon after my arrival, and during my stay I paid a visit to a friend who keeps a music and piano shop. He was lamenting the fact that his stock of instruments was getting very low. Suddenly a woman of the working-class type appeared in the doorway and began an inspection of the pianos. "What can I do for you, madam?" asked my friend. "Oh," she said, "I want a piano." "Sorry, madam, but I have none for hire." "But," she went on, "I want to buy one." After he had shown her two or three, her eye settled on a full-sized grand, and on being informed the price—one hundred and forty guineas—she bought it, and paid cash on the spot. The joke was that the address where the piano was to be delivered was in a particularly squalid part of the city, and the men who delivered the piano reported that neither the woman nor any of her family could play the piano, nor, as far as they could make out, could any of their friends or relatives!

I was astonished and filled with admiration at the manner in which the women of Britain were acting in every conceivable capacity—train, tram, tube and omnibus conductors, and even as drivers of big motor-lorries!

The Government had placed a fixed price on bread, potatoes and milk, well within the means of the poor. I must say that I found the standardized bread appalling stuff, brown and coarse, and no baker was allowed to sell any under twenty-four hours after its baking.

I had the good fortune to be shown over a shell-filling depot. The buildings, all single-storied, covered some twenty acres of ground. And there I received the biggest shock since my arrival in wartime Britain. There were 10,000 women working—all at full pressure, three shifts in a day of twenty-four hours. The organization and the general routine simply held me spellbound. I paid many visits to the various military hospitals and sang to the poor wounded boys. How grateful they were, and how happy it made me to sing to them!

But I was not content as the war went on and on, and the end seemed to get farther away. I felt that I ought to be doing something more, so I decided that I would return to Australia and join the forces.

I arranged for a short tour of South Africa on my way home, and then a tour on behalf of the Australian Government for war loan purposes; then I joined the Army. The *Adelaide Herald* announced it:

"The news that Mr. Peter Dawson, the noted singer, has enlisted, was received regretfully and yet with a certain amount of pleasure by the people of Adelaide. They will miss Peter Dawson, singer and artiste to his finger-tips, but are proud to know he will help represent them at the front.

Mr. Dawson enlisted at Market Square last evening. The announcement was received with cheers. Mr. Dawson was one of the speakers, and he related phases of the war as he had seen it in England, where he used to visit the hospitals and sing for the wounded. After a spirited appeal Mr. Dawson delighted his *alfresco* audience by singing a little soldier song which cheerily predicts that the sunshine will break through the dark clouds."

And so I was now a private in the Australian Army. I joined the 'foot sloggers'—the Infantry. (I think this experience must have been responsible for my immediate interest a few years later in setting the Kipling lines "Boots" to music.) Although I was something of a man of note in my country, I wanted no favouritism, and I certainly did *not* get any. My first duty was the inevitable fatigue of all new recruits—the latrines. A couple of days at this made me appreciative of a camp-bed at night. One day I passed the O.C. of the depot. He was an old friend of mine. He was alone, and I had an opportunity of saluting him and whispering: "You ——! This is your doing." He returned my salute, and answered, "Well, Peter, you must go through the whole lot of fatigues or the others will hate your guts." And then he added, "When you're finished, come to my office, and we'll have a drink." I felt better after that. And was I glad of that drink in the privacy of his office!

My next fatigue was 'spud barber'. I had a couple of days at that. Peeling potatoes for forty million men, or at least that's how it felt to me. On my first day I honestly thought I was helping peel potatoes for the whole population of Adelaide. I could not believe that a camp could possibly consume so many hundreds *of tons*!

Anyhow, the time came when I had completed my 'training' in fatigue duties, and I was going through real infantry training. I enjoyed every minute of that, and pretty soon I was a fully trained private.

A little later I was asked by the C.O. whether I would help in a recruiting drive. I gladly accepted, and with an officer and a couple of N.C.O.s we set out to gather in recruits. In the camp an American boxer, Jimmy Clabby, a great fighter and a most popular fellow, used to give boxing exhibitions, and when he heard about the recruiting drive he asked if he could accompany us. He would give exhibition boxing, and help bring in recruits. This permission was granted and off we set.

And what a tour it turned out! We marched over the iron bark ridges, across the stringy barked flats, here, there and everywhere. In a fortnight we enrolled 1,500 men. But the standard was high, and we had to reject a number, some because they were doing more important work and others because of health reasons. We had a grand batch of 600 men and everyone at headquarters was delighted.

Incidentally, Clabby was a brilliant heavyweight. He lost to Les Darcy, the Australian heavyweight, after a terrific fight. Clabby went on to beat Tommy Uren, heavyweight champion of Australia, and Albert Lloyd, who challenged him for the title. In 1919 he beat George Cook, who afterwards became heavy-weight champion of Australia.

I used to sing, Jimmy Clabby to box, and then we talked. I recounted my stories of how even the women of Britain were working, and how every man Jack in the old country was doing his bit to pull off a victory.

On my return to camp I was congratulated by the Army authorities, and was put into the Corporals' school. In this I came out on top and was proud. I cannot tell you how 'cocky' I felt when Nan sewed my stripes on to my sleeve. I felt that I had earned them, and I knew that I was proficient in my training as an N.C.O.

I finally left Australia for France as a Battalion Orderly Sergeant in the 7th Division of the Queensland Infantry, but just as we were approaching the Panama Canal I was called to the Commanding Officer's cabin. He said, "Well, Battalion Sergeant, I don't know whether you have noticed anything about the ship, have you?" I replied: "I have, sir. I believe we have turned about." "That's quite right. The war is over, and we are now returning home. Line up the men on deck and tell them, but keep a firm hold on discipline."

I addressed the men in this way—they were a tough lot, I assure you: "How many of you cock-eyed birds have noticed anything about how this ship is travelling?" Apparently none had noticed that we had turned about, so I continued: "I have here"—and I pulled out a small pocket-book—"what is known as a bullet-proof pocket-book. This sheet of metal which I have taken out is supposed to stop a bullet. I am now going to throw it into the sea." I suited the action to the word and threw it overboard, then faced them again.

"That means," I said, "we have just heard than an Armistice has been declared, and the war is over." My announcement was received in absolute silence. I have never seen a bunch of more disappointed men. One of them shouted, "I'd like to kill that ruddy wireless operator." And another, "Six months' flipping training for a flipping sea trip!" And finally, from a man who had been through the Gallipoli landing: "You silly lot of cows, you ought to be bloody glad. I was the only 'so and so' left out of my company. Fighting ain't funny. You ought to thank Gawd you're out of it." I dismissed them, and they went below very quietly, and very disconsolate. The majority were heartbroken with disappointment.

At the next parade two men who had been missed from the very first roll call after the ship left port reported on parade. They were a couple of men who had also been in the Gallipoli fighting; both had been wounded, and were returning to fight in France.

When I asked where they had been, I received broad grins. "Look, Sarge, we've been through it all before. You wouldn't want to make trouble for a couple of old sweats. We'd 'a' bin on 'and if anything was 'appening." I learned afterwards that these two 'old sweats' had been running a 'Crown and Anchor' board throughout the whole voyage. It says a lot for their popularity that there was none among their comrades who gave them away. In any case the war was over, and why make a fuss about a couple of men who had already suffered physically and mentally?

My last important job as Battalion Orderly Sergeant was to take 250 men from Sydney to Brisbane. When I was given the job I realized that with the war over I should be darned lucky if I got there with fifty men. Anyhow, I hit upon a scheme. Although I had their pay for the journey, I told them that I wanted their help for a few hours more and begged of them to 'play the game' and travel to Sydney. When they asked for money I replied, "You will receive no money until we make Sydney, because I haven't any." They all arrived at Sydney!

After my demobilization there was a bad slump in the concert world. Nobody was interested in booking dates. My brothers persuaded me to join the firm, which was now a big business. I cannot find any explanation why I decided to throw up my career, but the vagaries of the concert world in wartime probably had a lot to do with it. Anyhow, I did join the firm!

After six months at the factory I realized that the monotony did not suit me, and in order to avoid any embarrassing explanations of my desire to return to my life as a professional vocalist I decided to send myself a cable from London. I sent a cable to our housekeeper at our London home and instructed her to send the following cable to me:

Return to England immediately stop Now war is over must hold you to contract stop Please cable urgently stop Gramophone Company.

The reply came in six hours! At first my brothers pooh-poohed the idea that the Gramophone Company could hold me to such a contract, but when I mentioned that it was a question of my promise to return when the war was over, they no longer opposed my departure.

Then a most extraordinary thing happened. The day after the cable arrived I received a request from Charles Thring offering me a four weeks' engagement in Melbourne at £85 per week, with a possible extension to six weeks! This was followed almost immediately by a wire from Hugh D. MacKintosh:

Understand you are returning to England. Will you accept offer from African Theatre Trust to play a twelve-week guarantee, two first-class fares Sydney to Durban, and then Durban to Southampton. £75 per week. Wire urgently.

I had almost lost all my capital as a result of the war, and the few months at the factory had begun to depress me. I loathed the idea of asking for a loan, but the call was too great and I was determined to raise the money for our fares somehow in order to get back to England, where I knew I could start my career at the point I had left off before my departure to join the Australian Army.

These two offers blew my depression sky-high. I shall always remember a letter that also arrived from England at this psychological moment. It was from Tom Noble. In it he said: "Don't be a ruddy fool. We want you over here. Remember that old song of Billy Williams:

> *'Just keep on jogging along, keep on jogging along.*
> *Your luck will change some day, something will come your way.*
> *Things will be all right, though today they're all wrong.*
> *Keep on, keep on jogging along.' "*

Yes, in a few hours my future was assured. I played the six weeks for Charles Thring, and then left for England *via* South Africa. In South Africa I played the twelve weeks and accepted a further eight weeks at most profitable terms.

CHAPTER VIII

BACK TO WORK

MY first engagement after the war was at the Albert Hall to sing at Mme Tetrazzini's Farewell Concert. Supporting Tetrazzini were her accompanist and solo pianist Count Cimara; Albert Sammons, violinist; and Lenghi Cellini, the Italian tenor.

I had always been a great admirer of Tetrazzini and we had known each other for some time. She was a charming soul, with a heart as big as her voice—generous beyond reason. Her manager, Signor Tato, was often 'tearing his hair' in despair at the news of some further act of munificence on the part of the Diva. When he remonstrated with her in his voluble Italian she would just smile, pat his cheek and say in Italian: "Poor Tato, but don't you see it makes me happy? Tato would not like me to lose any happiness, would you, Tato?" And 'poor' Tato would kiss her hand and dismiss the matter with a shrug.

What a ghastly tragedy was her end! Poverty-stricken, she died a pauper. Her great fault—if you can call it a fault—was being too big-hearted and too easy a prey to the craft of the unscrupulous.

She possessed a glorious voice, which was heard the world over. It was a pity she did not have a little of Dame Melba's business acumen. In point of fact it was Melba who, through her insistence in barring other sopranos (unless she, Melba, agreed) from appearing at Covent Garden, prevented Tetrazzini's earlier triumph in Britain.

It was a pleasure also to renew my acquaintance with Lenghi Cellini. He was a fine tenor. He knew but a word or two of English when he first came to London, but was fortunate in meeting Guy d'Hardelot, the song-writer, who helped him a great deal. In a very short time he spoke fairly fluent English, mastering the language so well within four months of his arrival in this country that he took part in "The Messiah" with me. Later he made a great success in *Carmen* at the Royal Opera House, Covent Garden. 'Lenghi', as he became to his friends, was most popular. He grew very 'English' in his ways, but with one important exception—his method of 'attacking' food.

This was an intriguing sight to watch. He would sit down at the dining-table, grab a napkin, tie it round his neck and spread it across his bosom. With a knife and fork in each hand he would then proceed to attack whatever dish of food was placed before him. First the fork, then the knife, up and down, up and down, alternately, head well down over the plate, the distance between the plate and the mouth never more than six inches! But the most amusing performance he gave was in his assault of a salad. First he would pour darned nearly a bottle of olive oil into the dish, then carefully measure out salt, mustard, vinegar, pepper, and mix them together in a large tablespoon; then with the greatest care he would distribute this mixture over the salad. With knife and fork held firmly in his hands he then entered the fray. Somehow he worked faster with the knife and fork against a salad, but he also 'splashed' very much more! When the contents had disappeared he grabbed a spoon and proceeded to drink up the liquid. This he did to the accompaniment of raucous breathing noises. How I laughed! Lenghi didn't mind. "You people do not understand how to enjoy your food. You eat just like a duchess, making it appear as if eating ought never to be indulged in. Bah! Enjoy your food, Peetare, and to hell with the duchess!"

Albert Sammons was my very old friend, and of course we had many war experiences to talk over. . . .

That concert cheered me immensely. There was plenty of money about in those days—the war slump had not yet been envisaged. For the next twelve months I was kept busy with concerts all over Britain, and did a number of songs for the Gramophone Company. In the summer I found myself again on the same programme with Lenghi Cellini, in the Isle of Man. By this time his English was excellent and he was singing a number of English songs.

On the night of the concert a letter addressed to all members of the Concert Party, which included Flora Woodman and Margaret Cooper, arrived from my old friend Florrie Forde, asking us to join her in a picnic she was giving the following day. What a party that was! In addition to the members of our troupe, Florrie Forde brought her husband, Laurie Barnett; Lawrence Wright, song-writer and publisher, and his wife, Betty Warren, and a host of others whose names I cannot recall.

Within ten minutes Lenghi was 'Antonio' to Florrie, and when Lenghi did not get the joke Florrie obliged with her song "Antonio". At my home a week or two later Lenghi sang "Antonio" right through as a lark. I think it was Ernest Butcher who played the accompaniment for him.

I remember that Florrie Forde pulled a good joke on the

party after the 'picnic' lunch she gave. Incidentally, what a lunch! It was more a feast of Lucullus: lobsters, salmon, chicken, duck, beef, lamb, veal and ham, strawberries, peaches, apricots and lashings of cream; grapes, William pears and apples. She told her husband to ask everyone which liqueur they would like. This took a few minutes, and the list was handed to Florrie. Then she said: "Well, it's nice to have the names of your favourite liqueurs, but I haven't got any. You'll have to be content with 'bubbly'." A great-hearted soul. Her popularity in the Isle of Man was astonishing. She was called 'Our Queen' by the locals, and she certainly merited the title.

Shortly after this I made another important step forward in my career, when I was asked to join the small company of artistes making up the new 'International Celebrity Concerts'. These concerts were designed to give excerpts from the operas; that is, each artiste sung an *aria* or song from one of the famous Italian, French, German or Russian operas. In addition to myself were Rosina Buckman, Maurice d'Oisley, Edna Thornton and William James, the Australian pianist.

We did a three months' tour of England, Scotland, Ireland and Wales. The concerts were very successful, but they were in the nature of an experiment to find the reaction of the public to songs from the opera without orchestral support or scenic background. The Press criticism varied. For the artistes there was nothing but praise, but for the 'idea' there was a wide difference of opinion.

One critic wrote:

"An operatic concert, though a dozen excerpts from different operas may be rendered, has not the merit of one opera. However brilliant the singers, it has the annoying defects of a stump orator whose stories have neither beginning nor end. Many good qualities and much enjoyment were undoubtedly, etc. . . ."

On the other hand another critic wrote:

"One is at loss to understand why a concert of this nature should be so much more popular than those at which the less showy but more natural songs are chosen. The fact remains that this is the case, and until the public at large demand a good deal more from their favourite vocalists than an ability to sing dazzling scale passages and so on, the showy operatic airs will continue to be the chief stock-in-trade of our best vocalists. Of course there are two distinct ways of viewing the question of the operatic concert, for while it may be argued that the operatic air loses its particular worth from being cut out of the opera, one has also to remember that the majority of us have to rely almost entirely on the operatic concert for our acquaintance with opera."

The *Daily Mail* wrote during the sixth week of the tour:

"Though opinions may differ as to the attraction of operatic *arias* shorn of their atmosphere and native setting, there is, nevertheless, a public for them, and especially so when the singers happen to be of the repute of the quartet of the International Celebrity Concert Organization."

Encouraged by the success of this tour, I decided to produce my own concert of what might be termed today 'highbrow' songs. That there was an audience for the good classical songs I felt sure, and so on 9 May, 1924, I gave a recital at the Wigmore Hall, in London. I sang the *lieder* in German.

FIRST PART

(a) *"Sei mir Gegrüsst"*
(b) *"Erstarrung"*
(c) *"Wasserflut"* } SCHUBERT
(d) *"Die Krähe"*
(e) *"Ungeduld"*

SECOND PART

(a) *"Die Mainacht"*
(b) *"Botschaft"*
(c) *"Ständchen"* } BRAHMS
(d) *"Der Tod, das ist die kühle Nacht*
(e) *"Blinde Kuh"*

THIRD PART

(a) *"Nun wandre Maria"* . . . WOLF
(b) *"Verschwiegene Liebe* . . . WOLF
(c) *"Frühlingsnacht"* . . . SCHUMANN
(d) *"Du bist so jung"* . . ERIC WOLFF
(e) *"Traum durch die Dämmerung* . STRAUSS

FOURTH PART

(a) "Down by the Sally Gardens"	.	HERBERT HUGHES
(b) "Must I go bound?"	. .	HERBERT HUGHES
(c) "White in the Moon"	. .	ARTHUR SOMERVELL
(d) "The last Revel"	. .	JULIUS HARRISON
(e) "In Prison"	. . .	JULIUS HARRISON
(f) "Four Elizabethan Lyrics"		

Set to music by ROGER QUILTER

I had Gerald Moore as my accompanist. He did his job brilliantly. I have already told of my good Press notices of this concert, but I must confess that, although I thoroughly enjoyed singing these fine songs, I was convinced there was not in London at that time a large enough audience to appreciate that sort of programme.

And now I come to an event which completely changed the normal planning of our future.

Driving with my wife in my big Renault saloon from Glasgow to Newark on a Saturday afternoon, I had a dreadful collision at a crossroads about seven miles from Leeds. The Renault turned turtle and skidded about twenty yards upside down before it stopped! But for the fact that the strong wooden frame of the saloon did not crumple we should certainly have been killed.

I will not dwell on the details of this disaster except, first, to pay a tribute to a Leeds Infirmary doctor, who by the grace of God happened to arrive on the scene after a few minutes and decided to take a chance and rush my terribly injured wife in his small Morris Cowley to the Leeds Infirmary, where he knew that she could get the necessary attention if her life was to be saved. I had a miraculous escape, thanks to the stability of the car and because the steering wheel did not break. Nan was terribly injured, with several broken ribs, a broken left shoulder, deep lacerations in her leg, and her head half scalped. Two days later the leg developed gangrene. Dr. Gordon, who had rushed her to Leeds, told me that only my wife's determination to live kept her alive. "She is a miracle, Mr. Dawson." But the news of the infection was a terribly blow. And here I must pay my second tribute—to a brilliant surgeon, Mr. Richardson, also of Leeds Infirmary. He performed an operation on the septic leg which proved her salvation. I was not aware that an operation had been performed until it was over. My brother-in-law went to see Mr. Richardson, and to find out the real position of the gangrene trouble. "I shall have to make a drastic incision, and

A picture of Peter Dawson taken in 1920 when recording at the H.M.V. studios. (Note the old-time recording funnel behind Mr. Dawson's back)

Presenting a huge laurel wreath
to Battistini on behalf of British
and Commonwealth baritones

Peter Dawson parting with
regret from his dogs when
leaving for Australia, 1935

Recording marching songs with a choir of other distinguished singers,
including Webster Booth and George Baker. Ray Noble (*left*) conducted

even so, there is no guarantee that it will stop it. But we shall know within twelve hours after the operation whether it is successful or not." Tom Noble and his sister, Mrs. Fred Groves, then asked, "If it is not a success, does that mean . . ." "Yes," replied the surgeon, and went on: "You had better stand by all night. If things go the wrong way I will have you called, and you must then tell Mr. Dawson."

That night I was persuaded to rest. They stayed up all night, although I wasn't aware of the reason. They dreaded a telephone call. At 2.30 a.m. the telephone in the hotel rang, and the call was for Mr. Dawson. Tom rushed to the 'phone expecting the worst, but it was not from the hospital; it was from an agent who wanted to persuade me to sing two nights later at a concert he had already arranged, but which of course now had to be cancelled.

I don't know what Tom told the agent, but it was hot enough to melt the 'phone. Anyway, a few days later the agent did speak to me and he said: "Who was that spoke to me the other night? My God, I've never been spoken to like that in my life. He told me to go to hell the quickest way, and that I was something worse than a rat!" I explained the reason and he realized his mistake.

No 'phone call arrived that night, and in the morning I learned of the operation and of its success. "It's up to your wife now, Mr. Dawson," the doctor said, "and if I know her she'll win the fight. She really ought to be dead now, but she has no intention of giving in."

Nan was in that hospital three months, and then brought to London. It was twelve months before she was able to get about again, and then only very slowly and carefully.

The biggest blow of all! It meant she would never be able to make any further public appearances on the concert platform. The accident left her a semi-invalid, but worse than that it had affected her nerves and, as she put it, "I have lost my nerve for performing in public."

Fortunately Tom had succeeded in getting me a bonus cheque of £4,000 'for services rendered' from the Gramophone Company. This was a blessing, following Nan's long illness. I remember what joy I had taking Nan to town and buying her presents and pieces of furniture for our home near Ealing Common, West London.

I had arranged a tour of Australia for both of us, but this too had to be cancelled. I decided on another tour of Britain under the

G

auspices of Mr. Stephenson, who was making a big reputation in the North for promoting 'Sixpenny Concerts'. These concerts were a terrific success—so much so, that Mr. Stephenson was well on the way to making a fortune. I saw him in Sheffield in 1948. He has retired, an extremely rich man. "And it all started with Sixpenny Concerts," he told me, and he went on reminiscing: "I used to make £50 out of the sale of the programmes alone."

I did not pay another visit to Australia and New Zealand till 1931. That was my sixth tour of those countries. I paid further visits in 1933, 1935, early 1939 and 1948–9. And, as in the first war, I was in Australia when World War Two was declared.

There is a good explanation why I toured Australia so much.

The concert world is the most sensitive in its reaction to any kind of crisis. A bad strike in the industrial world, the death of the King, the financial slump of 1931, the abdication—all these events hit the concert world hardest. Whereas the theatre and music-hall will suffer a slump for a few weeks, the concert world suffers for months.

Directly these various slumps made themselves felt, I knew that I must get away to places not so affected. In addition, it is good for an artiste not to stay too long in one country, for however popular you are there is always the risk of becoming 'over' popular. And so I paid a visit to India.

CHAPTER IX

INDIA, BURMA AND STRAITS
SETTLEMENTS

BEFORE leaving for India I had made three tours of Australia, two of New Zealand, and two of South Africa, so I can speak with some knowledge of ocean-going travel. Hitherto I had found the atmosphere on board ship cheery, companionable and entertaining, but not so during this trip to India.

The aloofness of many of my fellows I put down at first to nervousness in the face of a new experience—travelling on an overseas voyage—but their aloofness persisted. I soon discovered that I was meeting the Anglo-Indians at their best, or worst, in this ship. Gone was the spirit of good fellowship one meets everywhere on ocean liners—that is, if they are not travelling to or from India. I have been called a good mixer. That's true. It's probably a fault of mine that I like talking to my fellow men and women, but I shall go on doing it.

These Anglo-Indians, made up of Indian Civil Servants and Army officers in mufti accompanied by their wives, were, I must admit, the strangest bunch of people I have ever had the misfortune to run up against. Probably, if I had met any of them away from the rest of the crowd, they would have been normal intelligent people, but in the 'clique', oh, what a wretched crowd of snobs! One or two important business men were *en route* to make contracts with Indian merchants, and we compared notes. These business men could make no approach to the Anglo-Indians. One, who hailed from Manchester, told me he did get into conversation with one of the higher standard civil servants, but "directly I mentioned I was going to Calcutta to negotiate some contracts for cotton wear I received the cold shoulder, and he quickly left me. Because I had not spoken with a Lancashire accent," he added, "he did not believe I could be 'on business'." Then he said with grim determination, "I'll make the 'so-and-so' sorry he snubbed me before this trip's over."

It was quite ludicrous the way those people behaved. They were always anxious to get 'a four for bridge', and were not amiss in condescending to approach any one of their own type, or any other 'presentable' person. I had been clumsily cross-examined by several of them, and I deliberately told them "I am going to

99

India on business." Later, when the news got round that I was Peter Dawson, the singer, it was really darned funny how they tried to become friendly. But by this time I was too disgusted with their general snobbery. I did, however, make many friends on board, and had a thoroughly pleasant voyage. I sang a few songs of an evening to my ship friends, and won the 'ship's run' prize once.

The captain of the ship was also bitten by the Anglo-Indian complex, and I was amused to notice that he, unlike any other ship's captain I had ever met, had red carpet for about twenty yards outside the approach to his cabin-office.

Naturally I was worried about my tour of India if we were going to encounter this class segregation, but a Scottish jute merchant assured me I must take no serious notice of the snobbery practiced by these 'nitwits' on board. "They're poor folk, who are to be pitied. They're part of a system which stinks in the nostrils of folk like ourselves, but we can do nothing about it." The greatest bore in the world is the ex-Anglo-Indian who perpetually bores you with, "When I was in INDIAH . . ."

We became friendly with an Army colonel, and he explained that it was paradoxical how these little people, with such warped minds, could do such good work at their jobs in India. Their peculiar brand of snobbery just suited the work they were called on to do among the Indian people.

The women were the worst offenders. The colonel explained it in this way: "In India these women have several servants to whom they are goddesses. They imbibe this adoration to such an extent that when they travel outside India they cannot dissociate their Indian life from life with other Nationals. The result is they develop a complex. The complex is helped by the life they lead in India. They don't work, they are spoilt darlings—that is, the majority of them—and they revel in it. What is this complex? Power! In India they are 'important people'; outside India they are just ordinary folk. Once they get on the boat to return there from a holiday (or leave) they become once again the Anglo-Indian." He finished with this remark: "Don't forget, it's a boring life for the vast majority of them. They need our sympathy more than our derision." Later experience confirmed his remarks.

But one incident on board I must relate to show how even the children of these Anglo-Indians become heirs to the same snob complex. The young son of a well-known barrister (who was going to Calcutta on an important law suit) met the young son of one of the more snooty Indian Civil Servants, and greeted him with a cheery "Hullo, would you like to have a game of some-thing?" To which the young snob answered, turning away with an unfortunate leer: "Who are you? I don't know you." The barrister's son was not accepting this rebuff and kicked the other boy's behind with the remark, "What are you, anyway—a monkey or a boy?" This was duly reported to the snooty I.C.S., who sought out the barrister, of whose identity he was unaware. When they finally met, the I.C.S. protested vigorously that his son had been 'kicked' and insulted, to which the barrister replied: "My boy tells me that your son was extremely rude, and that, like any boy with spirit, he kicked his behind. Is that the story as you received it?" This staggered the I.C.S. "No, that is not what happened. My boy merely told your son that he did not know him, and therefore did not wish to play with him," replied the irate I.C.S. "In that case," replied the barrister—remarking aside to his son: "Jack, what you told me is quite true. Good lad! —if you wish to bring your boy up as a little snob it's no business of mine. If you don't go away at once I shall do to you what my boy did to your son. Now get out!" The I.C.S. did just that. But he went straight to the purser. The purser, however, explained that the man in question was a well-known barrister and advised the I.C.S. to forget the incident.

All very unpleasant, but not unusual on ships going to India in those days! I was not sorry when we reached Karachi and said good-bye to our friends on board. We were on Indian soil.

Our itinerary included Karachi, Quetta, Simla, several Hill stations, Patna, Allahabad, Bombay, Calcutta, Madras, Bangalore and Delhi. At Delhi, during the concert, an officer in resplendent uniform knocked at my door, and very respectfully asked if I would please have the room cleared because "His Excellency, the Lord Lloyd, wished to speak to me". Lord Lloyd and several members of the Governor's suite entered.

Lord Lloyd expressed his appreciation of my singing and chatted about my visit. He showed an exceedingly good know-ledge of music, and was kind enough to say that he knew my records very well. He asked me whether I would sing him a certain song, which I did, but it meant a quick trip back to the hotel for my accompanist to get the song he had chosen. I think it was "The Lute Player". There is no man quite like the cultured English gentleman. They are so sincere, lacking in 'side', and are so wonderfully natural to all—whatever class—they meet.

Three weeks later I met another charming man when Lord Ronaldshay called to see me during the interval of my concert in

Calcutta. He was a Scot, and of course we 'got on' famously. We chatted about songs, Scotland, my tour, and he finished up by asking me to sing a couple of his favourite Scottish songs. I believe Lord Ronaldshay was then Governor of Bengal, although I am not sure, but I do know he held a very responsible position.

After travelling about India, and singing with success, I am pleased to say I came to one definite conclusion. It was this: *India is a fine country to tour through, but not to live in.* The great social gulf between the Army, the Civil Service and the business men was most distasteful to me. The segregated clubs, and the segregated dances, just made me writhe. The colour question also irritated me. In order to take out a millionaire Indian who owned the music monopoly in almost all India, was a manufacturer and the leading perfumery exporter, I had to have a private room at my hotel because "it would be embarrassing for me and my guest to dine in the hotel restaurant". Despite these distractions the tour was a big success, personally and financially. I sang in seven concerts in Karachi, thirteen in Calcutta and thirteen in Bombay.

Soon after my arrival I was advised to learn a little Hindustani. Almost immediately after this I found cause to take the advice. On my arrival at Bombay I indicated in English and by signs to my 'boy' that I wanted to be awakened at five o'clock in the morning. I suited my actions to the words. I held up five fingers, pointed to the clock, and made a noise like a man sleeping. But it was no good. In less than five minutes the boy was back carrying five bottles of soda water! He thought I could only mean five bottles of something to drink, and that my idea of sleeping and pointing to the clock meant I wanted the soda water in a hurry. I quickly picked up a smattering of Hindustani after that. My wife said she thought the boy was quite ingenious in taking my imitation of a man sleeping noisily as soda water.

India is too well known to need my observations on the beautiful scenery one covers on a tour north, south, east and west. But I certainly gloried in the wonder of the Taj Mahal, the snow-capped heights of the Himalayas, the amazing kaleidoscope of colour to be seen in the northern cities, where the merchants from Central Asia mix with the local natives and those from other parts of India. I found India totally different to any other country I had seen. I am referring to the scenery, for naturally a country of four hundred million Indians of various castes would strike a difference to the eye and the mind. The scenery was older in some inexplicable way. It was grandeur without the freshness one sees in Australia, New Zealand, South Africa and Britain.

And, of course, there were many inconveniences not met with in the other countries I have mentioned. In one place we stayed rats ran over the latticework which hung below the ceiling. It became so disturbing that I unpacked my catapult (I never travel without it) and, using the stoppers from mineral-water bottles, started potting them. After about twenty minutes' shooting they decided to stop their perambulations over the latticework, and I ultimately enjoyed a sleep.

We had one or two scares. The first happened when we were awakened at 5 a.m. in the train for a medical examination before proceeding on to Madras. When this was over somebody rather foolishly told us we had been tested for plague! The company was naturally very disturbed. And when on arrival in Madras the pianist fell ill we all immediately came to the conclusion she must have plague, and the poor girl herself cried to my wife that 'it must be plague'. Fortunately the doctor soon put our minds at rest: it was a touch of sunstroke. Although she had been advised to wear proper headgear, she had considered a lace hat sufficient protection against the sun. Not in Madras, as it was proved!

In Madras, too, we were in the thick of a political upheaval. Bombs were thrown into the mills not more than 300 yards from where we were staying. A certain section of the natives were very hostile, and we were advised to keep indoors at night. A native policeman and two rioters were killed in the gardens of the hotel where we were living. A very distressing incident, particularly as a couple of shots ricocheted into the bedroom next to mine.

At Quetta we were awakened by wild dogs entering our room. Nan and I thought they were wolves. We kept very quiet, but presently the night porter came along and 'shushed' them away. "Wild dogs," was his laconic remark as he left the room.

At Rawalpindi we had an amusing experience. The hall was next to the railway shunting lines, and I was approached by a handful of white engine-drivers for permission to 'park' their engines outside the hall, and "Would you please open the windows as far as possible?" Of course I was only too glad to oblige. The concert proceeded on its way but presently the shunting engines 'approached' and stopped outside the hall. The noise of escaping steam was deafening, making it impossible to go on with the concert, and unfortunately I was obliged to send a message to the drivers that if they could not turn off the steam I should have to ask them to move away. A few minutes later the reply came. Three loud blasts of the whistles from the three engines and away they drove.

I found the heat rather trying, especially during the concerts. The fact that we had four *punkas* going over the platform did not seem to ease matters. Immediately I had finished one set of songs I used to come off the platform and take my collar off, and have a good rub down. The mosquitoes were particularly trying in some places. At the hotel in Cawnpore there were no mosquito nets in the bedrooms. The pests were so irritating that we sat up all night, after wrapping our feet and lower limbs in paper. It was a case of swatting the little devils all night. That, I think, was the most distressing night of the whole tour, and I vowed I would never return to India, or if I did I should cut out Cawnpore!

Two incidents happened at Bangalore, a charming little place in the hills outside Madras where officers and their wives used to come for a rest during their long leaves in India. In the middle of a song I was singing a woman's scream tore through the auditorium. I stopped my song and the audience rose to see what it was all about. In the stalls the woman was screaming in agony, holding her ear. I climbed down and went to find out what had happened. A flying insect, something like a beetle, had apparently lodged in her ear and was causing agonizing pain. She was rushed to hospital for attention. The concert was held up for twenty minutes. The incident had a very serious effect both on the audience and on the members of the company. I personally was very glad to be handed a little cotton wool when I got off the platform. All the company accepted it too. When I went on for my second set of songs I noticed that several of the audience had left, too upset by the agonized cries of the woman to stay. But that was not all. Driving home after the show we came across a party of six policemen hitting a white man over the head and arms with their canes. A white woman was with the man and doing her best to protect him. I jumped out, as did my manager and Selwyn Driver, and as I remonstrated with the police the manager knocked one of the policemen down. I thought that would be the signal for trouble for all of us, but it wasn't. They immediately stopped attacking the man and listened to my protests. We learned that he had 'been rude' to a native woman—how, I did not worry to ask—but I called them aside and said: "You do not want make trouble. Here, take this, and you go away. I will take the man into the city." And I gave them a rupee each! The following day we left Bangalore, and we were not sorry.

One of the most exhilarating experiences I had was at Simla. Most of us have read or heard the Kipling lines from "Route Marchin'":

Oh, there's them Indian temples to admire when you see.
There's the peacock round the corner an' the monkey up the tree,
An' there's that rummy silver-grass a-wavin' in the wind,
An' the old Grand Trunk a-trail' like a rifle-sling be'ind.
      While its best foot first . . .

Imagine the thrill I got when I actually saw the incident described in the second line. I saw a monkey frisking about, and watched his antics. He suddenly stopped, kept quite still, and looked round stealthily. I turned to see what was attracting his attention and there, less than twenty yards away, a peacock was rounding the corner of a flower bed.

When you hear me sing "Route Marchin'" you will now understand why I always stress that particular line. I actually see the monkey and the peacock out there in Simla.

Everywhere I travelled in India I kept recalling Kipling. Every animal, scene, incident, cow, bird and elephant reminded in some way of the great man's writings.

*   *   *

From India we went to Burma for a series of concerts. Here again I was anxious to see the country and the people I had been singing about so much. "Mandalay" had constantly featured in my repertoire throughout my career. Rangoon conveyed more to me than it would to most other people at first sight, because I felt that I already knew it through the song. I was not disappointed. When I first approached and entered Rangoon I thought: There is 'the old Moulmein Pagoda, lookin' eastward to the sea'. And there, too,

      I saw a Burma girl a-settin',
      And I know she thinks o' me!
      The wind was in the palm trees,
      And I heard the temple bells.
      And I saw a Burmese girl,
      'Er petticoat was yeller,
      An' 'er little cap was green,
      An' I seed her first a-smokin'
      Of a whackin' white cheroot,
      An' a-wastin' Christian kisses
      On an 'eathen idol's foot:
      Bloomin' idol made o' mud—
      What they called the Great Gawd Budd.

Yes, I saw this on my first day. And I saw more of Kipling's Mandalay. 'When the mist was on the rice fields an' the sun was droppin' slow'. I also watched the elephants piling teak.

I have always been a passionate admirer of Kipling's works, but my visit to Burma and India inspired me to set more of his lines. To date I have set "Boots", "Route Marchin'," "Cells", and arranged a song scene of four songs on "Mandalay". No man knew or saw more, in and about India and Burma, than Rudyard Kipling, and my advice to any visitors going to these places is to study Kipling. When you arrive you will find his pictures continually and forcibly recurring to your mind. A thousand times better, this poet, than all the guide books you might buy! I met the man himself as he was leaving a private dinner party held at the Café Royal in Regent Street, London—he had been dining with Baldwin, Balfour, and, I think, Bonar Law—and he was kind enough to express his appreciation of my setting of his lines "Boots". I told him I was hoping to do one or two more, and he said, "Well, Mr. Dawson, if they are as good as 'Boots' we shall not quarrel."

One thing Kipling did not mention, as far as I am aware, is the profusion of bats in Rangoon. The first night of my concert there I could not at first imagine what the terrific din was I could hear above my head in the flies. It was so bad that I appealed to the audience, "Can you hear that noise, coming from up there?" I received several replies. "Yes, it's the bats." I decided to ask the audience to let me have a few moments while I tried to do something about it.

Ten minutes later I restarted. I hadn't sung more than half a song when I suddenly saw a huge cockroach—the mother of all cockroaches!—ambling across the stage in front of me. When I had finished I pointed to the crawling thing, which of course was easily visible to most of the audience, and said, "That's the first insect I've ever known that had an ear for music." That did it. We all laughed together, and the rest of the concert went off without further incident.

The audience in Rangoon had their own ideas what they wanted me to sing, and I thoroughly enjoyed the shouts for different items. I sang fourteen songs at my first concert, and gave four concerts in all. Then I moved on to Penang, Kuala Lumpur, Malacca and down to Singapore. Had anyone suggested to me that twenty-four years later this territory would be overrun by the Japanese, and that Singapore would be taken by assault, I should have considered it the ravings of a lunatic. But, on reflection, I do remember being told that "there would soon be as many Japanese as Chinese in Singapore". I don't know whether my informant was commenting on this as a menace, or just a passing view of the increase in the number of Japs entering the city. I wasn't interested.

My most potent memory of Singapore was something quite different. But for a miracle I might have been killed or badly injured. . . .

The weather during our stay was glorious, and because of this we made up our minds to take a car over to Sea Point after the show and do some bathing by moonlight. We had covered the climb over and round the hills, and were about to put on speed down towards the Point, when one of the ladies became enthusiastic about the view. We asked the driver to slow down and then stop, for we had decided to get out and enjoy the beauty of the scene. The driver walked on a pace or two and then turned back and said to me in a whisper, "Come with me a moment, sir." He pointed about ten yards ahead and continued, "Can you see what be strung across the road?"

I looked and at first could see nothing, but going nearer I found a strong wire had been drawn across the road at a height that would have caught our heads, and probably have decapitated those sitting in front, for the car was—like most in Singapore—an open one. Unfortunately we could not keep the incident from the ladies, and there followed a few grim moments, waiting until the driver succeeded in cutting the wire and putting it into the car to take to the police on our return to the city. But the men, luckily four of us, were more concerned in contemplating what would be the next step of the bandits who had set this ghastly trap. We made a brave show, creating a great noise and the manager brandishing a pistol, shouting, "I'll shoot the first swine I see!", while I got out an iron bar from the tool-box and 'pretended' to be seeking the bandits. But all was quiet and we could neither hear nor see any sign of men. We came to the conclusion that they must have seen us stop, thinking we had observed the wire ahead of us, and quickly made their getaway.

Nevertheless, we went on our way very carefully, and enjoyed our bathe. But first we reported the matter to the local police, who sent out a patrol at once. When I remarked to the manager, who luckily had a revolver, "Lucky you had a gun with you, old man," he replied: "Gun, my foot. That was my pipe!"

Because of the number of white foreigners in Singapore I

gave a mixed programme, which included a French and an Italian song, and two songs from operas. But here, as everywhere, the audience asked for their own favourite songs, and I was only too willing to oblige. One in great request was "Roses of Picardy". The war was still fresh in their minds, and "Roses" was a favourite all through the East.

We found the hurried travelling to and from Penang, Malacca and Kuala Lumpur most trying but, although terribly tired and worried by the heat and insect bites, we were cheered by the enthusiastic greetings we received everywhere. As a lover of the open country I was thrilled by the astonishing variety of trees I saw. A British official explained that I would find several hundred varieties in almost any square mile in the forest area. The glorious flora, however, really had me in wonderment. Australia has a huge variety, but here . . . The same official told me that there are over 9,000 known species of flower-plants and ferns. If I had only had more time I should have been very happy exploring the territory. And what an astonishing number of different animals! In a four hours' drive from Kuala Lumpur we saw elephants—I mean the wild variety—a tiger, several wild cats, mongooses (many), rhinoceroses, and at a distance of sixty yards a couple of huge alligators.

The expedition (confined to men) was spoilt by the heat, the 'millions' of flying insects, and the number of snakes that worried us every time we alighted for a walk. A great pity, because there was so much to see and hear. Even so I did see a wonderful collection of birds.

What a paradise of a country Malaya would be if only they could rid the air of the insects, the ground of snakes, and the pools of malaria! There are over six hundred species of birds, but also over one hundred various kinds of snakes. But the worst pest is the bat. They are everywhere. You can never escape them; if you don't see them, you can hear or smell them.

From Singapore we returned to Madras. But the political troubles were still on, and we left almost immediately for Ceylon, where we were to give a number of concerts, including a fortnight in Colombo. Colombo I know very well, for I have always paid a visit there on my trips to and from Australia. It was with great pleasure that on this occasion I should be staying for a series of concerts. In addition to singing in Colombo I took the company in to the Hill stations, and also managed to arrange a most enjoyable visit to that lovely place, Kandy.

What a beautiful spot! I had been told that, before I gave up my travelling, I must see Kandy. It is not merely a lovely spot to view from the outside, but is surrounded by scenic beauty unparalleled in the world. In the centre of the view of the town from the railway is the charming lake that was artificially constructed early in the nineteenth century by the last King of Kandy. The small town lies in a basin on the lakeside, surrounded by indescribably beautiful hills.

A short distance from Kandy are the Royal Botanic Gardens at Peradeniya. These are world famous and need no comment from me. But I do suggest that Ceylon is one of the most beautiful lands in the world, and ought to be seen. Perhaps, with air travel progress, the time may come when it will be possible for almost anyone to visit this scenic paradise for a few pounds sterling. Today is it too expensive except for the few.

After our trying time in Burma it was a great relief to find the atmosphere of Ceylon almost free from the wretched flying insects and bats of Burma. The concerts were most successful, and we left Ceylon regretfully for home. With regret, because we had struck the country at the right time of the year, and were able to enjoy a rest and admire its beauty.

CHAPTER X

MY IRISH TOURS

I WELCOMED the opportunity of singing in Dublin. I have a considerable repertoire of Irish songs or songs about the 'ould Country'.

But before I sang Irish songs I made a careful study of the brogue. I know nothing more irritating than to hear vocalists massacring a song through faulty pronunciation. In studying Irish songs I was fortunate in being born of Scottish parents. It is very much easier for a Scot to speak or sing the brogue than it is for an Englishman. I quickly discovered that I could sing Irish songs with ease, and I thoroughly enjoyed enunciating the brogue. There is something particularly satisfying in singing real Irish songs—or is it the 'blarney' in me? Begorra an' I wouldn't know.

My advice to all singers—amateur and professional—is to master the dialect of a song before singing it in public. The same advice should be followed in rendering songs in a foreign language. If you wish to sing in Italian, German or French, try to find a native teacher of the language to coach you in the correct pronunciation. In this way you avoid the remarks you have all heard —or uttered—at some time or another: "Wasn't his French atrocious? Much better to have sung in his own language!"

And so before sailing for Dublin I was well equipped to sing a number of songs and a few encores of Irish songs. I should not have been so confident of doing this successfully had I not been aware that my records of Irish songs were popular in Ireland.

My first visit was during the usual trouble of political strife. The concert party included Margaret Cooper, and the brilliant 'cellist, Suggia. On disembarking at Kingstown we had to pass through the ranks of 'Black and Tans' who were on guard at the port, and on the way into Dublin we heard the sound of desultory firing, which, although fairly distant, had the effect of terrifying Mme Suggia. I must confess that I did not relish the ride into the capital, for occasionally the firing was, or appeared to be, less than a couple of hundred yards away. But I was able to reassure Mme Suggia that she had nothing to fear, for the authorities would not have allowed us to go ahead if there had been the slightest risk. Although I comforted the Italian, Margaret Cooper and myself were scared at one point when a couple of police came running out of a side turning obviously being shot at.

On arriving in Dublin I found things much quieter, and, in fact, everything appeared normal. Nevertheless I was apprehensive about the prospects of the concert. But it would take more than a political scrimmage to upset the equanimity of the Dublin Irish, so the concert was a big success and passed off without incident. But when we returned to our hotel we were advised not to venture forth again. My accompanist, Hubert Barth, and myself thought there would be no harm in taking a short stroll before going to bed, and we sallied forth.

We hadn't gone a hundred yards when we were stopped by a couple of big fellows of the Royal Irish Constabulary who advised us to go back to the hotel. When we protested that we were not a couple of old women and needed some fresh air, the boys became tough—very tough—and we wisely followed their advice. In the morning we heard that a wild shooting affair had taken place about fifty yards from where we had been stopped by the constables. It occurred exactly ten minutes after we had returned to the hotel. We tried to find the constables the following day but failed. We wanted to thank them for their good advice, and apologize for our stupidity in questioning their caution.

Curiously enough my next appearance in Dublin was to sing at a concert in aid of the widows and relatives of 'The Martyrs who died in the fighting'. That was the most extraordinary concert I have ever seen or heard. And in addition to the character of the concert, had it not been for a split-second and fortuitous brainwave of Hubert Barth's we might have been lynched—and, considering the purpose of the concert, rightly so!

But first let me tell you about the concert, and how it differed from any in which I had participated.

In between my two appearances in the programme a distressingly painful and grim scene had been enacted. When the curtain went up, the stage revealed a setting of the gaol gates in which the martyrs had been incarcerated. Presently a dear old woman slowly walked on to the stage, and rang the prison bell. This was answered by a particularly vicious and arrogant warder. "Well, what do you want?" shouted the man. "I have come to see my son. He is to be executed in the morning for a killing he knows nothing about," cried the poor soul. "Well, you can't see him now. Come back in the morning," shouted the man, banging the gate in her face. The same kind of incident was repeated when the wife of one of the prisoners made an effort to see her husband.

Then the stage was blacked out for a few minutes and was lit again. It was the same scene the following morning. The mother appeared, and made a request to see her son. Without enquiring the name of her son, he brutally shouted: "You're too late. He was executed an hour ago." And the same arrogance and tragic news was received by the widow.

That piece of stark realism was the main appeal of the concert, yet, so mercurial and unpredictable are the Irish, I received so many demands for encores that I turned to my accompanist, Hubert Barth, and said, "I really can't sing any more, better go on and play 'The King'. (The National Anthem!) Hubert replied, "All right," and he walked to the piano. But fortunately for both of us he quite suddenly realized what a ghastly mistake it would be, and instead of playing anything he closed the lid of the piano, and gave the audience a most dignified bow. And the curtain fell.

When we told the manager what had almost happened he said, "Oh, may the good God be praised, may the good God be praised." And a little later, when he had recovered from the shock of what might have happened, he said: "D'you know, Mr. Dawson, I don't believe any power on earth would have stopped you from being lynched. Some of the boys would have believed you had done it deliberately." And I replied, "We should have deserved it."

On my next visit to Dublin I sang for a very different society. This was 'The Brotherhood of the Kingdom of Christ'. But on this occasion I did get myself into serious trouble with some of the tough boys of the I.R.A.

During the interval in the programme a couple of Irishmen, smiling, pleasant-faced fellows, came to my dressing-room, and asked me if I would sing a song in the second half of the concert, which, they said, would make everybody in the hall very, very happy. And they handed me a copy of "The West's Awake", which is a stirring song, full of patriotic Irish fervour, and which includes a striking passage cursing England. I told them I would sing it, and proceeded to rehearse it with my accompanist. The song was a little too long and I made a cut here and there.

Unfortunately I did not mention the incident to the manager, Mr. Tim Murray, but proceeded to study the song. I sang the two items in the programme, and for an encore sang "The West's Awake". I could sense that something was wrong before the song was finished; that indefinable mind wave that comes from an audience to a singer when something untoward is happening. When I finished the song there was utter and complete silence. Not even the men who had asked me to sing the song applauded. When I reached the side of the platform Tim Murray, with a face as white as my shirt front, gasped, "What in the name of heaven made you sing that?" I explained the incident and went on to say, a little testily, that I thought I was obliging the audience. "Ah, well, what's done can't be undone." Taking hold of my arm, he said that he wanted me to go to the band-room with him for a few moments. "I have a little food and refreshment, and I want to talk over a future engagement. I think I can explain what happened tonight."

Well, we stayed in the band-room for nearly two hours. Both Tim Murray and a friend of his who joined us kept us amused. And when I made any effort to go, they made some excuse. But finally I intimated that I must get back to my hotel at midnight because I had a timed 'phone call to London. When we made our way to the dressing-rooms all the lights were out and we lighted matches to find my music case and overcoat. Instead of leaving by the stage door we were escorted through the darkness of the hall to the front entrance. After a few minutes' wait in the dark behind the entrance doors a car drew up outside, and we were literally rushed into the car and off to the hotel.

On the way back to the hotel it was explained to me that a small bunch of very angry citizens had been waiting for me at the stage door. I had offended the audience of the 'Brotherhood' but they were not hostile: they realized that I must have been ill-advised. But I had also deeply offended the two men who asked me to sing "The West's Awake" by cutting out that part which curses England, and as Tim Murray put it, "Better not to have sung it at all, than leave the part out they badly wanted to hear you sing."

But on my next visit to Ireland and Dublin I was greatly honoured by being invited to lunch by President Cosgrave, at Templeogue. It was just a family affair, which pleased me immensely. The only other guest was the Irish poet, Padraic Colum.

To meet Mr. and Mrs. Cosgrave and their two delightful children in the privacy of their home was an unforgettable occasion in my life. I have sung before many private parties, but in that happy home at Templeogue I experienced one of the most pleasing of all family gatherings. I sang two songs that the President especially liked.

H

I remember being a little surprised to find framed photographs of Kreisler and John McCormack on the piano, which were moved immediately I said I should like to sing the songs the President had mentioned. During lunch the conversation, led by Mr. Cosgrave, turned to music, and I was very agreeably surprised to find that both Mr. and Mrs. Cosgrave were music enthusiasts. It does not take an artiste more than a few minutes to discover when a conversation on music and singing is perfunctory, and when it is sincere. Which reminds me that I do not recall meeting any Irishman, north or south, who did not have a taste for music in some form or other.

After lunch I was shown over the beautiful gardens around the house. I have always been a lover of nature. It was pleasant to note the surprise I gave Mr. Cosgrave with my knowledge of flowers.

"Where did you get all your learning?" asked the President. "Why, in Australia," I replied, and went on: "There is not a flower, or for that matter a bird, in Australia that I cannot identify. I am a great lover of my native country, and in my travels nothing gives me greater pleasure than to talk of its beauty. Not solely about its plethora of flowers, but about its glorious scenery, its trees, birds, the huge potential of its mineral wealth, and the certainty of its limitless future." Mr. Cosgrave then chatted to me at length about Australia. After a while he said, "Well, Mr. Dawson, you have greatly awakened my interest in your fine country, and I shall do my best to see it." Then with a whimsical look he added, "And I only wish we had more Irishmen who could sing the praises of his country with the same enthusiasm as you do of Australia."

The conversation then turned to Irish music and musicians. Padraic Colum asked me whether I had heard the Irish Army Band under its famous conductor Fritz Braza. I was glad to tell them that I had an engagement to sing with the band, and was looking forward to it with interest because so many people had spoken to me in high praise of it.

"Has the band made any gramophone records?" I asked. And the President replied: "I have asked the same question. But I am sorry to say that no records have been made—to my great regret. I understand that there are certain difficulties, but I am not aware exactly what they are."

I signified my intention to have a word with the gramophone people on my return to London, and would let Mr. Cosgrave know the result of my inquiries. (Later I did take the matter up with H.M.V., and they explained that they were anxious to record the band and other items in Dublin, but the custom restrictions on their portable recording apparatus in and out of Dublin were insuperable. I immediately 'phoned Mr. Cosgrave and explained the deadlock. "Well, Mr. Dawson, I will get that matter cleared up satisfactorily. Please tell the Company to send their recording apparatus as soon as they like, and I will personally guarantee that there will be no further trouble of the kind you have outlined. And thank you for taking the matter up so promptly. I know the band and the Irish people will be delighted to know that this fine band will soon be recorded.")

Fritz Braza was a magnificent conductor and a brilliant musician. I knew him by reputation—from his career in Germany.

It was from his great experience of bands in Germany that Braza had gained his innate knowledge that enabled him to make such a truly remarkable success of the Irish Army Band.

One of the great faults with Army band players—and what I am about to say must not be taken in any derogatory sense—is the perfectly normal thirst that is engendered by brass instrument blowing. Although the caricature of lager-swilling German band players is greatly overdrawn, it is an axiom that they like their glass of beer—and why not?

With this knowledge in his mind, Braza caused a stir in Irish Army circles when he laid down certain startling, almost staggering, conditions to the members of the Army Band he was to take over and conduct.

In order to ensure that the members of the band were in tip-top condition for an important concert he instituted the system which was received with approbation; he had the members of the band *confined to barracks two days before the concert*!

They were allowed no alcoholic drinks and debarred from smoking.

Although this savoured of interference with the liberty of the subject the members were quick to appreciate Braza's ruling after he explained to them just why he had introduced this revolutionary and seemingly dogmatic order. They were quick, too, to realize that it was Braza's intention to make them into the finest band in any army of the world, and to appreciate the truly remarkable results that Braza achieved. In short, the result more than justified the restrictions, and the band became world famous.

I have never heard a better band. Each man had been instructed by the great musician how to blow his instrument to improve the quality by using less energy than was his custom. The lipping was improved tenfold. It was a band that the President had every right to be proud of. But how about the members of the band and the restrictions placed on them? Every man Jack of them accepted the system of training with commendable spirit. I got to know them all very well, and they all expressed the greatest admiration for their conductor, who had instituted the system of training. "At first we rather resented this German telling us what we were to do and what we were not to do, but it did not take us long to understand the wisdom of his idea," was how one member of the band explained it to me.

And today the band is as keen on training before an important engagement as a football team is before a cup-tie.

I remember being brought up suddenly against the peculiar set-up in the political montage of Irish politics when I suggested to the President that it would be a fine idea to send the band round the town.

"Ah, Mr. Dawson, you don't know us yet. In one part of this fine old city the band would receive a great welcome and have flowers thrown at them, but in another part of the city they would have brickbats thrown at them." I did not pursue the subject.

It was in the garden that Padraic Colum (now living in the United States) asked me, "Have you seen the Arnold Bax setting of my 'Rann of Exile'?" It was only then that I realized that this quiet-spoken reserved Irishman, whose name I had not really gathered on the President's introduction, was the famous Irish poet. Of course I knew the song, also his "Cradle Song" and "Rann of Wandering".

Here is the lyric which Arnold Bax set to music:

Nor right, nor left, nor any road
I see a wonderful face,
Nor word to life the heart of me
I hear in any place
They leave me, who pass by me
To my loneliness and care,
Without a house to draw steps,
Nor a hearth that I might share,
O Con!
Before our people knew
The scattering of the dearth,
Before they saw potatoes
Rot and melt black in the earth,

I might have stood in Connacht,
On the top of Cruachmael Inn,
And all around me I would see
The hundreds of my kin.

I had always admired the song, and it gave me particular pleasure to meet the man who wrote the poem. When some years ago I appeared in a special programme in the larger music-halls, "Rann of Exile" was one of the most popular of my numbers. It is a fine tribute to any song that it is acclaimed both by the more discriminating musical audience of the concert hall and the critical audience of the music-hall.

It was Padraic Colum who, when I commented on the portraits of Kreisler and John McCormack on the piano in the drawing-room at Templeogue, remarked: "You probably don't know that John has political ambitions." When I expressed my astonishment Colum went on: "I assure you that John has already achieved one ambition: to be Ireland's greatest tenor. His other ambition is to be the President of his country."

And in response to my look of incredulity, he said: "John is absolutely sincere in his idea. And why not? There is a precedent. How about Paderewski?"

What a tragedy that John McCormack's life ended so soon. To think that the young tenor I had met in 1906 singing phonograph records for 7s. 6d. a round, was to become one of the world's greatest tenors, and certainly Ireland's greatest ever, might have achieved his other ambition of becoming the President of his country had not his life been cut so tragically short.

Shortly after meeting the President I met a man of an entirely different character, but a man that only Ireland could produce.

He was a king. Yes, the uncrowned 'King' of Kinsale. In all my wide experience never have I met such an astonishing personality. And I am convinced that nowhere in the whole world is there a man in whom is vested so many and diverse responsibilities. He appeared to own all the utility companies—including the waterworks. He owned the brewery, the best hotel; in fact everything that mattered in the town.

An example—*par excellence*—of the power he could wield (a power he enjoyed demonstrating to any visiting notability, and he must have placed me in that category) I will show in the following story.

On the night of my departure I was in his company at the hotel—his, of course—and he had insisted that he would drive me from Kinsale to the boat leaving Cork (Cobh) at six o'clock that night. At five, I suggested that as it was roughly an hour's drive to the port we had better be starting. I also knew that he proposed driving me to the ship in his particularly dilapidated old Ford car. I wanted to allow reasonable time in case of a breakdown. "Listen to me, my dear sor. The boat will not leave without you. That's a promise. A promise, mark you, from me!" And this was marked with such a tone of finality, backed by assenting nods from his friends round the table, that I accepted the situation, and we continued chatting and swopping stories— that is, when the 'King' gave us an opportunity.

But at six o'clock I was worried. The party was getting very gay, and I was losing a little faith in the ability of any man to hold a ship for more than an hour. "Don't get excited, my dear man. The boat daresn't leave without my consent!" And again I received nods of affirmation from the others.

We finally left the hotel at seven-thirty for Cork to catch the boat that was due to sail at six o'clock! We arrived alongside the ship at eight-thirty.

The captain could be seen on the bridge looking down on to the dock, and the crew were all standing by, obviously waiting for the arrival of the 'King'.

Cupping his hands to his mouth the 'King' yelled up to the captain, "We're coming aboard to the haberdashery department." And aboard we went. The haberdashery department was, of course, the bar. But here I wished my irrepressible host farewell, and made my way to my cabin, where to my surprise I found a present from the 'King' on my bunk.

I made my way to the haberdashery and thanked him for his very kind thought. This remarkable man did not leave the ship until ten-thirty.

His final words to me were: "Well, Peter, what did I tell you? They daresn't leave without my permission." And away he went, laughing, and shouting valedictions to one and all. A bluff, cheery soul, with a fund of reminiscences, and as witty a *raconteur* as it was ever my pleasure to meet. I never found out how he was able to hold up the sailing of the steamer, but I assume he must have held certain rights—harbour rights. Quite frankly, if I had not been aware that the ship was owned by the G.W. Railway, I might have been persuaded that he owned the line. He must have possessed extraordinary powers or possessed the mother of all blarneys!

The meeting with the 'King' was fortuitous, for just before

I met him I had remarked to John Fay, my accompanist: "How quiet it is here. There is very little to see, and nothing to do."

Overnight I had sung to a crowded and appreciative house, but in unusual circumstances. When I arrived—fortunately early —at the Opera House, there was no piano on the stage. When I asked "Where's the piano?" I was informed that the ladies' choir objected to a piano being on the platform. All my insistence went for nothing. If a piano was on the stage, and 'so obscure some of the dresses of the choir', they would not appear. I was told that other artistes had sung with their accompanists behind the scene and it had worked satisfactorily.

It was too late to continue the argument, and I decided to submit to this strange Irishism. So I sang with my accompanist out of sight. At the commencement of the concert I made a short statement to the audience: "No doubt you are wondering why you cannot see my accompanist or the piano. The fact is he is very shy. But I promise I will let you see him before the programme ends." And I did.

I literally carried a most embarrassed man on to the platform. And of course a great roar went up, for John Fay was a well-known and popular figure at all concerts in the town.

John was to have another embarrassing experience the following morning. We were outside a tobacconist's shop making some harmless remarks about a particularly nauseating-looking twist of tobacco in the window before entering the shop to buy some cigarettes. When I asked for a particular brand the man behind the counter, with a demoniacal expression on his face, hissed, "You can get out of here, you ruddy Englishmen." I thought it wise to say: "We are not English. My friend here is real Irish and I——" But I got no farther. "Get out, the both of yer. If you don't I'll hit yer with this," and he lifted a heavy counter weight to suit his action to his words. And that was that. Outside, John said, "Well, be jazers, and that in my own town."

That incident, and what had happened about the ladies' choir, taught me a lesson about the Irish I have never forgotten.

Ever afterwards I took particular care not to upset the susceptibilities of my Irish friends. I have always found them hospitable and friendly, but they are inflexible in their political and religious beliefs, and take these things far more seriously than we do in the old country or in my own country of Australia.

Paradoxically I am delighted to be able to state that I found no audience that resented the singing of English songs or songs about England.

Having made a success with "The Floral Dance" in Dublin,
I announced, with a little trepidation I must confess, "The
Sergeant of the Line". It went marvellously. And they shouted
for more!

I sung "Up from Somerset". I shall not be exaggerating when
I say that they showed their enjoyment of these songs with as
much enthusiasm as any audience in England. Which reminds
me that I sang "Drake" at Cork in the first part of the programme.
In the second half I sung it again because I had been requested
during the interval to sing it again in the second half. Another
song I received a large number of requests for was "Glorious
Devon", and of course "Boots".

These successes in Ireland of purely English songs recalls
to my mind a visit I paid to the London Palladium during the
I.R.A. troubles in Ireland, and the shooting of British officers—
and *vice versa*. An Irish tenor sang a number of Irish songs,
including the "Wearing of the Green". He was a howling
success! We met later, and I heard him say to a man who had
obviously asked him the question that I had in mind: "Those
people in the audience come here to be entertained. They don't
care a damn about politics."

How right he was. Had I not proved the truth of his observation in the reception accorded the English songs I sang in Dublin
during the trouble?

Yet despite the Irish songs, the poets, and the fine actors
and those fine Irish tenors—Joseph O'Mara, Alfred Shea and
John McCormack—Ireland only produced one soprano of
world-wide repute—Margaret Sheridan. Most of us know
that Signor Foley, the grand bass singer whose fame travelled
throughout the world, was Irish. In his prime Foley was
the absolute idol of London. Like many other artistes Foley
decided to add the prefix 'Signor' to his name because he
believed that a singer with a foreign name stood more chance
of securing engagements and more money! Foley was a dynamic
personality and possessed what is so often found in the Irish—
a frightening temper. On one occasion he was lunching at a well-
known restaurant and was annoyed at the way in which a certain
dish had been prepared. Not receiving satisfaction from the head
waiter to his complaint, and resenting the waiter's "I really
cannot understand what you are complaining about, sir," Foley
fumed, and getting hold of the dish shouted, "I'll show you what's
wrong with it," and taking the dish across the restaurant opened
a window and threw the contents and the dish out of it. "That's

what's wrong with it, and now what are *you* going to do about it?"
Fortunately the episode caused so much laughter that Foley
regained his normal *bonhomie*, the head waiter thought that
discretion was the wisest plan, and peace reigned once more in
the restaurant.

That was typical of Foley. After the storm he was as docile
and as charming as only the Irish can be.

Yes, Ireland has given many fine contributions and con-
tributors to the world of music. It has also produced a wonderful selection of songs of every class and variety. Out of the many
thousands of programmes I have sung, I should say that less than
ten per cent did not carry an Irish song, a song about Ireland, or
a song written by an Irishman. Among the songs that I invariably
sing as an encore is one of the following: "The Kerry Dance",
"Phil the Fluter's Ball", "Molly Branagan", "Lanagan's Log",
"The Pride of Tipperary", and let me add that I have sung them
with the same success in England, Scotland, Wales, Australia,
New Zealand, South Africa, India and the Straits Settlements!

I have often been asked to name my favourite Irish songs,
the Irish songs I most enjoy singing. Well, they are "The Kerry
Dance" and "The low-backed Car". Irish songs are wholesome,
stirring; and of course many of them are plaintive, reflecting the
great character of the race. But they must be sung with the
correct tang of the brogue, if not they will jar on the ears of the
Irish. The right intonation is vital, otherwise your effort will be
received with silent, respectful toleration.

Let's look at the lyric of Glover's delightful song "The low-
backed Car":

> *Sweet Peggy round her car, sirs,*
> *Has strings of ducks and geese,*
> *But the scores of hearts she slaughters*
> *By far outnumber these.*
> *While she among her poultry sits*
> *Just like a turtle dove,*
> *Well worth the cage I do engage*
> *Of the fair young girl of love.*

And the refrain:

> *While she sits in her low-backed car*
> *The lovers come near and far,*
> *And they envy the chickens,*
> *That Peggy is picking*
> *As she sits in the low-backed car.*

What a delightful song, and how I enjoy singing it!

A chapter about Ireland must not end without a reference to that magnificent Irish baritone, Denis O'Sullivan.

My memory of the first time I heard Denis sing will never fade. It was at the Caxton Hall, in London. This hall, by the way, is better known for its registry office weddings than as a concert hall today!

Denis sang "The Kangaroo and the Dingo", from Rudyard Kipling's *Just So Stories*, set to music by Edward German.

He sang the song with such clear understanding I could *see* the race between the kangaroo and the dingo dog!

The amazing clarity of his enunciation impressed me very considerably and I have never failed to pay tribute to his brilliance. In those days it was unusual to hear a singer 'live' in the song he was singing. Denis not only gave us the race but we heard every word of the text. Such diction was exceptional and I have always remembered it.

I shall be referring to Irish singers, song-writers, and other things Irish in other parts of this book, for the Irish, like the Scots, are ubiquitous. I shall be giving, too, the words of my favourite Irish song "The Kerry Dance", for this is the perfect example of the song with a story well told.

Part Two

CHAPTER XI

MORE ABOUT RECORDING

NOW back to recording. I was making many records under other names so that I might record songs in a different class with a *nom de plume* for each type of song:

PETER DAWSON: Art songs, Operatic, Choral, Ballads.

HECTOR GRANT: Scottish songs of the Lauder type.

FRANK DANBY: Light popular songs.

WILL STRONG: Music-hall hits.

For each song I changed my dialect. I have always been a good—I might say accomplished—copyist. Probably because I started doing so early in my recording career.

But I was not sorry when this singing of a variety of songs under several names stopped. Agents were asking for the addresses of Frank Danby and Hector Grant with a view to auditions; and the whole thing was indecorous to the future of Peter Dawson. I remember one well-known agent acclaiming the voice of Frank Danby, and saying to me: "Peter, d'you think you could put me in touch with him? He has a fine voice, and knows how to sing a song. He sounds like the type I want for a new musical comedy in preparation." I dared not tell him the truth.

Here are the names I used for songs I set: J. P. McCall, Peter Allison, Evelyn Byrd, Denton Toms, Charles Webber, Arnold Flint, Gilbert Munday, Geoffrey Baxter and Alison Miller. But during the past few years I have changed this. I have dropped these several names and retained one—J. P. McCall.

Despite my sales I was not receiving the commensurate fees I felt I was entitled to.

I was fortunate therefore in having a brother-in-law, T. J. T. Noble, who had had very considerable experience in the gramophone world, to boost my fees. At the age of eighteen he was recording superintendent of the Edison Bell Company, and later assistant superintendent for the whole of Europe for the famous French firm Pathé Frères. He served directly under Russell Hunting, the man who nearly wrecked the start of my recording career.

Writing of his adventures in his exciting life recording

artistes all over the world, he entered Fleet Street as a cub reporter and recently retired as Managing Art Editor of the largest group of newspapers in Great Britain.

As a result of Tommy Noble's first effort I received a contract for a minimum of £1,200 per year.

Before going into the matter of further increases in my fees I should like to return to my actual recording experience during these years, and also to tell you about the hard fight the H.M.V. Company had to persuade famous artistes to sing for them!

Yes, in the early days the gramophone record, like the early cinematograph picture, was regarded by the leading members of the musical world as something mechanically dreadful!

But the brothers Gaisberg, of the H.M.V., were prolific 'go-getters', and it was their clever persuasiveness and the help of Landon Ronald that won Madame Melba over as the first of the prima donnas to record for a gramophone company in this country. Very often once the first bather enters the water others quickly follow, and this was the case with the celebrities of the musical world.

Although the victory was with the Gaisbergs, they suffered much torment from the extraordinary behaviour of the stars. For quite an appreciable time Melba and the others regarded recording with disapprobation. And this attitude, quite undisguised, was particularly galling to Will and Fred. It also irritated the members of the orchestra, who by this time were most appreciative of the potentialities of gramophone recording. One well-known British conductor, G. W. Byng, remarked on one occasion when Melba had been disagreeable and patronizingly contemptuous: "Really, that woman behaves as if we were scum. I've a damned good mind to walk out."

That reaction was shared by the whole orchestra.

Genial Will Gaisberg stepped into the arena and managed to placate the ruffled musicians. He treated singers and musicians like little children.

The success of the disc record was astonishing. In a few months the demand for machines and records was a revelation even to the gramophone company itself. With the tremendous improvement in the art of recording came the world's celebrities. Chaliapin was one of the first. He had the most powerful voice of any singer I have ever heard. He was a tremendous man physically. Imagine such a voice and such a presence raging and roaring in a room of smallish size—for the studio room in those

days in which the recordings were made was about thirty by
twenty-four feet! Chaliapin liked nothing better in those days
than to give full vent to his powerful voice in order to impress his
audience, whether ten or twenty, or three thousand, but in a small
studio it was a strange, fearsome experience. One felt like a child
in the cage of an infuriated lion. At other times—for Chaliapin
was genial, friendly, and only terrible when he was actually
singing—everyone was fascinated by his extremely pleasant personality. Naturally, like all great singers, he had his temperamental
outbursts on occasions.

I remember at one session he was singing the number "The
Calf of Gold", from *Faust*, when suddenly he stopped in the
middle of the solo, raised his arms, and yelled out an avalanche
of words that nobody in the studio understood. He tore up his
copy of the music, made his way through the other artistes and
musicians and walked up and down obviously cursing, but just
what he was raving about we could not guess. Ultimately he
stopped, and explained that he had completely forgotten he was
singing in French, and after the first page had continued in Russian.
I knew one phrase in Russian which refers to a dog. I shouted
out: "Never mind. It's G—— S——" in Russian. Chaliapin
stood amazed. "What you speak? What you say?" I repeated the
expression in my best Russian. I have never heard a man laugh so
much, so loudly and so sincerely in all my life. He had us all
joining in. "That is goot, vary, vary goot. But you know what
it is? I tell you." He explained that I had more or less used the
words that called him 'Dog's body'. How he laughed! The
session was not continued until he had told a number of friends
whom he had invited to the studio to watch him record. That
was a curious innovation of Chaliapin's. He always brought a
bunch of people to hear him record. On this occasion Lady
Diana Manners and her friends were present. I always remember
how beautiful Lady Diana was. And what a keen knowledge
she has of music, and the operas! She was a great friend and
supporter of the Opera and music generally.

Chaliapin partially undressed before singing in a recording
studio. "I must be free," he used to explain. And free he certainly
was. Like myself, this great man really enjoyed making records.
He was almost childish in his unrestrained delight every time he
heard his voice played over. And in Russian he would say many,
many times: "But it's wonderful. I can still learn. I find mistakes.
I make many, too many mistakes. Here I can correct them." He
often repeated, and in English: "Recording is the best teacher for

us singers. I will try all my best numbers on a record until I am satisfied with my renderings." He did this for many years.

It was about this time that Chaliapin had caused a stir in the Press by advocating a change in sartorial attire for men singers on the concert platform. "The idea," he said, "of standing on the concert platform dressed in a stiff white shirt, and a stiff, evil-choking collar, trying to make the audience believe that you are Mephistopheles or a Volga boatman, is to my mind quite absurd." John McCormack, however, was strongly opposed to him. I recall that John said: "I certainly do not despise evening dress. On the contrary, I prefer it. I consider it extremely comfortable, smart and always suitable. In fact my disappearance from the world of Opera was partly due to my dislike of the costumes. I don't think we want any sartorial revolutions in the concert hall: clothes don't really matter."

I gave my own view that I have always considered it absurd to have to stand up before an audience, which is chiefly composed of men in lounge suits, dressed up like a tailor's dummy, half choked by a stiff collar! One gets accustomed to it, and it is a 'safe' suit. Safe insomuch that there might be a curious innovation if lounge suits of various hues were introduced. The dress suit is a convention, and convention must be obeyed.

If the costumes were to be worn as a habit, beards and moustaches would assuredly follow. That would mean special scenery.

Chaliapin conceived his idea through the unconventional atmosphere of the recording studio. I began to find wearing dress a constant annoyance for the same reason. When recording I was able to remove my collar and loosen my shirt. It was a great boon. If I had to sing at a concert following a recording date, the stiff shirt became a perfect bugbear to me.

That's where women have a decided advantage over men.

One of the most important steps forward in the art of recording occurred in 1912, when under the conductorship of George W. Byng, who was then conducting the orchestra at the Alhambra, Leicester Square, we recorded the Gilbert and Sullivan operas. The artistes taking part were: Bessie Jones, Violet Essex, Gladys Jones, Nellie Walker, Edna Thornton, Robert Radford, Harold Wilde, George Baker, Edward Halland, Ernest Pike, Walter Glynne, Derek Oldham and myself.

George Byng later made some grand records, conducting the Covent Garden Opera Orchestra, of the 'Ballet Music' from *Faust*.

These records of the Gilbert and Sullivan operas were made

on the old style, using the metal recording trumpet with insulating tape tied round it to eliminate vibrations and rattle!

In a photograph I have preserved, the old style funnel can be seen. One trumpet was used when a solo was being recorded, and two for a duet or a quartet.

It is interesting to note that no special chorus was used. We made up the chorus ourselves. If I was singing a solo with chorus, then the rest of the company would be the chorus. If Derek Oldham was singing a solo and needed a chorus I helped the others as a chorus baritone.

The money, if I remember rightly (1912), was one guinea per solo, and ten shillings for a duet, quartet or part. We made several of the operas, and worked regularly for about ten weeks. I must have averaged thirty guineas a week, which was very satisfactory in those days. We became a very happy family, and many lasting friendships were established. Soon afterwards I left for Australia for my second tour.

On my return Tom Noble had negotiated a new contract which gave me a minimum guarantee of £800 per year for three years.

About this time the Columbia Company were making a reputation in the gramophone world. That was not surprising when it is remembered that Louis Sterling was the manager, and Arthur Brooks the chief recorder. As a matter of fact, it was in the rivalry of these two companies that Tom Noble saw his opportunity of getting better fees for my work with H.M.V. On my return from Australia in 1920 I signed a five-year contract at a minimum guarantee of £1,200 for each year.

There was a sensational boom in the sale of records in those five years from 1920 to 1925. The recording had improved, the reproducing machines were being sold to the public with many innovations, but particularly a truer recording toned reproducer. The H.M.V. people were spending big money on advertising in the national Press, and, most important of all, the public were keen on buying records. I was fortunate in being one of their favourites.

The famous 'His Master's Voice' picture was appearing everywhere. The story of how the painting gave the name of H.M.V. to the Gramophone Company is well known, but it is not equally well known that the Company gave the painter of the original picture of the dog listening to 'his master's voice' a job for life painting originals, and paid him a special retaining fee for doing so. Those paintings were sent to every H.M.V. agent

throughout the world. I once saw the painter at work in the
factory at Hayes, Middlesex. I asked, "Why don't you paint
another kind of dog for a change?" He was an extremely shy man
and all I got in reply was: "I don't know. I haven't thought
about it." Perhaps he was bored. I know I should have been,
painting the same picture week after week, month after month,
and year after year.

Between 1920 and 1925 my records were selling in hundreds
of thousands. By 1920 I was informed that I had reached the
5,000,000 mark in the total sales of my cylinder and disc records.
By 1925 my sales had rocketed to over 8,000,000.

It was obvious that I was still not getting the fee commensurate
with my enormous sales, so Tom Noble began a campaign with
the H.M.V. Company for a bonus. Knowing the gramophone
business from the inside, he was in a much better position to
argue than I ever could have been. In the midst of the negotiations
I had my terrible motor-car accident.

The only ray of comfort I had during this worrying time when
my wife was so dreadfully injured and fighting for her life was
when Tom 'phoned me in Leeds, where I was staying to be near
my wife, that he had succeeded beyond his highest hopes.

For the first time I was to receive a royalty on every record
sold. This meant that I was to be paid five per cent of the retail
price of every record I made that was sold. Five per cent does not
sound a lot, but when it runs into hundreds of thousands it
becomes a very respectable total.

In the midst of my domestic trouble this was indeed a solace.
By this time, too, a great advance had been made in the recording
art. The result was that the public were not merely buying new
records, but renewing their old ones to a very considerable extent.

What a change from the first cylinder records, the first
records and the first phonographs! The reason why the phonograph was, in its infancy, regarded as an instrument of torture
can be traced to the fact that only very loud noises could make
any impression on the very early recording machines. On that
account the original 'artistes' selected were an auctioneer, a street
lecturer, an Indian medicine man, a railway porter and a
newspaper seller!

They were all iron-chested men who could make themselves
heard in a boiler factory, and, in order that there could be no
discussion about the understanding of the words, the favourite
items recorded were the Lord's Prayer, nursery rhymes and songs
that were known to every child.

Although tremendous advance had been made in the art of recording and reproduction of sound, the gradual improvement in wireless reception was beginning to give the Moguls of the gramophone world a real 'headache'. With the passing of the 'cat's-whisker' reception to the wireless receiver, plus the clarity of tone, it was obvious that broadcasting was to become a very serious rival to the gramophone industry. I was not surprised, therefore, when H.M.V. suddenly turned over to electrical recording, and the use of the microphone instead of the old-fashioned metal funnel. The difference in the tone quality was a revelation. So much so, that the company decided to remake most of the important records on their list.

The menace of wireless to the gramophone caused a change in the 'atmosphere' of the recording studio. For a few years, now, recording had become rather a grim business, just as the selling of gramophones and records had become. Hitherto we had enjoyed a great deal of fun. There was a fine spirit of *camaraderie* among the artistes, orchestra and the recording staff. There was always someone in good form with a joke or a prank, which kept us in good humour.

For instance, I remember a joke I played on that brilliant conductor Albert Coates. When rehearsing, Albert put physically everything he had into his work—to such an extent that he found it necessary to have two sets of underwear conveniently on hand.

After about an hour's exertion—correcting, rearranging, timing, and conducting his orchestra—he would be in a muck sweat. He would then break off for a few minutes, have a rub down, and make a complete change of his underwear. He would do this regularly on two occasions at each full session of three hours.

I have never been able to resist the temptation of playing a joke, and when I saw Albert's underwear hanging on a line in the dressing-room, well, my hands itched to 'have a go', and of course I did!

Borrowing stencil plates from one of the men in the despatching department, I printed on the pants PASSED WEAR TEST, and on the vest, TECHNICALLY REJECTED.

I considered it advisable not to wait to see his reaction, but I was told later that Albert roared with laughter and yelled out: "Where is he? . . . There's only one 'so-and-so' would do that. . . . Where is he? . . . If I find him, I'll kill the —— ——."

And Albert Coates enjoyed the joke until he learned from his

I

wife that it was indelible ink, and the laundry could not get the words out. But Albert was blessed with a sense of humour, he continued to use the underwear at recording sessions, and enjoyed showing friends "what Peter did to my undies".

On another occasion we were using a larger orchestra than usual in a small studio, and the musicians were closely packed. They sat on high stools and chairs. The trombone players sat immediately behind the cornets. There were a number of 'collisions' during the rehearsal, but everyone managed to find an opening playing towards the recording funnel. When the artistes in front moved to take up their positions it compelled the musicians in the front to press back on those behind.

The signal was given to start. Almost at once I was flung forward by the weight of the violinist who had been hurled forward by a cornet player, who had been knocked off his seat by a trombone player. The accident was caused by the valve of the trombone catching the ear of the cornet player and hurling him forward off his high stool.

At another session I had a narrow escape from a nasty accident. We were recording a dramatic production called "The wreck of a troopship". The assistant recorder was so busy with a huge hammer smashing at a thunder sheet he succeeded in wrenching the sheet from its moorings in the ceiling, and with a tearing crash the whole contraption, including the heavy hook, fell on me. Fortunately the iron bolt missed my head, or—but why temporize? It hit me on the shoulder, and after a few minutes' wait, during which the 'thunder' was reassembled, we continued to founder on the troopship. That was not the last incident in that particular session. An electrician was arranging one of those electric lights which depend on a counterweight for their varying height when he tugged too hard, and the whole lot fell. Yes, again on me! No damage was done, and we all enjoyed a laugh. When I felt my head after the session was over I had a lump about the size of a squash ball.

I recall an incident that concerned Harry Lauder. He was having trouble with the orchestra that was accompanying him. He took exception to the flautist who was standing very close to him. Lauder thought that the musician was taking liberties with the score, and he told him twice, "I want you to play only what's written." But on the third occasion he rather rudely shouted, "I want you to play only what is in the music, and nothing more." Once again the orchestra played the melody, and the flautist solemnly moved his fingers over the keys, but he wasn't playing a note. "Thank you, that is exactly how I like it," said Harry. Then he wondered why, from a quiet smile, the whole orchestra broke into laughter. On being told what had happened, he became 'verrry, verrry angrrry'. I don't think he ever forgave the orchestra, George Byng, the conductor, or the recorder; as for the flautist, he insisted that the man never played again for him in any orchestra.

A well-known music-hall comedian, who must remain anonymous, was a heavy drinker. When he arrived at the studio his chauffeur brought in a large case of beer bottles, and in another five minutes another case—twenty-four pints altogether! One case was for the members of the orchestra, the other for the comedian himself!

The eagle eye of Fred Gaisberg spotted the beer, which was taken away. "The orchestra can have the beer after the session, but not during the recording." The comedian, however, kept going to the next room and imbibing. By the end of the session of three hours only two bottles remained of his dozen!

Another amusing incident happened during the making of a record with Chaliapin. I was standing on a small stool in order to sing over his shoulder into the recording funnel when the recorder gently pushed me forward, but he had forgotten that I was standing on the stool, with the result that I overbalanced and fell. I could not grab the funnel to save myself for fear of smashing the recording apparatus, and as I fell I grabbed Chaliapin. When I landed on the floor I found I had the big Russian's watch and chain in my hand. And in Russian he said: "You don't have to go to all that trouble to get the time. I would have told you if you asked." When that was translated it caused a two-minute break in the session because one of the cornet players laughed so much he fell off his very high chair and was knocked out for exactly ten seconds. His colleagues had counted him out, not realizing that he was in fact knocked out.

Let us now return to the new recording and the task of re-making the best of the records in the Gramophone Company's lists. When we remade the Gilbert and Sullivan records in the new recording, Dr. Malcolm Sargent was the conductor. He had been doing quite a considerable amount of recording, but it was not until we did the Gilbert and Sullivan sessions that I got to know him well. Somehow, at the start of our acquaintanceship, we did not hit it off too well.

We had our first 'breeze' during the recording of the *Pirates of Penzance*. The other artistes were Derek Oldham, Leo Sheffield,

Elsie Griffin, Dorothy Gill, George Baker, Nellie Briercliffe, Nellie Walker and Stuart Robertson.

Malcolm Sargent liked to hear all voices at strength even when 'running over' for timing. Most of us knew our parts and words to perfection. During one of these rehearsals I sang *sotto voce* to save my voice. Suddenly the conductor cried to me: "What's wrong, Dawson? I can't hear you at all." "There's nothing wrong, I know the part backwards, I'm just saving my voice for when we really make the record." "I like to hear the voices at all times," was his reply. The rehearsal was a lengthy one; and the alterations, changing and timing were a little annoying to all of us. I again conserved my voice where it did not matter. When the session was over, Billy Manson, the recording manager at the time, asked: "What's been happening, Peter? Sargent says you don't know your part, and that you are not co-operating." I explained exactly what I had been doing; not using my full voice where it was not necessary—in my mind—to do so. Billy understood in a moment, and added: "That's what I thought. I knew darned well you knew your part, and had some damned good reason for your attitude." Then he added: "You know, Peter, you are the only singer in this series not a member of the D'Oyly Carte Company, and the representative out there probably 'hates your guts'. I expect he has been complaining to Sargent, and that does not makes things any easier." It was a fact that the D'Oyly Carte people had representatives or a representative, whose job it was to listen in to all performances of the operas. Any mistakes by the artistes were reported to the head office. It was the first occasion in England of snooping in the musical world. It was naturally resented by the artistes; but let's be honest, it was a good idea, because it kept the company 'up to scratch'. There is nothing worse than a slack company singing opera. We certainly resented a 'representative' at a recording session, although we knew how very particular the D'Oyly Carte Company were about 'cuts' in the score.

Sargent and I are now good friends. I have a great admiration for his work, and a wholesome respect for his musical erudition.

I was kept very busy for the next six months recording my best sellers on the new electrical recording.

By 1934 or thereabouts the slump in the sale of records had set in. I remember that when I toured South Africa at this time the biggest gramophone dealers in South Africa, Messrs. McKay and Co., had been selling records in 'bargain' bundles at a cash price, and that they had turned their attention to the sale of household goods!

In London, in 1935, Louis Sterling, now chairman of the great E.M.I., told me that sales in the gramophone industry were so poor that his organization were switching their enormous factory over to the manufacture of wireless receivers (including radiograms) and that the gramophone side of the organization was worrying him.

I was aware of this because, in an effort to recapture sales, we had been making records of songs that were popular on the stage. Two of these songs were "Saddle your blues to an old Mustang" and "We saw the Sea".

I received hundreds of letters abusing me for singing such songs. Nevertheless they sold very well. At this time another idea was tried out. A young assistant at Chappell's, in Bond Street, had written lyrics to some of the fine old marching tunes played by the military bands. They were so good that the Gramophone Company decided to have them sung by myself, with a chorus made up of distinguished singers. The conductor was Ray Noble, and the singers with myself were John Turner, Edward Halland, Webster Booth, Jackson Potter, George Baker and Walter Glynne. These really fine marching songs should be heard; they are most inspiring, and with such a distinguished company as 'male chorus' what more can one expect? The titles we made were "El Abanico", "Sons of the Brave", "Punjaub March" and "With Sword and Lance". Fortunately they sold very well. I only hope that the unknown lyricist at Chappell's received his just reward for a very good idea and excellent lyrics.

With this same chorus of stars we made Stanford's "Drake's Drum", "Outward Bound", "The Old Superb" and "Devon, O Devon", all on the new electrical recording, and using microphones.

It was a delight to record under the new conditions. All the old recording gadgets had been scrapped. In place of the recording horns or funnels were sound (acoustic) correcting contraptions, and instead of bunching round the recording apparatus we sang into microphones; one for the singer, another for the accompanist, and a third and fourth when they were required for chorus work. No more packing round the funnel, but plenty of room to move in freedom.

I consider that the present recording is as near perfection as one can reasonably expect. In addition, the reproducing diaphragms supplied with the new gramophones and radio-gramophones are really very good indeed. Therein lies the secret of good reproduction in the home. If the reproducer is 'tinny', 'hard', 'sensitive', or 'barrelly', change it at once. Remember to keep a careful eye on the needle you use. Fortunately they are not expensive, so you need not over-use them. And if a record sounds strange when you start to play it, stop it and change the needle, or see that it is held firmly in the slot.

I have heard records 'murdered' through a faulty needle. Once when I called this needle question to the notice of a hostess, she replied: "Really, I can't believe it is the needle. I bought them only yesterday." It had not occurred to her that it is possible to have a faulty needle or that it can be loose in its socket.

I have not inquired about the total of records of mine that have been sold, but before the Second World War the number had passed the 12,000,000 mark. Today, despite the restrictions on the number of records permitted for sale during the war, it must have passed the 13,000,000. During the latter part of the war and the following post-war years there has been a terrific boom, and I am proud to say that I am in the forefront of the sales.

I still receive five per cent on the retail price of my records. This would be quite satisfactory if I did not have to give the best part of it back to the collector of Income Tax!

Now to try to answer the question that is so often posed: "What is your best record?" Here is my reply: "The next record I am going to make."

What are my favourite records? Here are a few that I really enjoyed making, and incidentally I like singing: Stanford's "Songs of the Sea"; "The Lute Player"; "*Largo al Factotum*" from the *Barber of Seville*, which is the easiest to sing, as it comes tripping off the tongue, and I revel in it; the Kipling songs: "Boots", "Cells" and "Route Marchin' "; "The Floral Dance"; and that rollicking and delightful Irish song, "The Kerry Dance"; "The Song of the Flea", for I enjoy putting my own interpretation into it. Then I like to sing the Prologue of *Pagliacci*, and in my own way; "Lover in Damascus", which Ray Noble, that versatile musician, conducted; "I am a Roamer", which Mendelssohn wrote when he was sixteen. The exuberance of youth! And that's how I sing it. I must include that Maori song, "*Waiata Poi*" (Tiny ball on end of string), because I can let myself go in the true Maori fashion. I prefer the romantic to the traditional songs. There is too much of a sameness of tempo and traditional 'rendering' in the latter. There is no scope for the individuality of the singer. The only man who ever attempted to break away from the traditional tempo was my old friend Tommy Beecham. He put "The Messiah" into double time! It was a splendid innovation, but the old diehards in the musical world resented it and said so. Sir Thomas Beecham had the right idea. It made the performance 'alive' and was welcomed by the singers. A well-known tenor told me that he thought the only reason some objected was because it prevented them having their usual doze during the performance!

In the romantic songs the artiste can put his own rendering forward; he is not tied down by tradition.

Finally, I do like singing the religious songs, or semi-religious: "The Lost Chord", "The Holy City", "There is a Green Hill far away", "Christ is Risen", "Jerusalem" and "Nazareth". Then "Little Prayer I Love", "Bless this House", "I heard a Forest praying" and "None but the weary Heart".

Those are the songs I have enjoyed recording. But of course there are many, many more; and of the 3,500 songs I have sung for record purposes I can say that I have certainly enjoyed singing five per cent of them, which represents 175 songs. Of the songs I have recently made I would mention "The Snowbird" and "O Lord, Thou art my Shepherd". The former I made some time ago, the matrice was destroyed, and I recorded it again.

Looking back over my life as a phonograph and gramophone artiste I realize that my experience is unique.

I am the only artiste recording today who made records for the cylinders of the Edison Bell Company in 1904.

I have sung under five different names because I acquired the ability to understand thoroughly the art of recording.

If you ask how and why, I can only answer because I have always put diction, or if you prefer it, enunciation, in the forefront of my rendition. I have from the beginning studied the lyric of a song until I knew it. In this way I 'lived' every song I recorded— no matter whether it was a trivial or a classical number.

I did not waste any of the instruction given so patiently to me by Sir Charles Santley or the advice of my Scottish teacher, Mr. Bamford; and, finally, the hints and teaching of Professor Kantorez, the man who turned me from a basso into a baritone with exceptional range.

Finally, I have never taken my recording lightly. Every song I recorded received my full attention and study. In short, I never 'pigged' my work, however unimportant the song may have been.

Like the gramophone industry, I have survived two bad

slumps, and it is a great comfort to me that today my voice and my records are in greater demand than ever.

Yes, I do reverently 'Count my Blessings' for my good fortune.

There is another popular vocalist who must thank the gramophone for establishing him in the music world. I can claim a share in his success as I was responsible for taking him to the Gramophone Company and arranging that he should be given an audition.

My old friend Ernest Butcher came to see me when I was singing in a concert at Blackpool; he had a 'Pierrot' show in another hall. Ernest Butcher, in addition to being a very excellent comedian, has a very good voice, is a witty *raconteur* and can write songs.

When I asked him about his company he told me that he had a tenor of whom he thought a very great deal, so much so, in fact, that he begged me to come along and hear the fellow sing. Ernest was, and still is, a good judge of a voice. So I went along and heard the tenor sing "On with the Motley". He certainly had a remarkably good voice. And he had a good presence. I congratulated him on his voice, and asked whether he had ever thought of making records. He had, but, like many other artistes at that time, found it was extremely difficult to get a trial. I therefore arranged that when he was next in London he should give me a 'phone call. Later this was done, and I took him along to Fred Gaisberg, and asked for a trial. "This fellow has a good voice, and I think a good one for recording. You know I wouldn't bring along anyone I wasn't sure of, Fred." A trial was duly made, and Fred told me that "He is inclined to bleat a bit, but you are right, he has a voice. I'm going to try him on the Zonophone." The Zonophone was a subsidiary of the H.M.V. Bleating is a common fault, and it did not take Webster Booth—for that's who it was—a few minutes to correct it, once he heard his own voice. After that he never looked back. From the Zonophone he was promoted to the H.M.V., and from there he went on into more and better-paid engagements. I asked for him when I made the series of marching songs with chorus, and generally watched over his progress until he was fully established. Once again, in 1948, I was able to persuade him and his charming wife, Anne Ziegler, to make a tour of Australia. In letters to me from there he expressed his delight of the people, the country and the success they had both made. "How right you were once again, Peter," the last letter ended.

Yes. A chance meeting; a successful gramophone *début*, and another reputation is launched to success.

Most of us have seen and heard Albert Whelan and his whistling entrance on to the stage, but I wonder if any of his numerous admirers knew that he took part in the recording of twenty hymn records for H.M.V.? Albert had been making records, and was present when the question of finding a good falsetto or treble was discussed.

There was a deadlock, and we could not find what we wanted. Suddenly Albert interrupted and said, "It will probably surprise you, but I can sing treble or falsetto, and I am quite prepared to do so in your choir if you like." Naturally this caused a good laugh, and we went on with the discussion. Albert insisted, "Look, I am serious about it, and if you like I'll do a trial right away."

Albert, like most Australians, was always 'pulling our legs', but he finally convinced us that he was indeed serious. A trial was made, and Albert Whelan sang the treble in the chorus of twenty hymn records for H.M.V. The soloists included Harold Wilde, Stewart Gardiner and myself.

Another man I found extremely versatile was John Barbirolli, the British conductor. I had heard many flattering opinions about John's musical ability, and was therefore very delighted to find that he was to conduct the recording of Sir Edward Elgar's "Caractacus".

I knew that he played the piano expertly for his work, but at the famous party given at the Savoy by Sir Louis Sterling (to celebrate his knighthood) John played the viola superbly. He gave a couple of solos to the astonishment and delight of everyone present. Later he became world famous, conducting, in addition to his own Chamber Orchestra, the New York Philharmonic, the Royal Opera, the London Philharmonic and the London Symphony orchestras.

Barbirolli, like Toscanini, is no copyist. His success and the rapidity of it can be traced to his creative genius. Britain can be proud of her John Barbirolli.

To return to Sir Louis Sterling's party. What a party! In addition to John Barbirolli I remember Eva Turner, Lawrence Tibbett, Lauritz Melchior, and that remarkable performer on the 'harmonica' or, as it is better known, the 'mouth organ', Larry Adler. What a sensation he caused among the 'heads of the musical world'! Then Richard Tauber, who sang "You are my heart's delight", and who at the end of the song went over to

Diana Napier and made a delightful bow. The American 'Harmony Boys' performed valiantly, considering that a pretty serious mistake had occurred in the drinks they had consumed just before they sang. The waiter had served them with two double whiskies instead of two plain ginger ales. The boys thought the ginger ale 'rather nice' and had a couple. Fortunately they took it all in good part, and made a big success. On the other hand that irrepressible American comedian, Harry Richman, who had just flown the Atlantic with the wings of his plane filled with ping-pong balls in case of a 'forced landing on the ocean', was very merry.

When he walked on to the platform he announced, "I've been waiting so long to get to this piano that I knocked back a few drinks and here we are." And with that he started singing "*La Donna è mobile*" in a good tenor voice, before starting on his inimitable story-telling. Sir Louis Sterling is not likely to forget his party, and neither are those who attended it.

It was immediately after my session with John Barbirolli that I listened to the inimitable Gracie Fields making a record. Gracie, like the rest of the established recording artistes, wants to be at ease during the singing for records. Her method was to take off her shoes, and sing in her stockinged feet! "High heels make the legs tired," Gracie explained to me, "and if your legs are tired, you can't sing at your best."

That was something quite new to me, but it was nevertheless a darned good idea.

Leonard Smith, who was recording at the time, whispered to me: "From what I hear, it's a pity that Melba didn't have the same idea. It might have softened her temper!" Then he added, "Do you remember what John McCormack told Melba that time she thought he had arrived late for a session?" I did. Melba said, "You're damned late, you young ——." And young John, who had been very patient, like all of us, at Melba's rudeness, flared up and shouted, "Mind your own business, you interfering b——!" He walked out of the recording studio refusing to sing with her ever again, and he did not.

For years Melba was referred to by the musicians as "Madam Sweet and Low". A sweet voice, but low language.

I have told earlier that she did improve after a while. Like all people of that kind, she changed immediately she was answered back.

Before concluding this chapter I paid a visit to the gramophone library at Hayes, Middlesex, and asked to see the first catalogue on which my name appeared for H.M.V. Miss Matthias, who knows everybody and every title ever made—she is an encyclopaedia of the record world—showed me the catalogue. It was dated October 1904, and my name appears as follows:

> Peter Dawson.   (Comic).
> "Navajo."
> "Long ago in Alcala."

One month later the second catalogue reads:

> Peter Dawson.   (Comic).
> "Navajo."
> "Long ago in Alcala."
> "Calvary."
> "The Old Bull and Bush."

I expect the inclusion of "Calvary" in the repertoire of a 'comic' must have brought protests, for the next catalogue gave me my right title of 'Basso'.

For those who might be interested, here are the songs I sung in my first two years on Zonophone and H.M.V. records: Those above, and "When the Stars were Young", " 'Tis I", "Asleep in the Deep", "Lanagan's Log", "Oh, for a Sail in the piping Breeze", "True till Death", "Blow! blow! thou Winter Wind", "The Gallants of England", "The Bedouin Love Song", "Anchored", "The Bellringer", "Let me Love Thee", "Hybrias the Cretan", "O Star of Eve", "In Cellar deep", "Unless", "Sincerity", "The Shipwright", "I fear no Foe", "The Admiral's Broom", "White Wings", "Little brown Jug", "The place where the old Horse died", "Wrap me up in my tarpaulin Jacket", "Clementine", "Memory of the dead", "Tommy Lad", "The West's asleep", "The Singer was Irish", "A Nation once again", "Good-bye, little Sister", "The Powder Monkey", "At the bottom of the deep blue Sea", "Rule Britannia", "Young Tom o' Devon", "The gilded Popinjay", "The Oddfellows' Song", "Rip Van Winkle", "Marna", "The Palms", "Three for Jack", "Bonnie Banks of Loch Lomond" and "The Bandolero".

As an indication of the demand for my Hector Grant records here is the list of songs appearing in the early 1907 catalogue— less than eighteen months after I started to record under this name: "I love a Lassie", "Foo the Noo", "Bonnie Mary of Glengary", "Sandy you're a Dandy", "Sister", "Dougal" (New Aladdin), "I wish I had someone to love me", "Arra Wanna", "Tramp, Tramp", "The Referee", "Jean McNeill", "Calligan", "I took the Prize", "Tobermory", "Wedding of Lauchie McGraw", "Lassie dinna sigh for me" (the biggest seller—

my own song), "John McKay", "A Trip to Inverary", "Boy
Blue", "She's my Daisy", "Saftest o' the Family", "Ticklie
Geordie", "Rising early in the Morning", "Killicrankie", "David
Evans", "Jean from Aberdeen", "Sandy Boy", and "Mrs. John
MacFarlane".

All the above records were made within two years of my first
song for the H.M.V. Company. They sold many, many thousands.
My fee for each title was £1 1s. (Ten shillings for duets and
quartets.)

I do not regret for one minute that I have sung exclusively for
His Master's Voice Company. I feel like one of the family. And
I have many lifelong friends as a result of my association. Whenever I visit the Company either at Abbey Road, near Lord's
cricket ground, or the huge factory at Hayes, Middlesex, I meet
old friends, and that counts a lot. Like most Scots I enjoy a 'wee
drap', and it is comforting to find that the same brand of whisky
is served today as it was in 1905! No, I must not mention the brand
—that's advertising!

Some years ago I was good-humouredly challenged about the
statement that I had recorded 3,500 different titles for phonograph
and gramophone records. In the first years I was singing an
average of twenty songs weekly! I have just discovered a note-
book in which I noted the songs I recorded when singing
exclusively for H.M.V. and subsidiary companies. It starts on
13 October, 1916:

Oct. 13 Song with piano .. "Can't you hear me calling, Caroline?"
   ,,   ,,   ,,   ,,   .. "The Gateway of Heaven"
   ,,   ,,   ,,   ,,   .. "The Lute Player"
   ,,   ,,   ,,   ,,   .. "Chip of the Block"
   ,,   ,,   ,,   ,,   .. "Call of the angry Deep"
   ,,   ,,   ,,   ,,   .. "Invictus"
   ,,   ,,   ,,   ,,   .. "O Love because of You"
   ,,   ,,   ,,   ,,   .. "The Night Watch"
   ,,   ,,   ,,   ,,   .. "Rest, Soldier, rest"
Oct. 23   ,,   ,,   ,,   .. "Mother Asthore"
   ,,   ,,   ,,   ,,   .. "The Old Sacristan"
   ,,   ,,   ,,   ,,   .. "Lighterman Tom"
   ,,   ,,   ,,   ,,   .. "The Watchman"
   ,,   ,,   ,,   ,,   .. "A rolling rollicking Stone"
   ,,   ,,   ,,   ,,   .. "Death or Glory Boys"
   ,,   ,,   ,,   ,,   .. "The Armourer's Gift"
   ,,   ,,   ,,   ,,   .. "Three Bachelors"
   ,,   ,,   ,,   ,,   .. "The Requital"

Oct. 26 With orchestra   .. "The Tanks that broke the Ranks"
,,   ,,   ,,   .. "When you're a long way from Home"
,,   ,,   ,,   .. "If I could turn the Clock back"
Nov. 3 With piano   .. "The Skipper's Yarn"
,,   ,,   ,,   .. "The Mermaid and the Tar"
,,   ,,   ,,   .. "The Lighthouse Keeper"
,,   ,,   ,,   .. "My beloved Queen"
,,   ,,   ,,   .. "Brother Ambrose"
,,   ,,   ,,   .. "Daddy's Perplexity"
Nov. 6 Orchestra. Duet   .. "Order, please" (with E. Pike)
,,   ,,   Solo   .. "Somebody w'd shout out Shop"
,,   ,,   ,,   .. "At Finnigan's Ball"
,,   ,,   ,,   .. "You can't do without a bit o' Love"
,,   ,,   ,,   .. "Hullo, Hawaii, how are you?"
Nov. 22   ,,   Duet   .. "Blighty" (with Ernest Pike)
,,   ,,   Solo   .. "Taffy's got his Jenny"
,,   ,,   ,,   .. "The Cobbler's Song"
Nov. 23   ,,   ,,   .. "I am a Roamer"
,,   ,,   ,,   .. "The Blind Ploughman"
,,   ,,   ,,   .. "The Call"
,,   ,,   ,,   .. "Green Hills of Somerset"
,,   ,,   Duet   .. "Follow up" (with E. Pike)

The titles of some of the records may surprise you, but remember that I was singing under various names, including Will Strong, Frank Danby, Hector Grant.

You will also note that late in 1916 I was recording *forty* songs in *six weeks*.

In 1922 I did a series of records on 'Physical Culture' exercises. My note-book for 20 December to 29 December reads:

Dec. 20 "Off to Philadelphia"   .   .   .   .   . Solo
,,   "Blarney Roses"   .   .   .   .   . ,,
,,   "Young Tom o' Devon"   .   .   .   . ,,
,,   "Girl in Kildare"   .   .   .   .   . ,,
,,   "Nobody's Darling" (with orchestra)   .   . Chorus
,,   "PHYSICAL CULTURE"   .   .   .   . Talk
,,   "PHYSICAL CULTURE"   .   .   .   . ,,
Dec. 21 "PHYSICAL CULTURE"   .   .   .   . ,,
,,   "PHYSICAL CULTURE"   .   .   .   .   . ,,
,,   "Rock of Ages"   .   .   .   .   . Quartet
,,   "Jesu, Lover of my Soul"   .   .   . ,,
,,   "Nearer, my God, to Thee"   .   .   . ,,
,,   "Eternal Father"   .   .   .   .   . ,,
,,   "Pagan"   .   .   .   .   .   . Solo

Dec. 28 "Valley where the blue Birds" .   .   .   . Duet
  ,,   "Genevieve" .   .   .   . ,,
  ,,   "Fishermen" .   .   .   . ,,
  ,,   "Flow gently, Devor"   .   .   .   .   . ,,
  ,,   "PHYSICAL CULTURE"   .   .   .   . Talk
Dec. 29 "PHYSICAL CULTURE"   .   .   .   .   . ,,
  ,,   "Battle Eve" .   .   .   .   .   . Duet
  ,,   "Before the Battle" .   .   .   .   .   . ,,
  ,,   "Watchman" .   .   .   . ,,
  ,,   "Outpost's Vigil"   .   .   .   .   .   . ,,
  ,,   "Swanee River"   .   .   .   .   . Quartet
  ,,   "Silver Threads"   .   .   .   .   .   . ,,
  ,,   "Beautiful Isle"   .   .   .   .   .   . ,,

Twenty-seven records in ten days, and five different types!
It is difficult to work out the exact number of my records that
have been sold, but it is certainly not less than 13,000,000. This
does not include quartets, chorus or 'talking' records. Twenty-
five years ago I was told that the companies were one million
behind on the orders for my records.

CHAPTER XII

BROADCASTING

BROADCASTING, one might say, has educated the public into an appreciation of music without being aware of the process.

Before the advent of the talking machine the musical knowledge of the masses was extremely limited. Then with the improvement in the technical side of the gramophone industry, particularly the wonderful progress made in the art of recording, it literally drew millions of enthusiasts and the love of music began to spread all over the wide world.

The most famous artistes were engaged, the finest orchestras and the most brilliant conductors, and in a few years the classics of the great masters were given accurate presentation as far as tempo and orchestral colouring was concerned.

The advantage of the gramophone over broadcasting lies in the fact that one can select one's own special programme and become thoroughly conversant with the great masterpieces. Broadcasting, speaking now on behalf of the vocalists, is quite different inasmuch as the artiste is at the mercy of the technicians. He is unaware just how his efforts are being received by listeners. He is in the dark, and rarely gets the factual truth, however much he may try. I have often inquired, diffidently, when I have finished a broadcast session, "How did I go?" and received the assurance, "It sounded very good, Mr. Dawson." And I have to be content with that.

Whereas, when recording, a test is made and played back so that I can hear exactly how it sounds and where I can make improvements in my rendering of various phrases. The recording experts can alter the tone and the quality until the best result is obtained before the recording of the song is attempted.

By sheer experience I possess a knowledge of the gramophone recording microphone, which makes recording to me something that I could do, as the saying goes, 'on my head'.

I use the same technique when broadcasting, and I have no doubt that it helps the result on the receiving set in the home. But I have no real knowledge of how I am being broadcast. That is to say, whether the microphone suits my voice, whether it is too hard in tone, too barrelly, too thin—or, in short, whether it is the best for my particular voice.

In recording in a gramophone studio, I know: in a broadcasting studio, I do *not*.

I am passing no reflection on the technical experts of the B.B.C., they know what they are doing, and can make adjustments to get what they consider the best result. But it is a little disconcerting to me not to have any idea what I sound like.

Of course when I make a record I know that I can have a copy to play in my home. Once I have broadcast there is no guarantee that I shall ever hear a particular session again. If it is a programme that is recorded then I have the opportunity of hearing myself. But then only once!

Nevertheless, I heartily enjoy broadcasting. I am meticulously careful in everything I do. When I sing into the microphone I can 'see' the vast unseen multitude of listeners. The microphone is there, but I am able to eliminate everything extraneous to my mind except the listeners and the song I am singing.

Once an artiste is microphone-conscious his real personality never gets over the air.

I made my first broadcast on Australia Day, 1931. It was at a reception given by Sir Joseph Cook at Australia House, in London. The Prince of Wales graced the occasion with his presence.

Although it was not a broadcast from a B.B.C. studio, it was my first song 'over the air'.

It is interesting to read what I said in an interview at the time: "I remember very well how I felt when I stood in front of the 'mike'. I put my shoulders back and thought: 'Goodness, I can do whatever I like. I do not have to keep near the recording horn. This feels fine! But I soon discovered that what I had gained on the roundabouts was lost on the swings. I quickly learnt that the microphone is a very keen critic. It detects one's faults.

"The old recording apparatus covered a multitude of sins. Not so the 'mike'. It picks out all the flaws—and somehow seems to amplify them. Singing into it necessitates great care. It is so fatally easy to 'blast', to sing just a little bit too powerfully, and the effect is deadly."

I made those remarks after my first broadcast. Two years later, after I had become accustomed to singing over the air, both in London and in Australia, I said in an interview in New Zealand:

"The radio has taught people to listen, and from this fact there is evolving an appreciation of good music that, but for broadcasting, would never have been awakened in the hearts of the people."

And now for my first B.B.C. broadcast. Within an hour after I had finished my first programme I answered a 'phone call from Tommy Noble, and this is what he said:

"For the love of Mike, Peter, why in the name of heaven did you sing those German songs? Your first broadcast. Hundreds of thousands of people who buy records wanted to hear you over the air, and you sing them German *Lieder*. For pity's sake, Peter, why did you do this to them?" And before I had an opportunity of answering, he continued: "Exactly three months ago you said in the *Daily Sketch*, 'I can and have sung in German, Italian, French, Russian and Spanish, but I am never happy with a German *Lied* when I know that nine-tenths of my audience have no idea what it is about.'"

I think the reason I decided to sing German *Lieder* can be traced to the fact that at this time I was giving a recital or two of foreign songs. I felt that I wanted to show I was capable of singing these beautiful German songs, and I must say I enjoyed singing them.

Here is a list of the Germans songs I sang at my first B.B.C. broadcast:

"*Sei Mir gegrüsst*"	Schubert
"*Die Mainacht*"	Brahms
"*Botschaft*"	Brahms
"*Du bist so jung*	Wolff
"*Blinde Kuh*"	Brahms

Although I know I should have thought of the majority rather than the minority when arranging my programme, I received a large number of congratulatory messages on my German *Lieder*. But the most agreeable surprise occurred when I went out to post some acknowledgments.

A policeman approached and, touching his helmet in a salute, said: "Excuse me, Mr. Dawson, I should like to tell you how my wife and I enjoyed your broadcast last night. Particularly the Brahms and the Schubert songs." I thanked him for his compliment, and moved on very pleased. But I could not help pondering on what the gramophone and wireless had done to improve the public taste in music. Imagine, twenty years earlier, a policeman commenting on the beauty of the songs of Schubert and Brahms! For when I had asked my policeman whether he played a musical

K

instrument, he had replied: "No. I don't play any instrument, and I don't sing, but I am a keen listener, and I have a lot of records. My favourite is your record of Schubert's 'The Erl King'."

And today the wonderful variety of music being broadcast by the B.B.C. is designed to suit all tastes. Who would have thought at the time I made my first broadcast that within twenty years three different programmes would be produced, designed to interest every man and woman whatever their individual interest may be in music?

What a revolution has taken place in the musical education of the peoples of the world! And that the public in Britain and the Empire are now sincere music lovers is proved by the immense increase in the sales of gramophone records of the better-class music, such as piano concertos, orchestral symphonies, operatic *arias*, oratorios, art songs, and the fine songs of some of the modern composers.

Yes, we owe a great debt to the fine work of the B.B.C. in this direction, and for the magnificent recordings of the gramophone companies.

Mr. Oscar Preuss, the popular recording manager of the H.M.V. Gramophone Company, told me that proof of the appreciation of the listening public for music that is broadcast is reflected in the demands received from the public by the gramophone retailers for records of songs, concertos and symphonies, etc., a couple of days following the broadcast. He gave me an example of what followed my own revival of that cheery Maori song "*Waiata Poi*" (Tiny ball on end of string), which I sung at my first broadcast on my arrival in London, September 1947. "The orders came in thousands and from all parts of the kingdom," explained Oscar. And he added with a smile, "That's not because of your appearance in London, Peter, but solely because they heard you broadcast it and wanted a record that they could play whenever they pleased." He went on to confirm that broadcasting did positively help the sale of records, and that he was astonished how the demand had been most marked in what we can only describe as the better class of music.

What is most encouraging is the interest taken in music by the younger generation. My young nephew, Tommy Noble (junior), is typical, I am sure, of thousands of other children— he is fifteen. Here is how his taste runs: he has bought the following records 'off his own bat':

"Ride of the Valkyries", "Overture of the Wasps", Handel's

"Largo", Prelude from the film *A Matter of Life and Death*, Boccherini's "Minuet", Greig's "Piano Concerto in A Minor", the incidental music to the film *The Night has Eyes*, "*Clair de Lune*" (Debussy) and "Mars" from "The Planets" (Gustav Holst). But to illustrate his versatility of taste—and I hear of similar divergence in other youngsters of today—he also buys 'Rumba' records, and enjoys playing "Dark Town Poker Club" by Phil Harris, and Danny Kaye's records, "Minnie the Moocher" and "It's a quiet Town". He has bought, too, a good collection of the French records of Jean Sablon, including "*Sur le Pont d'Avignon*", "*Le Fiacre*", "*Pour vous J'avais fait cette chanson*"; Georges Guétary's "Magdalena" and "I dreamt I was back in Paris"; Georges Ulmer's "*Pigalle*" and Lucienne Vernay's "*Le petit souper aux chandelles*".

Compare this list with the knowledge of music held by boys of fifteen in 1918!

Let us pay tribute to the wonderful progress made by the gramophone and the phenomenal advance made by wireless broadcasting.

And let us be particularly grateful that both these mechanical marvels bring the music of the world's composers, players and singers into the privacy of our homes. Unfortunately—but there are some who might prefer 'fortunately'—the old-fashioned homely function known as the 'musical evening', when everybody must sing or play, has practically ceased to exist. I think it is a pity in some ways, for there are few pleasures like producing one's own music. Yet it cannot be denied that very often these functions were painful affairs. To this day I have dreadful recollections of one of my sister's suitors singing endless repetitions in a raucous voice of "My beautiful, my beautiful".

No doubt many of my readers can recall similar inflictions, which had to be borne because it was not polite to do otherwise.

Today the wireless is switched on and instantly the company is entertained by vocal or instrumental music sung or played by first-class artistes. True, that sort of thing has its limitations, but we live in an age of ease and comfort, and it is certainly easier, and generally more satisfactory, to adopt the new method.

I have made many broadcasts since 1931, but I have restrained myself from accepting too many because I believe it is possible to overdo it. For that reason I declined many offers to make advertising broadcasts from Luxembourg. I did two or three and left it at that.

That reminds me of a strange coincidence involving Vic

Oliver. He arrived at a concert at which we were both appearing and heard me sing the "*Largo al Factotum*". A few days later we were in the same programme at a B.B.C. broadcast and again I was singing the "*Largo al Factotum*". One week later he arrived at a broadcasting studio where I was just about to commence an advertising broadcast. The song I was asked to start with was the "*Largo*". When he heard me giving certain directions to Debroy Somers, who was conducting the orchestra, Vic cried: "Oh, no, not again! Is that the only song you know?" We had a laugh, and then he said he would like to take part in it. Turning to Debroy Somers, he asked permission to play the violin in the accompaniment. Debroy knew that Vic was a first-class player and agreed. And so Vic sat next to the first violins and accompanied me in the "*Largo al Factotum*". Too late we realized that we ought to have announced: "Orchestra conducted by Debroy Somers; leader, Vic Oliver." If I was agreeably surprised at Vic's performance, a few minutes later I was astonished by a performance of Debroy Somers.

During a break in the session Debroy was chatting about versatility and began the most remarkable demonstration I have ever seen in my life of instrumental playing. He played a short solo on the violin, cornet, bass, piano, clarinet, saxophone, and finished with a really brilliant number on the harp. That is why I am never impressed when I see American dance band leaders (earning colossal fees) playing alternatively a couple of instruments. What a sensation Debroy Somers would be in the States were he to play half a dozen instruments during one number!

It was at another B.B.C. 'party broadcast' that I met a man I hadn't seen for over twenty years. Where I used to sing baritone solos, he would sing comic songs and tell stories. We probably earned a fee of a couple of guineas each. And we often met. It was in the early days when I was singing at dinners. He became the most popular of the radio comedians, and deservedly so. I am referring to Tommy Handley. We had a long chat over the old times. Naturally the conversation turned to income tax—it always does! We spoke of the number of stars who only work about three-quarters of a year in order 'not to work for the Government'. Tommy was most emphatic. "That's wrong. You must keep before your public." And then he added, "When a popular artiste forgets he is a servant of the public his popularity will soon vanish." To which I heartily agree. It is the public that made you and they should be respected always. I listened to Tommy's broadcasts regularly when I was in Australia. There was no other radio comedian who talked so fast and yet so clearly. His diction at high speed was astonishing. What a tragedy that such a comic genius should pass from us so early in life.

The greatest and most pleasing success I achieved in a broadcast programme was the series in 1950 called "Our Pleasure to Present". The first programme was on Sunday, 4 July, and the twelfth on 19 September.

The public have always been kind in their appreciation of my broadcasting and I have received many letters thanking and congratulating me on my singing, but during the series of "Our Pleasure to Present" the number of letters sent to me through the B.B.C. was astonishing.

They came from all parts of the British Isles and from all classes of people, many from hospitals and nursing homes, and some from depots of the fighting services.

The idea was Doris Arnold's. She felt that at nine-thirty on a Sunday evening listeners would appreciate a programme of songs of a spiritual quality. She discussed the suggestion with me; and I agreed that in these troubled times, with the talk of war in the air, conditions grim, and the atomic bomb threat, a programme devoted to religious or semi-religious songs might prove a solace to many people on Sunday nights. And how right that very sincere and clever woman was. The response was remarkable in the extreme.

Letters started the first week and continued to grow in volume after each performance.

Doris Arnold chose the songs, the great majority from my repertoire. We had many discussions, and very great care was taken over the songs selected. Many of the letters asked for the names of songs that are in my repertoire.

There were one or two letters from some old admirers of mine, in which protests were made that conditions were so depressing that a 'brighter' programme of songs would have helped to lift the people out of the doldrums, but they represented less than one per cent of the letters. Doris Arnold's idea was overwhelmingly right. The people appreciated the spiritual tone of the songs, and their letters proved that they gave many thousands great comfort.

And let me say, too, that I enjoyed singing these lovely old songs. Every real artiste prefers to sing a song that is a 'song'. Take that grand "Edward" of Loewe's. It is a song in which I use two voices and the Scots dialect. That is what I call an 'art' song. I enjoy singing it.

Before closing this broadcasting chapter I must go back a little. It was about 1931 when I made my first broadcast that a considerable controversy developed throughout the English-speaking world over the popularity of the gramophone and the wireless. A certain number of people who disliked the gramophone enjoyed referring to it contemptuously as 'Canned Music'! And what a measure of scorn they succeeded in imparting to those two words.

I remember being asked to give my views on the subject by the *Melbourne Herald*. I looked it up, and because there are still, in 1951, quite a number of hard-boiled musical purists who dislike—or are prejudiced against—the gramophone and wireless, I want to quote what I said on the argument then.

Here it is, and unabridged:

"CANNED MUSIC

The musical world is divided into three classes: the highbrow (10 per cent), the would-be highbrow (10 per cent), those who like a good tune (75 per cent), the remaining 5 per cent is made up of the incorrigibles—the boogie-woogie-croony enthusiasts.

Now I am a man of the soil: I come from the people and what gifts I am fortunate to possess I want to give back to the people. My object is 'the greatest happiness of the greatest number'.

With this ideal the highbrow and would-be highbrow are constantly at variance. They would like to see music sharply divided at the point where the academic meets the popular.

They get a sort of sad pleasure from the belief that they can understand and appreciate what the Toms, Dicks and the Harrys, to say nothing of the Marys and Janes, can't understand and appreciate. And so their dislike of anything that reproduces music, that is not of the Simon-pure standard of execution on the spot, tends to become almost rabid.

'Canned music! Horrible—tinny—distorted—vulgar,' they cry, and shudder delicately, if a little ostentatiously.

Well, I must emphatically beg to differ from them. We eat canned fruit, canned vegetables, canned meats, canned fish, and we agree that such are necessities of civilization, enabling the distribution of products that would otherwise go to waste.

So it is with 'canned music'. Incomparable, splendid

harmonies that would otherwise be for the very few are canned for the people. Great!

Few musicians who can think straight and who are not musical Pharisees can fail to admit that, whatever may have been said in the past about the ability to make records of speech and music, today reproduction has been made almost perfect by electrical processes, which has enabled the song and the music of the great geniuses to be preserved for posterity; deathless, imperishable, for ever able to teach students and to charm audiences. To overlook this grand achievement of mechanical progress is to write oneself a fool.

Music has an effect on listeners that is far greater than mere aesthetic pleasure. It enters their daily lives; it gives them greater capacity for thought, and more to think of and with."

CHAPTER XIII

SONGS

Stories Behind the Popular Successes

WHEREVER I travel throughout the Empire I can never escape the question, "How does one set about writing a song that will be a success?" The query is not confined exclusively to song-writers; it is posed by all sorts and conditions of people.

Of course, a musical Socrates could not find the formula for that poser. It is fraught with snags. It is a subject so varied that I think the best way to deal with it is to tell the stories behind the popular successes, and in this way perhaps the difficulty will be conclusively dealt with. In a later chapter I shall deal more technically with the musical aspects.

But I do want to tell you the surprising stories of how some of our most popular songs came to be written and published. I shall mention only those that have achieved world-wide fame; I am 'including *out*' the drivelling songs we hear so much over the wireless through the invidious system of song-plugging. Let me first give you the story behind the song that has sold more gramophone records than any in the long list I have sung—and I have made over 3,500 different titles—the song that is 'called for' by the public, the song that concert agents ask me to include in my programmes, and the song in which I have *no* financial interest! It is "The Floral Dance".

This song owes its origin to sheer chance. Katie Moss, the composer, chanced to be in Helston, Cornwall, enjoying a holiday. And fortunately the famous 'Furry Dance' was held during her stay. She told me how she stood absolutely thrilled as first the gentry of the County danced, in and out of the houses, accompanied by the village band, and later the villagers and visitors joined in the processional dancing. For they really do dance in and out of the houses, and every house is joyfully left open as a welcome invitation to the merry throng.

Katie explained how strongly she felt the urge to join in the fun, but without a partner she was lost. Suddenly she noticed across the road a man she recognized as a certain Welsh baritone, David Brazel, whom she knew. She flung herself across the road and, to the bewilderment of the man, pulled him into the gay, laughing, dancing crowd, and in a few moments 'they were enjoying the time of their lives', as Katie put it.

But it was not until she was returning in the train to London that the inspiration came to her to write a song about the dance, in the complete picture she had experienced. Maybe the rhythm of the train set her composing brain into action—it often does with a song-writer. Whatever it was, by the time she reached her destination she had the rough outline of a song that was destined to become one of the most popular songs ever written in the English language. She afterwards explained to me that during the train journey she experienced the strange sensation of her sub-conscious mind persistently entreating her to write a song about the episode. "It became an insistent command. If my mind was distracted for a moment or two from the theme, back would come the subconscious order to keep striving," Katie told me.

And she wisely composed the song while the scene, the music and the enjoyment were fresh in her mind.

I first saw it almost immediately after Katie had shown it to Chappell's. Chappell's assured me that they had a 'winner', and I certainly was captivated. The quaint old Cornish melody had been revivified, and Katie Moss had achieved a real triumph with her *gaieté de cœur* lyric.

Thorpe Bates was the first to sing the song on the concert platform. I was the second. It scored a sensational success. The Gramophone Company were quick to see the selling potenti-alities, and I recorded it within a week of my first rendering.

But this song was not, and is not, one of those ephemeral ditties that are plugged out of existence in a few months. It is as popular today as it was when it was first launched. That is the irrevocable hallmark of the successful song. Yes, Katie Moss wrote a number of other songs, but never quite succeeded in evolving another 'Floral Dance'.

Another song which, but for the enthusiasm of Mr. Bowker Andrews—father of the Bowker Andrews of the B.B.C.—might never have been published, is Kipling's "Boots". I can be for-given a bleat of pride, I hope, when I confess that I set this song to Kipling's verse.

I have always enjoyed composing, and for that purpose I read a fair amount of poems. I remember putting a volume of Kipling's in my pocket to read in the train, travelling to a concert at Margate. When I read "Boots" I stopped reading any further. I knew the words were crying out to be put into a song. From that moment on everything else was obliterated from my mind and I rapidly began to compose a melody approximating to the tenor of the verse.

"Boots-boots-boots-boots movin' up and down again!"

What a fine song it would make! It must be in marching time, and as I cogitated, the rhythm of the train seemed to be appealing to me to get on with it! You know the sort of thing. The wheels go with a steady beat:

T'lum-T'lum-T'lum-T'lum-T'lum-T'lum-T'lum
Tee-a-lum tee-a-lum Tee-a-lum tee-a-lum.
T'lum-T'lum-T'lum-T'lum T'lum-T'lum-T'lum-T'lum.
And so I hummed a melody to:

We're foot-slog-slog-slog-slogging over Africa
Foot-foot-foot-foot-sloggin' over Africa
(Boots-boots-boots-boots movin' up and down again)
There's no discharge in the war!

By the time I reached Margate I had the melody well impressed in my mind. On arriving at the hotel I bewildered everyone by asking excitedly where I could find a piano. "Would you care to register first, please?" I remember testily replying: "Look, I can register any time, but I've got to find a piano quickly or a song I have in my head may be lost for ever!"

It was obvious the receptionist thought he was dealing with an eccentric; but he was taking no chances with the determined expression on my face, and he rather timidly led me up a flight of stairs into a room with a piano. And there I tried out the melody, the chords, etc., and commenced making alterations. I wrote out enough to satisfy myself that the foundation of the song was established, and that I could embellish it in my own study when I returned home.

But the song occupied my whole attention. I frankly do not recall what I sang at the concert: I was completely enmeshed in the web of my song.

On arriving home I went straight to the piano. I called to Nannie, "Come and hear a song I have composed to Kipling's words."

I played it with undisguised pride, but my wife's reaction was very disconcerting. "It's—well, it sounds a little ordinary." And then she added: "I don't like the introduction. It's too agitated."

From such a shrewd critic, it was a shock. Nevertheless, after reading the verse, Nannie changed her view, and I am pleased to say became enthusiastic. But she never liked the introduction. Here it is:

For once we agreed to disagree. And the introduction as above is the one published. It is the introduction I composed in the train going to Margate.

It was not very long before I tried it out. This was at a Promenade Concert. The song was a spontaneous success. In fact the ovation was so tumultuous that Henry Wood was peeved —he was like that, he did not welcome too much success to others on his programmes—and he made the disparaging remark that I have already quoted.

Chappell's were very impressed and approached me for permission to handle the publication. I gladly acquiesced. It was now a question of waiting to hear how Chappell's fared with Kipling's agents.

But many weeks passed and the song was not published. When I 'phoned Mr. Goodman, of Chappell's, he informed me that Kipling's agents were demanding such a high royalty it was not worth while proceeding with the publication. They were making one more effort, but Goodman warned me they were not optimistic. And a little later I learnt that the agents were adamant on their percentage.

It was then that the late Bowker Andrews came into the arena.

He heard me sing the song at a concert and came round to see me, asking if I had fixed up publication. I explained the attitude of Kipling's agents. He hesitated for a moment or two and then said: "Look here, Peter, I know Kipling—and his agents. Will you let me handle it?" I agreed, and at the same time told him how Kipling himself had given me permission to set his song to music and sing it.

"Yes, Mr. Dawson, sing the song with my best wishes for a success," Kipling had said. And he was kind enough to add,

"There is no one I should like to hear sing one of my verses more than you, Mr. Dawson." He then asked if I was contemplating working on any other of his verses. I was not, but I said quickly, "Yes, Mr. Kipling, I am studying some others." In another few months I had published my settings of Kipling's "Cells" and "Route Marchin'."

A week or two after Bowker Andrews took the song he 'phoned to say that he had made a satisfactory arrangement with Kipling's agents, and the song was duly published by the Swan Music Publishing Company. It was an instantaneous success, and I was receiving as much as £60 per month for royalties from the sheet-music sales. The song was also very successful in its sale as a record, and today it still is a good and regular seller. I have been fortunate enough to write several successful songs, but "Boots" is easily the most popular, both from the public demand and the sales.

That soldier song reminds me of that other popular number, "The Sergeant of the Line".

Some years ago W. H. Squire came to see me full of enthusiasm about a song he had written, which he said was a wonderful one for me. He played it over, and I agreed it was a really good rollicking song. "Well," said Squire, "no time like the present. Will you help me get it published?" And without delay we set out. But three music publishers turned it down. Finally we went along to Boosey's. They wouldn't entertain it either, the reason being that they regarded the song as semi-comic. In those days the music publishers wanted only what they term 'black and white' songs—that is, songs that are published with the regulation black type on a white background. Songs not in this category usually carried a picture or a drawing of some kind on the front of the sheet-music copy. It can be likened to a form of musical snobbery of the music publishers; and we had to accept the decision. "The Sergeant of the Line" was not a 'black and white' song, and that meant, in effect, it was more likely to suit the publishers of music-hall songs.

We were both very disappointed. Squire took the blow philosophically. "I'll put it on the shelf," he said, and then added: "It may be published some day." But only a short time after Harry Dearth, who was at the peak of his career at that time, called on W.H.S. Just by chance Squire played the song over to Harry. He was immediately impressed and started asking a lot of questions. The composer explained what had happened and Dearth, like myself, was so intrigued by the possibilities of the song that he took it round to Boosey's, told them he was going to sing it and more or less insisted that they should publish it.

He sang it at a Boosey Ballad Concert that week and it caused quite a sensation. It was, of course, a new type of song. It became an immediate success. I recorded it, and sang it all over the country and throughout my tours. But for Harry Dearth's call on Squire it is quite possible that the song would have been lost!

One of the most popular songs today, and one that is likely to retain its popularity for many years, was written by an officer then serving with the Scots Guards. His name is Major Alan Murray.

A few years after the First World War I was in the habit of receiving 'phone calls and a letter at regular intervals from a certain Major Murray, who was anxious to arrange a meeting with me to hear a song he had composed, which he 'was sure would interest me'. The first letters came from the Castle, Edinburgh, later from London. Like other singers who are in the limelight, I am worried a good deal by song-writers sending their compositions to me. These communications are invariably followed by a 'phone call, and always in the same strain: will I please make a record of it and/or broadcast it.

Now, with all the good will in the world, I could not possibly do any such thing. And I must be brutally frank, and say that quite ninety-five per cent of the songs are of poor quality and a waste of time to even play over, although I rarely do play them over, for I can tell by reading a song whether it has any attraction or appeal. If the song shows promise I then play it over and try it out.

Major Murray had a different technique. He did not send a copy of his song but asked whether he could not meet me to discuss a song he had written. Finally my wife said: "Why don't you meet Major Murray? He sounds like a reasonable man, and he obviously admires your singing." So I arranged to meet the Major at a West End restaurant. Here he showed me the song. I read it over and was immediately impressed.

I took him along to Weekes, the music publishers in Hanover Square, and he played while I sang the song. Without any delay we moved on to Chappell's in Bond Street, and after singing it to them they decided on immediate publication.

And that was how "I'll walk beside You" came to be published. It is now known and sung all over the world in every language. Major Murray lost the sight of an eye in the First World War, and gave up his career as a serving officer with his regiment. He is a splendid pianist, and is now an established composer of songs. I remember some years ago, when he was holding an official position at Dover Castle, what an enjoyable night we had singing some of his later compositions. After "I'll walk beside You" his most popular song is that stirring "Call of the Pipes". Others of his I have sung are "I'll go with You", "Phantom Fleets", and "Wandering Player".

Before leaving Major Murray I must tell the story of the surprise I had during the last war when I recognized his voice doing the war commentary to Australia on the B.B.C. Overseas service. At first I said to my wife, "I know that voice," and each time I heard it I became more annoyed with myself for not being able to place it. But it came one day when I was running over "I'll walk beside You". I was as happy as the proverbial schoolboy. I wrote to Murray, and he confirmed that it was indeed he. You will hear more good songs from this versatile man!

Another song which today is known to everyone who likes a good song is that popular Pat Thayer winner "I travel the Road". Thayer had no luck with it when it was published by Lorraine and Co., who went out of business some years ago. During my first week at the Palladium, Thayer came round to see me and begged me to read it over. I read it, and played it over, and liked it immensely.

Up to this time nothing had been done with the song and Thayer was a disappointed man. It struck me as such a good number, and one that I felt sure the Palladium audience would like, that I sang it as an encore on the fourth night. It was a terrific success.

This success created a demand for copies, particularly after I had made the record. Unfortunately the success came too late to help the original publishers, whose business had been bought by Keith Prowse, but the latter were very grateful for the 'plum' they had picked up. Today "I travel the Road" is an established song of the people, almost like a folk-song.

Which brings me to the one that has become an Australian folk-song and captured the imagination of the whole English-speaking race—that saga of the Australian Bush, "Waltzing Matilda".

All sorts of stories have been written and published giving the origin of this number. The supposedly authentic version issued on copies published by the Oxford University Press reads: "Waltzing Matilda, an Australian song", and gives the following extract from Thomas Wood's *Cobbers*:

"We mourned together that there were no folk-songs in Australia. The bullockies sang ribaldries to music-hall tunes; the shearers did not sing at all. In my own Essex and Suffolk I had filled a note-book. There was not enough here to fill one page. . . . The only Australian song, I said, that had the right sort of smack was 'Waltzing Matilda'. Did he know it? Did he not! It was written in the very town of Winton in Queensland; sung, for the first time, in this very room.

Yes. 'Banjo' Paterson used to come and stay with old Robert McPherson, out at Dagworth Station, years ago. They were driving into Winton one day, in the buggy, along with McPherson's sister and Jack Lawton, the drover. He's told me the tale, many a time. On the way they passed a man carrying his swag. 'That's what we call "Waltzing Matilda" in these parts,' said McPherson; and 'Banjo' Paterson was so struck with the phrase that he got a piece of paper and wrote the verses there and then. When they got to Winton, his sister, who was a bit of a musician, wrote the tune; and they all sang it that night."

This is probably quite authentic; but the melody of "Waltzing Matilda" was originally an old British Army marching tune, written for the purpose of encouraging men to sing and whistle on the march.

Marie Cowan heard this tune at Waonambull, Victoria, and played it over on her piano. Hearing the melody, 'Banjo' Paterson (A. B. 'Banjo' Paterson) was struck by its rhythm, and in a few hours they were collaborating on the setting of words to the tune Marie Cowan had memorized. A few hours later the song was set. Marie Cowan had very cleverly arranged the old British Army tune into what was to become an Australian folk-song of world-wide repute.

But it was not a popular success for some time. I remember taking a copy of it from Australia to London, where I made a record of it for the Gramophone Company. It had a big appeal, and a matrix was sent to Australia for the Australian branch to print and sell copies. All I got for my pains for the suggestion was to be shown a letter written from the Australian head of the company: "Please do not send any more of that sort of rubbish!" When, however, I returned to Australia and sang the song, the demand for records was sensational. I sang it many times to the American troops stationed in various parts of Australia, and they were very enthusiastic. The result was that my records of

"Waltzing Matilda" were sent to America in thousands. Wherever I go today, "Matilda" is called for.

That brings me to the story behind the other colossal success —a song that was first sung in the early part of the twentieth century, that lay dormant for forty years and became a huge popular success in 1947. This is the Maori song "*Waiata Poi*", or as the vast majority of the public call it, when they send notes asking me to sing it, "Tiny ball on end of string".

I first sang this charming little song in 1914. It flared up again into popularity after I sang it on my first appearance for the B.B.C. when I arrived in London in early September 1947. I was accompanied by the B.B.C. Theatre Orchestra, and the song had been arranged for his orchestra by that brilliant conductor, Walter Goehr. The chorus was made up of members of the Kentucky Minstrels. It was a big success, so much so that for the first time over the air I was asked to repeat it as an encore! I believe that is unique. Everywhere I sing in the United Kingdom I receive requests for "Tiny ball on end of string".

Actually there are three songs that I am almost compelled to sing through public demand. They are "The Floral Dance", "Waltzing Matilda" and "*Waiata Poi*". I sometimes feel I ought to change my name to "Floral Mat Poi". Yes, I do enjoy singing them! Having lived in New Zealand and met the Maori people, I naturally endeavour to put some of their traditional spirit into my rendering of "*Waiata Poi*", and I find that the public enjoy it that way. The same remark applies to my partiality for "The Floral Dance". I love Cornwall and the old Cornish folk songs. As for "Waltzing Matilda", well, I have an intense love for the Australian Bush and all it means to Australians. It is a truly wonderful place: the breath of the trees, the sound of the birds, the ever-changing beauty of the country as you move about it, the remarkable characters who are to be found in no other place on this earth—and that includes the swag man and 'waltzing matilda'.

As I am talking of Australia, I am reminded of a song called "The Waratah and the Wattle". An Australian magazine once published on its front page the picture of a girl and a spray of wattle; this picture inspired the editor so much that he wrote a lyric about it, and then wrote to me asking whether I would set his words to music. I duly did this, and the song found a ready publisher in Chappell's of Sydney. But when I called to show the finished article to the editor he had vanished. I learnt that he had gone to America, and I am not sure whether he has yet heard the

Presentation of a copy of the first and famous H.M.V. 'dog' model gramophone and the latest 1949 Record Reproducer to Peter Dawson by Sir Ernest Fisk, managing director of the Company, at the Savoy Hotel in December 1948

Left to right—Mark Hambourg, the late Sir Charles Kingsford Smith, Hugo Larsen (*impresario*), and the author

Toscanini

Sir Henry Wood

Pachmann

Chaliapin

song he inspired. It swept Australia, and is now an established success.

It is not always the professional song-writer who writes the successful song. One of my most popular songs, "The Dreamer", is another of those that might never have been published but for the sagacity of a music publisher in Australia. The man who wrote the lyric was a traveller in cosmetics! His name? Tom Siddle, an Englishman. He sent me the lyric with the request to read it. If I did not think it was worth a musical setting, would I throw it into the waste-paper basket! I read it and was instantly impressed and commenced composing. I wrote to Tom Siddle telling him what I was doing, and suggested that he come to London and hear it. He turned up the following day.

What happened to his sale of cosmetics for the next day or two I do not know. Anyhow, we went along to Weekes, and Hubert Greenslade played it over and I sang it. We all agreed that it was good, and off we went to Ascheberger's, the music publishers, and sang it to Walter Eastman. When I had finished, Walter, with a perplexed look on his face, said, "Yes, but what's it all about?" I felt as though a pail of water had been thrown over me. I was furious. And with the parting shot "It's a beautiful song!" I stuffed it in my pocket and left the place.

Although it was not published I sang it with success for years. On my return to Australia I sang the song in Sydney, and it was acclaimed both by the public and the Press. Ernest Lashmar, of the Australian branch of Chappell's in Sydney, rushed round to the stage door and asked me to let him publish it. I did, and Tom Siddle received the reward he deserved for his beautiful lyric. Doris Arnold, of whom I have very great respect for her knowledge and judgment of songs, paid a tribute to "The Dreamer" and included it in the series I did for the B.B.C. under the programme called "Our Pleasure to Present"—a series of twelve Sunday night programmes, which included those brilliant piano duettists Rawicz and Landauer, Herbert Dawson at the organ, and Hubert Greenslade at the piano as my accompanist.

Another man who sent me a lyric, with the request I should read it with a view to setting, was Henry Baxter, of Sydney. He called the lyric "Australia, Home of the Brave and Free". Baxter was a physical culture expert, with his own gymnasium. Yes, it is a little surprising, but there are many other instances of what we might call amateur song-writers making successes. Baxter's lyric was extremely good, and it went through Australia like wildfire. During the last war it was sung everywhere that Australians

L

were found. Let me confess that although I spent a considerable time on the musical setting, the stirring words of the song helped me in my work tremendously.

There is a little 'ego' in all of us, and I hope I shall be forgiven for telling you about the song I composed—words and music—inspired by Mr. Churchill's world-famous sign of Victory. It was the biggest seller of any song in the history of Australia. All the money received from the rights of the song were given to the Australian Comforts Fund which was sponsored by the Lord Mayor of Sydney, Alderman Stanley S. Crick. Chappell's published it, and gave their rights over to the fund. I had written only one verse, and it was pointed out that it would be a good idea to have another. I was with the Lord Mayor at the time, and I turned to him and said, "Come along, Stan, you'll have to help me with this." And he did. In quick time we had written a second verse.

This song was sung all over Australia—in the theatres, music-halls, picture houses, concerts, schools—and played by all military bands. The greatest thrill I got out of the song, and a thrill that pleased me more than anything I can remember, occurred when I was watching a military route march and the band suddenly struck up my "V for Victory" marching song. I nearly fell to the ground with surprised delight. And then, like a kid, I just had to march along with the boys to the sound of my own song. I feel the thrill of that moment even as I write about it.

Another man who wrote grand lyrics of Australian Bush history, particularly about the bushrangers, was Edward Harrington. I have set several of his lyrics to music, and yet I have never had the pleasure of meeting him. They include "Lassiter's last Ride", "The Bushranger" and "Black Swan". Yes, in recent years Australian writers are producing fine poems and lyrics of the history of the country. And we now have a goodly number of songs telling the Australian story in folk-songs.

I will conclude further reference to Austalian art with the story about a charming lady, Mrs. P. Carroll, who lives in the Blue Mountains of New South Wales. This is another author I have never had the pleasure of meeting. She sent me a lyric about 'Cobb' coaches, "Grey shades of Cobb and Co." When I started to set the lines to music the words formed themselves into fantastic chordings and melody, underlying the soul of the country. I worked very hard to do justice to her fine lines, which are of great historical interest to Australia. Here they are:

They footed trade ere roads were made,
The famous Cobb and Co.
Naught but a track in the great outback,
The dauntless Cobb and Co.
And still they race at breakneck pace
When dark clouds hover low,
Grey shadows drape a phantom shape
The coach of Cobb and Co.
Grey shades, grey shades.
Grey shades of Cobb and Co.
With an eerie wail haunt the trail,
The stage of long ago.
Grey shades, grey shades.
Grey shades of Cobb and Co.
They take the bend at Dead Man's End
A swaying as they go,
An eerie sight at dead of night,
Grey shades of long ago.
When shadows creep and bushmen sleep
They haunt the trails of old
Where natives prowled and the dingoes howled
And miners washed their gold.
The horses fly with blazing eye,
The drivers bending low,
With flying manes and dangling reins,
The stage of long ago.
Grey shades, grey shades,
Grey shades of Cobb and Co.

And to illustrate the trend of Australian lyricists, and the commendable effort to give Australians songs indigenous of their history, I should like to present the words of three more songs:

Whalin' Up The Lachlan

I've eaten bitter bread, mates,
In sweat that drenched my brow;
I've felled the red gum timber,
Scarred hands on axe and plough.
Now when the sun is shining,
With swag upon my back,
I laugh at soured selectors
As I pass down the track.

Refrain

Whalin' up the Lachlan,
By the waters grey,
Whalin' up the Lachlan,
All a summer's day
We'll see the camp fires redden,
By bend or sandy bar,
Whalin' up the Lachlan,
Where all my old mates are.

Some like to crack the greenhide,
And some to sow and reap,
And some to pink with B-bows,
A-shearing greasy sheep.
But some there are, sundowners,
Who take the easy way,
Nor care about tomorrow
If they make shift today.

Refrain

Whalin' up the Lachlan,
Done with axe and plough,
Whalin' up the Lachlan,
The billy's boiling now.
We'll fill our pipes an' yarn there,
And watch the world roll by,
Whalin' up the Lachlan,
Under a starry sky.

—LOUIS ESSON.

LASSITER'S LAST RIDE

Lassiter rode from his camping ground
In search of a golden lode,
But no one knows what Lassiter found,
Or the track that Lassiter rode.
He fared alone to the great unknown
And followed a phantom guide,
For only God and the stars looked down
On Lassiter's long last ride.

Now Lassiter sleeps in the great North-West,
  Where they say that the dead sleep sound,
But what was the end of Lassiter's quest,
  And where is the gold he found?
Others will go where the fierce winds blow
  And die as Lassiter died,
But only God and the white stars know
  The end of Lassiter's long ride.

Oh, some may jest at his fruitless quest,
  Or murmur his name in grief,
But somewhere out in the great North-West
  Lies Lassiter's golden reef.
And men will track to the great outback
  And try as Lassiter tried,
But only God and the stars looked down
  On Lassiter's last long ride.
                              —EDWARD HARRINGTON.

THE BUSHRANGERS

Four horsemen rode from the heart of the range,
Four horsemen with aspects forbidding and strange,
They were booted and bearded and armed to the teeth,
And they frowned as they looked on the valley beneath.
Their leader spoke grimly and shaded his eyes,
"The town's at our mercy, see yonder it lies."

Through gullies and creeks they rode silently down,
They stuck up the station and swooped on the town;
They bailed up the troopers and raided the bank,
They laughed and were merry, they ate and they drank,
Then off to the ranges they rode with their gold.
Oh, never were bandits more reckless and bold.

But the days are long past since the grim mountains rang
To the galloping hoofs of the wild Kelly gang.
They're gone from the gullies that knew them of old,
And nobody knows where they buried their gold,
For time brings its punishment, time brings a change,
And no more the Kellys will ride from the range.
                              —EDWARD HARRINGTON.

Yes, Australian song-writers are making their mark, but the country is still without a national song. It will surprise people living outside the Commonwealth that there is a great deal of

State or inter-State jealousy. That is the basic reason why we had
to create the capital at Canberra. And it is this strange inter-State
jealousy that is preventing what was for many years accepted as
the national song of Australia from being finally accepted as such.
"The Song of Australia" was composed in 1859, the year a prize
was offered for a song suitable for adoption as Australia's national song. Entries came from all over Australia, and from these
the judges selected the above. It immediately sprang into favour
and was acclaimed not only in South Australia and Western
Australia, but quickly took the public's fancy in other States.
Here is a verse:

> *There is a land where, floating free*
> *From mountain top to girdling sea,*
> *A proud flag waves exultingly—exultingly,*
> *And Freedom's sons the banner bear*
> *No shackled slave can breathe the air,*
> *Fairest of Britain's daughters fair—*
> *AUSTRALIA!*

I will not explore the whole question; it is fraught with
regrettable prejudice. However, another song has recently been
'promoted' in opposition to the "Song of Australia", called
"Advance, Australia Fair". This song springs from New South
Wales, and, despite the hold that the original had on the Australian public, the fact that a State is pushing another song against
the hitherto accepted national one is unfortunately sufficient to
retard the unanimous acceptance of the song voted in 1859 as
the national song of Australia.

As a child of seven I was taught to sing "The Song of Australia" at the East Adelaide Public School, and then some time
afterwards, when a scholar at a Grammar School, it was sung by
the whole assemblage. Later I made a record of it in London,
and it was sent to Australia for sale. I have often been asked to
sing the rival song, "Advance, Australia Fair", but not knowing
the words have had to decline. It is all very unfortunate, and I do
hope that one day the "Song of Australia" will win the right it
earned in 1859 to be Australia's national song.

Leaving Australia and her national song problem, I want to
talk about that very popular number which swept round the
world, "I hear You calling Me". Several publishers refused it,
and even Chappell's turned it down. It was hawked round the
publishers for months without success. It would never have been
heard but for the extraordinary chance that John McCormack

was asked by the composer, Charles Marshall, to try it. John did, and thought it was a winner. He wasted no time. In a few days he sang it at a Boosey Ballad Concert at the Royal Albert Hall. The whole world knows the result. Boosey's published it with alacrity. John McCormack had seen the appeal in the song and the result was that within a year the whole world was singing "I hear you calling Me". The record sold in thousands and it was a best seller in America as well as the United Kingdom.

But here's another fine little song that most of us will recall with pleasure, which might have been lost. Who has not heard, or heard of, "Little grey Home in the West"? It was written by that prolific writer of songs, Hermann Lohr. He sent it to me, and later 'phoned. "I feel sure you will like it," he said. "I haven't made any success with it, but I feel that it is probably the best I have written."

I played it over and then sang it. My wife apparently was listening and came into the music-room and said: "That sounds like a good song. What's it called?" "It's a song I heard Thorpe Bates sing at a Chappell Ballad Concert last Saturday; it didn't strike me as particularly good," I explained. I had many other songs to learn just then and put "Grey Home" aside.

A few days later Hermann Lohr 'phoned again and asked me whether I would be kind enough to try it out, and added: "You are about the only man who could sing it as I intended it. Please give it a try out. If not, I'll just have to shelve it." When I told Nan about the conversation, I said, "That's Herman Lohr asking me to sing that song you like so much." Nan was certain it would be a success, and so I tried it again, and sure enough took a fancy to it. I 'phoned Hermann and told him I would sing it at my next appearance at the Albert Hall. I did. And what a success! Lohr was in front, and the following day I received the following letter from him:

"My dear Dawson,
    I have just got back from the Albert Hall, where I had the great pleasure of hearing you sing. The 'Grey Home' was beautifully given—see how they loved it! And you held on that end as I like it—and you sang the song—Well! *Entre nous*, that's the first time I've heard it as I intended it. Thanks for your top note too—but hold it for ever!
    My very best thanks.
                                        Sincerely yours,
                                        Hermann Lohr."

I sang the song over to the Gramophone Company and it was recorded at once. Its success is well known. Yet, although it is a simple song, it must be sung with feeling, and the words of the story must be clearly heard. About six months after it was an established success I heard a famous contralto sing it. It was dreadful. She sang it in a monotonous depressing dirgeful style, and the words were almost unintelligible.

Herman Lohr, of course, was a great song-writer, and came second only to Fred Weatherley in the number of successes he wrote—and, like Frederick, if a song did not 'catch on' after a fair trial, he would shelve it, or pigeon-hole it, and start another. What a gold mine of good songs must be in the shelves of song-writers! Songs that have not been taken up by the right people, or did not suit the artistes to whom they were sent; songs that with just a small change in a difficult phrase could have been made into a winner; beautiful musical settings to poor lyrics, or bad musical settings to fine lyrics.

That 'atmosphere' is essential for the success of certain numbers was proved conclusively in the Maori number "*Waiata Poi*". When I first sang that song, I sang it as written. But after my visit to New Zealand, and my meetings with the Maori people, I was able to infuse the spirit of the Maoris into the song. And what a difference it made! The song was alive; and I must confess I love to acclaim the Maori *hakas*.

But why this little gem of a song was not a big success until 1947, after I broadcast it, I cannot guess. Perhaps songs, like fashions, have their appeal to different generations. I know I have told of the death of the Ballad song twice during my career. But the Ballad keeps reviving. I find myself singing songs 'by request' today that I had considered dead years ago. In 1948, there was a definite revival of some of the really old ballads—which reminds me that Chaliapin once considered "The Bandolero" as 'a grand song', and had a Russian translation made of it. Today requests are being made for this fine old number.

Talking of the revival of old songs, here is the history of another phenomenal song success—one that was written over forty years ago from the Maori. An Australian song-writer named Jim Darling heard the Maori song, and re-arranged it with his own construction. But it did not meet with success. Keith Prowse in London bought the rights of the song and it was just put aside. About a year ago Gracie Fields sang it over the air on her return from Australasia, and that started a demand.

Chappell's published the song, or were about to, when Mr.

Van Leer of Keith Prowse remembered that he had bought a number like it some thirty years ago. He looked it up, and sure enough there it was. He immediately got into communication with Chappell's and informed them that Keith Prowse held the sole rights in the new sensational hit *"Now is the Hour"*.

It is common knowledge how this song has succeeded, but I wonder whether anyone can realize what a furore it made in the United States. In August 1948 I was informed that the composer had just received his first cheque for royalties from that country— for 75,000 dollars! Why is it a success just now? I cannot explain. Probably it is the sentiment of the people after a war, and the simple words and melody.

A similar kind of world-buying of a piece of music occurred some thirty years ago. It was not a song, but a waltz—a waltz that was played in every country in the wide world, and is still being played wherever a waltz tune is heard. And the waltz was written in London by a British composer.

In the latest catalogue of H.M.V. it is obtainable on four different records, played by four different orchestras. In the States it can be bought on seven different records with a variety of orchestras and soloists. And it all started with a man who had an idea for the title of a waltz and nothing more! The late Bowker Andrews had the name: it was *Destiny*.

He heard scores of waltzes from composers, but could not find one that fitted his title "Destiny". Then one day he ran into his old friend Sydney Baynes in Regent Street, London, and casually asked, "You don't happen to have heard a new waltz being played anywhere that I ought to hear, have you, Syd?" Baines replied: "As a matter of fact I've just written one and am playing it at Drury Lane, and it's a big success. It's a simple, flowing melody and, although I say it myself, Andrew, it's a haunting tune."

With that, Bowker Andrews called a cab and back to his music-publishing office they went, where Baines played his waltz. "That's it. At last that's it!" shouted an excited Bowker Andrews. "That is the haunting melody I wanted for 'Destiny'."

Arrangements were agreed to for the publication and the terms were settled. Of course, fortunes were made. Nothing like the success of "Destiny" has been achieved since—that is, for a waltz.

I cannot leave a chapter on songs without a reference to the one I have sung throughout my life as a professional singer. I have, of course, songs in my repertoire that I have known all my life and sing occasionally, but that grand Irish song "The Kerry Dance" I must have sung more than any other. It has a charming lilt of melody, and look at the lyric:

O the days of the Kerry dancing,
O the ring of the pipers' tune,
O for one of those hours of gladness.
Gone, alas, like our youth too soon,
When the boys began to gather in
The glen of a summer night
And the Kerry pipers tuning
Made us long with wild delight.

O to think of it, O to dream of it
Fills my heart with tears.
O the days of the Kerry dancing,
O the ring of the pipers' tune,
O for one of those hours of gladness
Gone, alas, like our youth too soon.

Was there ever a sweeter colleen
In the dance than Eily More?
Or a prouder lad than Thady
As he boldly took the floor?
Lads and lasses to your places,
Up the middle and down again.
Ah! The merry hearted
Ringing through the happy glen.

O to think of it . . .

Time goes on, and the happy years are dead,
And one by one the merry hearts are fled.
Silent now is the wild and lonely glen
Where the bright glad laugh will echo ne'er again.
Only dreaming of days gone by in my heart I hear
Loving voices of old companions stealing out of the past once more
And the sound of the dear old music
Soft and sweet as in days of yore.

O to think of it . . .

Composers are remembered by one outstanding song that carried their name round the world. (In order that I do not annoy any sensitive song composers, I want to make it quite clear that in giving the list of songs that have become world famous in the English-speaking world, and stating that one song only invariably represents the composer, I am *not* suggesting that the composers concerned did not write other good songs. They all did. But I do claim that the songs I quote here are those that made the composer known throughout the world.) Let us take some of the older songs first:

Tosti: "Good-Bye" (made famous by Madame Melba).
Sir Charles V. Stanford: "Songs of the Sea."
Pinsuti: "The Bedouin Love Song."
Trotere: "My old Shako."
J. L. Molloy: "The Kerry Dance."
Herman Lohr: "My little grey Home in the West."
Landon Ronald: "Down in the Forest."
Leslie Stuart's *ballad* song "The Bandolero."
Sir Edward Elgar: "Land of Hope and Glory."[1]
Haydn Wood: "Roses of Picardy."
Katie Moss: "The Floral Dance."
Eric Coates: "The green Hills of Somerset."
T. Dunhill: "The Fiddler of Dooney."
Frances Allitsen: "The Lute Player."
Alan Murray: "I'll walk beside You."
F. Cowan: "The Border Ballad."
Coningsby Clarke: "The blind Ploughman."
Ernest Newton: "The Drum Major."
Alba Rizzi: "Little Prayer I Love."
Edward German: "Glorious Devon."
J. P. McCall: "Boots."
A. W. Finden: "The Indian Love Lyrics."
Hope Temple: "An old Garden."
Kennedy Russell: "Young Tom of Devon."
Alfred Hill: "*Waiata Poi*" (Tiny ball on end of string).
Oscar Rasbach: "Trees."

[1] I don't think it is generally known that this song was inspired by King Edward VII. After hearing Elgar's "Pomp and Circumstance" he was very impressed with the melody included in the work, and later suggested to Sir Edward that that particular melody would make a fine song. Sir Edward lost no time, and his song "Land of Hope and Glory" has become a national song of Britain. In fact it is no exaggeration to say that it ranks second only to the National Anthem. (Which reminds me that America tried to claim it as a national song referring to America, and a huge choir sang it in front of a background of flags of the U.S.A. The music critics of the Press, however, damped the ardour of the sponsors by revealing that Sir Edward Elgar wrote the song about Britain.)

W. Sanderson: "Up from Somerset."

Michael Watson: "Anchored."[1]

W. H. Squire: "The Sergeant of the Line."

Guy d'Hardelot: "Because."

Dorothy Foster: "Rose in the Bud."

J. Airlie Dix: "The Trumpeter."[2]

Charles Marshall: "I hear you calling me."

Pat Thayer: "I travel the Road."[3]

Peter de Rose: "I heard a Forest praying."

George Butterworth: "Is my Team ploughing."

S. Lover: "The low-backed Car."

Percy French: "Mountains o' Mourne" and "Phil the Fluter's Ball."

R. Wallace: "Old Father Thames."

A. Lockhead: "The Pride of Tipperary."[4]

A. B. 'Banjo' Paterson: "Waltzing Matilda."

Paul Reubens: "The Admiral's Yarn."[5]

Charles Willeby: "Bow Bells."

May Brahe: "Bless this House."[6]

I have sung nearly all the songs listed above, and am proud that I have helped to popularize them. Naturally I have not attempted the soprano songs like Tosti's "Good-Bye" or Landon Ronald's "Down in the Forest". I have a good range, but not that good! On the other hand, there are composers whom it would be difficult to credit with one outstanding success because

[1] This song was published in twenty-five variations—solo, duet, trio, etc. And all keys. Michael Watson also sung the song. His voice was so good he was reprimanded by a well-known critic for singing such 'tawdry' songs as "Anchored".

[2] Dix set the song to Francis Barron's lyric. Barron was a Guards officer, who later travelled over the seven seas. He finally became a traveller for Keith Prowse. He and Dix sold this popular old song to Boosey's and received *one* guinea each! Fortunately, in later years they cashed in for mechanical rights.

[3] Thayer has one or two other songs racing for first place—his beautiful song "Snowbird" and another song of the open road, "Walk down the Road". But I doubt whether either will ever reach the popularity of "I Travel the Road".

[4] Lockhead, incidentally, is a Scotsman. But many a good Irish song has been written by a Scot!

[5] This refers to Reubens's ballad songs, and not those he wrote for musical comedies.

[6] This lady may write a song even more popular than this, for she has a number of others, including "I'll pass by your Window".

they have written two or three equally popular successes; but this is just the exception that supports my initial observation.

The most prolific writer of song successes is undoubtedly that great song-writer the late Frederick Weatherley. Look at this list of successes:

"The Midshipmite."
"Nancy Lee."
"Thora."
"Nirvana."
"The Holy City."
"The Star of Bethlehem."

On the occasion of Weatherley's fiftieth anniversary as a song-writer, I had the pleasure of being invited to the celebration dinner given in his honour by William Boosey. It was held at Oddenino's Restaurant in Regent Street, London. The Right Hon. Sir Gordon Hewart, K.C., M.P. (later the Lord Chief Justice), was in the chair. The committee of four comprised Mr. William Boosey, Mr. Leslie Boosey, Mr. W. H. Squire and Mr. Hermann Lohr. The date was 11 December, 1919.

George Baker sang "Three for Jack", Philip Ritte sang "Roses of Picardy", Herbert Cave "The holy City" and I sang "Nancy Lee". But instead of singing "And there she stands upon the quay and waves her hand", I made a really awful musical 'spoonerism' and sang "And there she stands upon her hands and waves the quay". It caused great amusement: but very few believed I had not sung it that way deliberately. It was a genuine spoonerism, probably caused by a change-over that George Baker and myself had made a few minutes earlier. I was down to sing "Three for Jack", and we changed.

CHAPTER XIV

MY MUSICAL EXPERIENCES

FOR many years I received offers of engagements for special appearances on the music-hall stage. These I steadfastly refused because I thought it wise to let a certain number of years elapse in order to avoid the possible discovery of my Hector Grant episode. But when my brother-in-law wrote me a letter telling me that the London Palladium was offering me a good fee to make a special appearance, I decided to agree that he should open negotiations.

That was in 1930. A week or so later I arrived in London from a tour and was met at Waterloo Station by Tommy Noble, who greeted me with the news: "By the way, Peter, you're top of the bill at the Palladium next week. Val Parnell wants you to sign the contract right away, and I have fixed a lunch for you to meet George Black, the manager of the Palladium, tomorrow at Frascati's." It was Wednesday and I was due to appear on the Monday! "What about fees?" I asked. "Two hundred and fifty pounds for the week." And that was that.

A great amount of publicity followed. Certain diehards in the concert world resented my appearance on the halls, but the Press welcomed me. I duly met Mr. George Black, and was photographed signing the contract. We discussed the programme. I informed him of my appearance on the music-hall stage over twenty years earlier as 'Hector Grant'. That pleased him, for he was naturally a little anxious about the 'temperament' of an established concert artiste like myself making his *début* on the music-hall stage. I have always had a soft corner in my heart for the Palladium, and enjoyed taking Nan to enjoy the programmes there, when we were able to spare the time to go. The programmes were always full of variety to please all tastes. The perfect precision of the performance made me marvel at the expert organization that must exist behind the scenes.

And so I attended on the Monday morning for the rehearsal. George Black was there, and talked over the scene he suggested would be appropriate for my number. What a fine brain Black possessed! He wasted no time. In a few moments he had discussed the songs I had intended singing, and with his unique knowledge of the Palladium audiences suggested an alteration or two. And what an analytical mind he had! His explanations were always given with his beloved Palladium audience in his mind. "They would not appreciate that because . . ." or, "They'll love that one because . . ."

On the same bill with me was Sophie Tucker. And what a brilliant artiste! Here was the greatest exponent of the art of getting the maximum out of a song. It was a joy to watch and hear her sing a song. Two other fine turns were Cicely Courtneidge and the Palladium favourites, Flanagan and Allen.

Following the rehearsal, I pondered on how the smoke from the crowded house would affect my voice. In my earlier experience of the music-hall, when I sang as Hector Grant, I had some pretty grim times in singing through a barrage of tobacco smoke, particularly in the second-house performances. And on the second house on Saturday nights the atmosphere was occasionally shocking! On the opening night I made my way on to the stage and took a peep at the audience from behind the curtain. I saw masses of people—rows and rows of faces, and I realized for the first time what a really huge place the Palladium is. And I was very agreeably surprised by the clearness of the visibility in the auditorium. I failed to see any serious smoke clouds, and was very pleased.

My first shock occurred when I walked on to the stage and made my bow. I could not see any of the audience!

The spotlights from the back of the circle and from the side of the hall, shining directly on to my face, blotted out my vision completely. It was uncanny, and disturbing for a few moments. But the feeling immediately vanished when the orchestra struck up the opening bars of my first number, "Hey, for the Town's Factotum", from the *Barber of Seville*. But that I was thrown out of my stride was proved conclusively, for I commenced singing the great Buffo *aria* in Italian. And realizing my mistake, I changed into English (with a smile at the audience) after singing sixteen bars.

When the song ended I had another shock. The applause was so strangely piercing, deafening. It sounded almost exaggerated. I was mystified. During the few moments before singing my next number I was able to see a little more of the audience. The picture focused on my mind was a multitude of lighted cigarettes and cigars mingling with an occasional white shirt front.

Even when I was taking my calls the huge audience was still a blur to my eyes, for the house was in darkness.

I was quite astonished at the clearness of the atmosphere, for despite the red ends of cigarettes and cigars—which reminded me of a huge field of glow-worms—I was absolutely untroubled by tobacco smoke, and there wasn't a whiff or fragment of smoke on the stage. I learnt from the stage manager that *sirocco* fans carried the smoke out and away from the auditorium.

Back in my dressing-room I remarked on the difference between the music-hall and the concert platform. At the Palladium, because of the darkened house and the bright glare of the front 'spots', I could not see my audience. On the concert platform I can see the audience clearly and recognize individuals.

After a performance or two at the Palladium I became more accustomed to the lights, and to the sound of the applause that had sounded so unreal at the first performance. The explanation was given to me by George Black. "The applause of the music-hall audience is an expression of their real enjoyment. If they like you, well, they let themselves go and applaud wholeheartedly. They do not wait to see what others do, or wonder whether they should or should not show their appreciation—they just go ahead and applaud." Then with a smile he added, "If you happen to please the whole house, as you did, well, that means many thousands of hands joining together in spontaneous applause." And with a laugh he concluded, "The time to be surprised is when you *don't* hear it."

With the possible exception of the Promenade Concerts, the average concert audience is much less demonstrative in their show of appreciation as is the music-hall audience. Of course, the whole atmosphere is different. You will find a similar vast difference between the theatre and music-hall audience. But it is a fact that a music-hall audience is full blooded and knows exactly what it wants. If you give them something else there will be no polite applause, but just the silence of disapproval, and you might even get what is popularly known as 'the bird'.

There is a great deal of poise on the concert platform, but on the music-hall stage the artiste must be intensely human. He must be one of the people—on the other side of the foot-lights.

I regard myself as a singer of the people, and therefore understand what they need and expect. And let me say at once that their taste is not low. Sing good songs to them in the 'right' way and they will like and appreciate it.

They are impatient of mannerisms and affectations. Above all, they love words: a story in song. It is as easy to 'uplift' with your singing as it is to 'let down'. A suggestive after-dinner story may get shrieks of laughter from one quarter of the house (music-hall), but those who did not laugh and did not applaud are the people that matter, for they *do not forget*!

On the concert platform artistes are inclined to strive more to get the poise of a note than to sing the story of their song and thus get the maximum value from the words.

All the songs I sang at the Palladium were songs of high word-value as well as musical merit.

But where the music-hall scores most over the concert is in the organization behind the scenes. You have probably noticed that quite often on the concert platform a singer will walk on and exchange a few whispered remarks with his accompanist, and the audience is kept waiting. There is an air of casualness. But you will never find this happening on the music-hall stage. Everything goes like clockwork. There is organization with discipline and efficiency. An artiste has so many minutes, and he must get finished in that time. He must be ready to walk on the stage at the precise moment that he is scheduled to appear, and fully aware of exactly what he has to do, so that not a moment is wasted.

The audiences, too, seem to be disciplined. They are genuinely attentive, and very quick to respond to what they consider good. They expect much from a performer but reward him generously. They are, however, very hard and severe to the artiste they frankly don't like. That acclamation of disapproval known as 'the bird' is devastating to an artiste, and it is practically non-existent in the concert world.

The concert audience will show its disapproval of an artiste by a very restrained applause—or refraining from any applause.

Apropos of the politeness of the average concert audiences, I remember hearing the story told of a famous Italian singer, a soprano, who at one of her concerts received no applause whatever, except for a few polite hand-taps. "Vy, oh, vy is it?" she cried, at the side of the platform. Her agent, who chanced to be there, took her quickly and quietly aside and explained that she was very much out of tune. And he advised her to make a little speech saying that she was there against doctor's orders, and she hoped the audience would understand.

She did this very charmingly in her broken English, and the

M

whole audience applauded her speech and everything she sang afterwards—and I am told she continued to sing out of tune. That just could not happen on the music-hall stage.

I thoroughly enjoyed my first appearance at the Palladium, and accepted an engagement to sing there again the following year.

CHAPTER XV

SECONDS OUT

I AM devoting this chapter to talking about, and to, accompanists, conductors and song-writers—with a few remarks on diction. For that purpose I am heading the chapter 'Seconds Out' because I am coming in, punching, from the bell onwards.

ACCOMPANISTS

An accompanist should possess the instincts of a jockey, a navigator and a cricket batsman all rolled into one.

The jockey instinct will help to take his soloist safely over the sticks, the navigator will adhere to the proper course of *tempo*, and the batsman instinct will help to make a sixer when a singer requires help on a mountain top. The higher the note, the greater the muscular efforts from the jockey-navigator-batsman as he flails the ivory keys with his india-rubber fingers backed up by the wrists of iron.

At no time should the accompanist adopt mannerisms likely to distract the attention of the audience from the solo performer.

Sitting on the music-stool, obliquely to the audience, he will (jockey fashion), when the starting-gate is raised, read the voice track and follow the trail and lift his mount over vocal obstacles; should the mount falter for a word, the jockey-eye on the words will immediately, and like a ventriloquist, supply the elusive link.

An accompanist must be a quick sight-reader, and also be capable of transposing, up or down, any reasonable piece of music—even manuscript.

I once attended a vocal recital when the ccompanist played most difficult *arias* and songs from memory. Such a change, and what a boon to the artiste! The elimination of the irritating flashes of pages being turned during the progress of the song. And I have known occasions when the piece of music has dropped to the floor, causing embarrassment to the singer and the audience, not to mention the poor dishevelled accompanist.

Albert Chevalier, the costermonger comedian, had his pianist off-stage in order that nothing should distract his characterizations on the stage from his audience. What a pity I did not realize, as a young man, the advantage of such an arrangement!

Another point about accompanists. When they have ambitions to become solo pianists it is wise for them to forsake accompanying. Immediately the ambition to become a soloist bites the accompanist and he makes appearances as such, the result is that when he comes on the concert platform to accompany an artiste he instinctively realizes that he is a soloist, and can be forgiven for wanting the audience to know it. What happens? Instead of sinking his identity in the art of the vocalist and exemplifying the jockey-navigator-batsman, he is a solo pianist and wants the audience to 'feel' his presence.

One of the biggest disappointments I have with accompanists is that, although some of them have played a song hundreds of times, and scores of times for the same singer, they still persist in playing with a copy of the song in front of them on the piano. Compare this with the brilliant pianists who can play whole concertos from memory!

My last word on accompanists: I have seen no progress in their art during the whole course of my career.

CONDUCTORS

In the concert world a conductor has the whip hand. He can either beat you to it or drown you.

It is regrettable, but true, that a great majority of them have the complex of the musical snob. They are unique, inasmuch as they wield absolute power and control over all artistes. Their word is law, their decisions are sacrosanct and there is no appeal. It follows, too, that this majority to which I refer are wrapped up in their own importance, to the inevitable detriment of the singer; and as a result of this peculiar state of affairs it is not surprising that this same majority of conductors are not brilliant exponents of the art from which they have derived their reputations and their livelihood.

These men have no real constructive genius in their study of the great orchestral works. One does not discover any brilliant or even clever changes in euphony, construction or emphasis denoting musical erudition in their interpretation of the composers. No, this majority can be classified as common or garden musical copyists. For many years it has been possible to buy the recordings of the world's famous conductors, conducting the world's finest orchestras. Whole symphonies can be purchased. A conductor can, with the aid of gramophone records, master any work to the manner born!

A student conductor is very fortunate today in that he can hear all the great ones at his elbow—just pull out a symphony, place the records on the robot player, and then with the full orchestral score in front of him he cannot go wrong. Today one can recall the old question: "Which came first, the egg or the hen?" and pose another question: "Which came first, the score or the record?"

Now let me say at once there is no harm whatever in studying the records of the old masters. In my early days I studied most carefully the renderings of songs as sung by men like Albert Coates, Ben Davies, Charles Tree and others. *But* I used my own renderings after I had heard their interpretations. The trouble with the conductors in my majority list is that they follow the recordings to the letter, and make no attempt to translate their own reasonings into the score. And quite frankly many of them are incapable of such musical acumen. The proof of this can be found in the difficulty conductors find in conducting the *Apprenti Sorcier* as recorded by Toscanini.

I have been asked what to look for from a conductor. I can only say, 'the final beat!'

One final comment on conductors and their attitude towards vocalists. The vast majority have no time for the average singer. They regard them as non-musical, in their sense of the word, and obtrusive. The hours I have wasted in the early part of my career—hours thrown away waiting until the conductor thinks fit to give the unfortunate vocalists a run through with the orchestra!

SONG-WRITERS AND MUSIC PUBLISHERS

And now a word of advice to aspiring song-writers, particularly the amateur of the species, and those amateurs who hazard both 'words and music'.

Would-be composers should never attempt to use their own lyrics unless they have been favourably reviewed by someone who is an authority on the subject. Then, when they have given it a musical setting, they must have it scrutinized by an accredited musician, who will put the time-spacing and chordings into legitimate academic order. Rather like a man with a good voice seeking the help of a teacher. Having composed a song that is considered favourably by an authority, the next step is what to do with it.

There are two ways. If you have written the song as a song, without having any particular artiste in view, then take it to a music publisher. If, on the other hand, you have written the song with a certain singer in mind, then try to find a way to get the composition considered by that singer. But let me warn you, a singer of note is inundated with new songs. I have received songs from would-be composers quite unsuitable for a baritone—songs that tell of the flowers and the birds, and therefore suitable for female voices. Others have sent me songs of a range more fitted to tenors. This is a mistake easily remedied. It is a mistake the established song-writers never make.

A famous song-writer, who is writing fine songs still, told me that he was helped to his success by a clever music-publisher friend. When the song-writer, in the early days of his success, took a song to his friend for 'vetting', the publisher would keep it a day and then tell the budding song-writer: "You have something there, but it's not quite right. Go home and see whether you can't improve on it."

The song-writer went home, studied it, and almost reconstructed it. When he returned the new effort to his music-publisher friend, he was informed that he had written 'a damned good song'.

The music publisher repeated the advice on the first three occasions. Finally the song-writer 'got the idea', and today he follows the system. He writes a song, rewrites it, and he has often rewritten a song three times before he has satisfied himself with the result. But now no publisher can say to him: "I don't like this song. It's loosely constructed."

I have set over thirty songs. I write and rewrite until I am absolutely satisfied I cannot improve on my composition.

Judging by the number of crudely constructed songs I receive, a large number of would-be song-writers are under the impression that composing a song is easy. Others seem to be obsessed with the notion that so long as a lyric is about a 'road', the 'open air' or the 'sea' it is sure to be a success. Yet others have the mistaken idea that they only have to write a successful song to put them in the lap of luxury.

Let me disabuse them right away, and tell them about the music publishers. These are what we call in Australia the 'Ned Kellys' of the music world. The 'new' song-writer is up against a system that gives the composer little chance of making a fortune the quick way. The publisher is a past master in the art of the 'knocker'. Your song may be really a winner, but the publisher will not let you know that. He will pull a poor mouth, and get the composer down so low that he will gladly sign on the dotted line below a maze of small print overlaid with innumerable 'buts' and 'ifs' that would take a clever man a week to understand. The poor composer is so pleased with the fact that his song is to be published he does not realize until he writes further successes that the publisher rakes in the shekels and the composer the fame.

Still, that is the custom of song publishers, and has been as long as I can remember. Naturally, once a composer has 'established' himself then he can make his own terms—*but*, that is, providing he has not signed on that dotted line for a number of years. I suppose the music publishers have published large numbers of 'losers', and the successful song has to compensate for those failures. But it's darned hard on the young composer who may have written a 'winner' at his first attempt.

In the chapter on 'Songs' I have explained how some publishers have been sadly amiss in their judgment of a song, and also how a clever music publisher can find a winner after it has been rejected by others.

DICTION

I now want to say a few words about diction.

A famous tenor, who was noted for his bad enunciation, was singing one night in Gounod's opera *Romeo and Juliet* when he completely forgot his words. Instead of 'cracking', however, he continued singing like this: "Oh, deuce take it . . . I have forgotten my words . . . My damnable words . . . I have forgotten," and so on, extemporizing as the melody progressed to its end! And believe it or not, the audience did not notice that anything was wrong. Neither did the manager of the company who was listening to the performance.

Whether this story is true or not I can't guarantee, but it does illustrate the point I wish to make, the fact that the greatest fault of modern singers is in their words—or lack of them. If further proof were needed, it is only necessary to mention that the words of a song are now almost invariably printed in a concert programme—the audience is never expected to understand the singer's pronunciation of them!

This fault, however, is intensified when the songs are being broadcast. For one thing, the listener has no programme of words, and the artiste is not seen. Yet in my opinion the words of a song are quite as important as the music.

After all, if it is merely a meaningless tune that people want to hear, why worry to get a vocalist, who has spent many hundreds of pounds and many years on his or her training, to sing it?

The *vox humana* stop of an organ or, for that matter, a bassoon, would do equally well. But a song is meant to tell a story—however simple it may be—and if the listeners cannot hear the words they will certainly not appreciate the song.

Words are becoming even more important now that impressionist songs are so popular. The impressionist song differs from the old ballad in that its music sets out to paint the words—and without words it is not even a 'tune'. You cannot, as a rule, whistle a modern song as you could "Annie Laurie" because there are a dozen little shades of rhythm and accent which are meaningless without the words. Broadcasting has made apparent the sins of these singers of songs without words. Wireless is no worse than others, but the 'ether' seems to emphasize the faults. Actually, broadcasters should find it easier to make themselves understood for, being close to the microphone, they have a great advantage over the concert artiste who has to make himself heard in galleries perhaps 200 feet away, and overcome certain acoustic difficulties.

Some voices by their very nature are not musically clear. Compared with Canadians, Australians or Americans, Englishmen, for instance, seem to be smothering their voice when they sing. I have noticed that most Dominion artistes have a slight drone in their speech which enables them to sing more clearly than people in England. The same remark about clarity of speech is found in the Scots, Irish and Welsh. But of course in the end it is experience that counts in putting a song across.

The old school of singers, of which I am now a member, gained their knowledge at smoking concerts and Masonic dinners. I often used to sing at some function every night of the week, and on occasions two or three times a night. Today, young singers do not get the same opportunities, and practice, however conscientious, cannot take the place of singing to a real audience.

People have not much money to spend, and dinners and 'smokers' are becoming comparatively rare. Wireless will remedy this, for an artiste could broadcast quite often and yet not be heard twice by the same people. This applies particularly in America, where there are so many different stations broadcasting different programmes.

It is only by experience that a singer learns to give to the story that he sings the same attention that he gives to the voice in which he is singing it. To make a success—on the concert platform or in the broadcasting studio—a singer must get inside his song. His voice must become subconscious—almost automatic —and his whole attention must be focused upon the story of the song.

When I am choosing new songs I do not trouble at first to read the music. I simply read the words aloud, and if they sound nonsensical—as they do, I am sorry to report, nine times out of ten—I turn the song down. You can tell after a fair experience almost by the first two lines whether a song is going to be good or otherwise. My advice to a young singer—whether he aspires to the concert platform, broadcasting, or only wishes to sing to his friends in the drawing-room—is, "Read your song, commit it to memory, and then start worrying about the music."

I often think that if you can recite your song you can sing it, and this appreciation of the value of the words is one of the vital differences between the mere singer and the artiste.

Concert singers have still a lesson to learn from music-hall performers. The music-hall artiste who did not make his word clear would quickly 'get the bird' whether he (or she) was singing at a West End hall or a North Country Empire. The hall is in darkness, so that his audience cannot follow the words in their programme even if they were printed—which is most unlikely anywhere these days. The music-hall artiste depends on his enunciation and personality to get the song across in an 'easy-on-the-ear' manner. Of what use would a comedian be if his words were aerated like some concert artistes we all know of?

I hope that broadcasting will teach singers to be more pains-taking in the enunciation of their words—but that, I am afraid, will not be for some time, as many of those engaged in broad-casting are inexperienced and it is, I repeat, experience that counts in singing songs. I often say that a man cannot sing until he is forty!

To my mind, the only disadvantage of wireless is that you cannot see the singer. Television may overcome this difficulty. I hope it will, because good singing is fifty per cent facial expression. But even without television, broadcasting must make artistes appreciate the value of words. The listener must be gripped by the story or sentiment of a song or his attention will be distracted—there is not the same 'atmosphere' about listening to a loudspeaker as there is in listening to a singer in a concert hall. Listeners will insist on having artistes who make themselves understood, and if they do that they will have rendered a signal service to music.

Unfortunately, the microphone has created a new type of artiste—the crooner. The proof of that is in the fact that most of the very successful crooners have never sung in a large hall or theatre without the use of the 'mike' and loudspeakers!

A few years ago I caused a great flutter among crooner fans in Australia by referring to Bing Crosby and others of the same type as 'Moo-ers'. That was not meant disparagingly, for it is obvious to all that Bing is an artiste at that particular type of crooning. But the success made by crooners must have a deleterious effect upon youngsters who, finding they are possessed of vocal potentialities, will be persuaded to earn a living the easy (crooning) way rather than the hard way—through the concert world.

And let me give this warning to those young people who have been advised by a singing authority that they possess an exceptional voice: if you neglect your training as a concert vocalist in order to make an easy living as a crooner, you may regret it for the rest of your days when as a result of the vast number of applicants your life as a 'crooner' lapses prematurely. For, believe me, almost anyone with personality, good diction and a voice of mediocre quality can become a successful crooner, *but* not necessarily a financially successful one!

And this brings me to the choice of songs. I expect that many singers and others interested in singing will disagree with me, but I must say I am convinced that in England songs should be sung in the English language. Forty years' experience of British audiences has satisfied me that the vast majority of the British public like, or prefer, to understand the words of the song to which they are listening. I can, and have, sung in German, Italian, French, Russian and Spanish. In each case I made a careful study with native teachers in those languages, so that my pronunciation was clear and the words scrupulously enunciated; nevertheless I am not completely happy about it because I am conscious of the fact that nine-tenths of the people sitting in front have not the remotest idea of the language, or (unless the song is particularly well known) what it is all about.

After a concert at which I sang the "*Largo al Factotum*" from the *Barber of Seville*, in English, a charming Scotswoman wrote saying that she had often heard the song before, but how happy I had made her by letting her know what it was about. From the great number of letters I receive I am assured that the public prefer to understand the words and the meaning of the songs they hear.

The young men and women of today demand sincerity about everything, and, unlike some of the concert-goers of thirty years ago, they will not feign interest in what they do not understand. If they are attracted to opera, opera must be sung so that they can really understand what it is about. Our old British habit of singing opera in every language but our own is quite extraordinary.

Good vocal translations of songs, of course, are easily made. I recall how Sir Thomas Beecham took infinite pains over those of his opera seasons some time ago. And an artiste should begrudge neither time nor trouble to ensure his, or her, audience getting the maximum amount of enjoyment.

But except in the case of opera, why trouble to learn all these foreign songs? We have British *Lieder* everywhit as good, as tuneful and musically profound as that of the German; and a dozen or more composers who have written and are writing songs of a standard which has probably not been reached in Britain since the Elizabethan era.

The songs of John Ireland, Arnold Bax, Armstrong Gibbs, Thomas Dunhill, Roger Quilter and others are well known to the discriminating, but they are too rarely given the prominence they deserve on the concert platform.

Some time ago, when the old-time ballads passed out of fashion, many singers filled up the gap in their repertoire with an increased number of foreign or old songs. They looked abroad for what they could unquestionably have found at home, for British composers, who have an acute sense of discernment, were quick to realize that the ballad had degenerated into maudlin sentimentality and were replacing it by a type of song that is best described as the 'music cameo'.

The object of these song-cameos is not so much to tell a story as to paint a picture. Where the old songs used to describe an incident or a series of incidents, the new songs put suitable music to words which created an 'atmosphere'. Walter de la Mare's "Silver" was a perfect example. A couple of others that spring into my mind are H. Balfour Gardiner's "Rybblesdale" and Dear's "Sherwood".

These cameos cover all moods from tribulation to exultation, from grief to gladness. And every year new songs are being written, if anything, more beautiful than their predecessors.

I have made a speciality of songs by British composers, and

I find that audiences really enjoy them. They appeal irresistibly to the intelligence, and although they demand a great deal of patience and practice I am sure that other artistes would find it well worth their while to give good British songs a more prominent part in their repertoire—and in their programmes.

Here I append a few titles of some of the songs I have in mind. The list is not complete by any means, and I have probably left out a number that I ought to have included, but the list will give a good idea of the type of song I have in mind:

Arthur Somervill's "Loveliest of Trees" and "In summertime on Bredon"; Parry's "A Fairy Town"; Edward Elgar's "Big Music"; C. V. Stanford's "The Fairy Lough"; Roger Quilter's Shakespeare Songs; Vaughan Williams' "Orpheus with his Lute"; Frank Bridge's "Isobel"; Thomas Dunhill's "Full Fathom Five" and "The Fiddler of Dooney"; Edward German's "Just so" songs; Armstrong Gibbs' "Five Eyes"; D. M. Stewart's "No answer"; Robert Ainsworth's "On the idle Hill of Summer"; Peter Warlock's "The Birds"; Edgar Barratt's "Coronach"; Gustav Holst's "Lovely kind and kindly loving"; Alison Travers' "If Music be the food of Love"; George Butterworth's "Is my Team ploughing"; Julius Harrison's "Sea Winds".

But—and here's the rub—many of our modern composers are more or less compelled to write less-intellectual songs because many of our music publishers require the more popular type of song that sell better. It is a truism in this country that the sale of songs to the more discriminating fall far below the sale to the lovers of the mediocre.

CHAPTER XVI

MEMORIES OF CELEBRITIES, FRIENDS AND COLLEAGUES

THROUGHOUT my career I have been very fortunate in meeting a grand variety of people from every walk of life.

I have often been chided on my habit of chatting haphazardly to anyone I chance to meet. It may be a liftman, a shop assistant, a peer, a postman, a waitress, a knight or an M.P. This lifelong habit of mine has given me many very happy hours. It is too late to stop now, should I wish to—but I do *not*.

I must start with my meeting with their present gracious Majesties when they were the Duke and Duchess of York. They attended a concert given by the Royal Amateur Orchestral Society at the Queen's Hall. I sang Roger Quilter's lovely Elizabethan Songs.

After the performance the Duke and Duchess were kind enough to thank me for my singing, and commented most favourably on my rendering of Quilter's songs. The Duchess expressed her fondness for that charming type of old song, but added that she enjoyed all forms of music. The Duke agreed that he too liked almost every kind of music.

When I sang on Australia Day over the air from Australia House, the Prince of Wales expressed his very warmest appreciation of my singing and said that he knew my records from his collection of them.

Apropos of the Royal Family and my records, King George V had a good selection of my records, and expressed his fondness for them to Mr. Billy Manson of the Gramophone Company. Which reminds me that after a dinner in the City—a Guild dinner, I believe—Austen Chamberlain came round and introduced himself to me. "I have always wanted to meet you, Mr. Dawson. You see, I have a big collection of your records and I have always thought I ought to meet the man that gives me so much enjoyment—away from the House of Commons," he said smilingly.

Then he surprised me by saying, "My father really started my collection and my interest in your singing, for he possessed a goodly quantity of your cylinder records." We enjoyed a long talk on recording and my concert work, and before he left he wrote down a number of records I recommended.

Others who were kind enough to go out of their way to call on me and talk about their collection of my records were the late Lord Asquith (H.H.A.), Bonar Law, Lord Baldwin and Ramsay MacDonald.

Mr. Oscar Preuss, of the Gramophone Company, tells me that one of the finest collections of my records is owned by Mr. Winston Churchill.

To return to the concert at the Queen's Hall attended by the Duke and Duchess of York. In the orchestra was a young gentleman who appeared on this occasion to have celebrated in advance, and in order that there should be no mistakes it was decided by the other members of the violin section to put petroleum jelly on the peer's bow so that no sound should come from his efforts. So all went well.

Of the musical celebrities I have been fortunate to meet I must mention Dame Nellie Melba first. I have already given some inkling as to her character, but there is no doubt that she possessed a glorious voice. The trouble was that she was unable to get 'down to earth' again after her rave notices. From the nice Australian girl she became the spoilt social snob of the music world.

Only to fellow Australians did she remain—more or less—her natural self. But that vanished after a few years. I cannot forget how she grumbled to me at length when she heard about the success of Florence Austral, that magnificent soprano who made a sensational overnight success when she appeared in *Aïda* at Covent Garden.

I remember that the *Daily Mail* gave her a flaring front-page boost acclaiming her wonderful voice. It also meant fame and fortune, for after that she was instantly booked for the United States.

Dame Melba's reaction was not against the success of Florence, but against her use of the name Austral (short for Australia), for her real name was Fawez. Melba's name was Mitchell, and she had adopted 'Melba' as a derivation of her native city of Melbourne.

"Why the devil can't they keep to their own names and stop copying my idea?" was her angry remark. 'They' meant the inclusion of Elsa Stralia, another fine soprano from Australia who had adopted a name associating her with her native country.

I had often toured with Florence Austral and her husband Amadio, the flautist. She certainly possessed a grand voice, but I must confess that I was astonished at her success following the *Daily Mail's* remarkable write-up. Nevertheless she deserved her triumph. She was a very 'large' woman, and I remember that on one occasion, in a very small hall somewhere in Australia, the entrance to the so-called 'stage' was about eighteen inches wide. The backcloth was roughly three feet from the front of the platform. We had quite a job steering Florence on to the stage to sing. When she did appear she looked like a giant, and many a titter was heard from the front when she sang a song which, unfortunately, told of a little wandering girl!

Elsa Stralia made her greatest triumphs in America, where she sang many operas with Titta Ruffo, the great Italian baritone of the day. Of the many fine female singers I met, the one that will always have a warm corner of my heart is Dame Clara Butt. What a fine artiste, and how charming she was to young singers! I remember singing in a cantata, "The Wedding of Shon McLean", at the Queen's Hall. Here was no posing, no temperamental storms, just a natural woman with a wonderful contralto voice. The cantata was conducted by Hubert Barth, who was my accompanist a few years earlier and figured in the incident in Dublin which I described in the 'Irish Tours' chapter. Agnes Nicholls also appeared with Clara Butt and myself.

I appeared some years later with Clara Butt in Australia, when she was a very sick woman and had to travel about in a bath chair.

In addition to her own affliction, she had lost one of her sons, and was to lose the second a few months later. What a tragedy for such a great person! She can be described as a real singer of the people. Faultless diction, glorious quality—in fact she possessed a voice unequalled before or, as far as I can find, since!

It was about this time that I was asked whether I could help a young man who had arrived in London from Canada. My friend Dixon Ryder, who at the time was chorus master at the Metropolitan Opera House, New York, was the young man's mentor. Dixon Ryder had been badly wounded in the war, a shell splinter had torn through the top of his head and resulted in paralysis of his left side, including his hand. I tried the young fellow out on an accompaniment, and decided to let him have the opportunity of accompanying me at three recitals I was to give at the Wigmore Hall of German *Lieder* and a number of French and English classical songs. By the time we were ready for the concerts I realized that he was indeed a brilliant pianist and that he had the exceptional gift of the art of accompanying. A most rare and difficult art.

That, I believe, was the first real chance Gerald Moore had of showing his remarkable ability. After that I took him all over the place as my accompanist. In the meantime, he was studying under Arthur de Greef, Mark Hambourg and also Harold Craxton. It is nice to know that today Gerald Moore is at the top of his class as an accompanist, and is of course a brilliant exponent of the piano. Accompanists would do well to study Gerald's methods; they will learn more that way than any teacher can tell them![1]

I must now tell you about my old friend Mark Hambourg. I have known Mark for over forty years. I first met him and heard him play at the Savage Club, in London. I was taken there by a friend, and had the great pleasure of hearing Mark play Dvořák's "Slavonic Dance". For a second number he gave us Chopin's "Mazurka". I was spellbound—for two reasons. Firstly I certainly did not expect to hear a piano played in a club in the West End of London; and, secondly, not by such an exponent of Mark Hambourg's class.

Although the performance was impromptu, he played superbly. I shall never forget the occasion, because he had a smile on his face the whole time, as though he was thoroughly enjoying himself.

Later I was to know him very well indeed. We appeared on a great many programmes together, also toured Australia and New Zealand, and we appeared again together on my tour of Great Britain in 1947–8.

Mark Hambourg is a brilliant pianist. He is not merely a brilliant exponent but possesses a creative brain, which is the hallmark of genius. He does not, for example, copy any other pianist in his readings of the masters. To listen to his interpretation of Chopin, Schumann, Beethoven and Dvořák is a complete joy.

One of my happiest memories during our long tour of Australasia was listening to Mark rehearsing the works for his next concert.

What pleased me so much about Mark was his capacity to relax. Always ready for a joke, he is a witty *raconteur*, is erudite, astute and a good judge of a cigar.

[1] I have made some criticism about accompanists in the chapter 'Seconds Out'.

I am not likely to forget how philosophical and undemonstrative he was after a particularly galling experience we suffered many years ago when he, Albert Sammons and myself shared the proceeds of a concert at Oxford that we had agreed to sponsor at our own risk.

After we had paid the expenses of the hall, printing, fares and hotel bills, Mark received *sevenpence*, Albert Sammons *sixpence* and myself *sixpence*! The local agent had forgotten that the date clashed with an important Oxford University Dramatic Society production. All that Mark said was: "Of course, it's stupid. But do you know, I have never played better in all my life. I'm quite content." Albert and I expressed ourselves rather more forcibly.

In our very successful tour of Australia and New Zealand, singing and playing in sixty concerts, there wasn't a dull moment! It might have been a nightmare for both of us; but fortunately we became friends. We both dread to think what would have happened had we taken a dislike to each other. More of Mark later.

What a different personality was that other great Russian pianist Vladimir Pachmann! He was the superb showman, the grand *seigneur*, a god in his own right, a musical paranoiac. Engraved on my memory was this carefully intoned declamation, made to me after I had congratulated him on his playing of one of Liszt's works: "I thank you. . . . In the last two thousand years there have been three great men . . . Jesus Christ . . . Liszt . . . and Pachmann—Vladimir Pachmann."

With that profound statement he moved away, his head in the air—and his mind, too, I've no doubt. Make no mistake, he was deadly serious. Previously he had set me agog with his extraordinary behaviour on the platform. As he came on to the stage he received an ovation but, to the astonishment of the whole audience, he turned and with hand upraised said in his deep ponderous voice: "Why you applaud me? I have not yet played." He then made his way to the piano, and immediately commenced testing the stool. It was obvious that he was not satisfied. He sat down, stood up, and again endeavoured to make an adjustment. Still not satisfied, he felt in his pocket and brought out a piece of white cardboard about the size of a visiting-card, folded it once or twice and put it under one of the legs of the stool. Once more he sat down, but was again disappointed with the result. Into his pocket again, and another piece of white paper was carefully, laboriously folded and put under a leg of the stool. This time, to the relief of the audience—and myself—he was

N

satisfied. This was not all. He looked at the keyboard, scowled, and peered closer, and with a grunt of disgust took a large handkerchief from his pocket and proceeded to dust the keys with elaborate ostentation. This done, he finally began to play. Of course, he played superbly. But his temperamental displays were not ended, for after a perfunctory bow he walked off the platform and demanded in an imperious tone for a man in the audience that was on the platform to be removed at once! "I cannot play. His face it is always there!" he shouted. And went on: "A white face, a terrible white face. It is always in my eyes. I like it not. It is terrible. *Please, please* move the poor man." Believe it or not, the manager had to go on the platform and make his apologies to the fellow—a harmless-enough, pale-faced individual—who took the *contretemps* in good part and took another seat in the auditorium.

Pachmann went on to the platform again, shrugged his huge shoulders and with the semblance of a smile sat down to play his next work. When this was over he received tumultuous applause. But the big fellow held his hand up, and with a deprecatory gesture explained that, "No, it was not good," and to the amazement of all, added, "I will play it again." And he did—magnificently. Only a genius could get away with these idiosyncrasies, and Pachmann's playing certainly compensated for them.

He was a man with a violent temper, and yet he could be as docile as a fawn. He was unpredictable, as this story will show.

He was staying at the same hotel as myself, and after his concert he entered the dining-room. To my astonishment I learnt that his food was prepared by his own man. He travelled with his own dinner service of gold. Sure enough he ate off gold plates in my presence. Presently there was a heck of a row, and he was spitting from his mouth—all over the floor—the contents of a glass of champagne that he obviously found distasteful. "Bring the manager!" he cried to the waiter. When the manager arrived, Pachmann asked him whether he had nothing better than that champagne to drink. The manager tasted the wine and, to his credit, was quite firm in his view that the champagne was "Quite good. In fact, Mr. Pachmann, it is very good." "Good!" yelled the big fellow. "I will show you what it is good for." And he proceeded to empty the bottle into flower vases that were around the room. "Now, sir," he said quietly, "what other wine have you?" The manager suggested a fine old port. This was brought. The manager waited while the *maestro* tried it. To the relief of the manager—and incidentally to all the other diners—

Pachmann smacked his lips and with a broad smile said: "Ah, this is indeed the wine good! It is beautiful, beautiful." And silence reigned over the room.

When the manager, commenting on the fact that Pachmann had his own chef, carried his own dinner service and drank the most expensive wines, remarked, "You live very well, Mr. Pachmann," the big fellow replied: "Why should I, Pachmann, not live well? Do not kings live well? What are kings but figureheads?"

And the other side of his remarkable character. The car in which he was travelling between Chesterfield and Mansfield broke down. This meant that Pachmann was held up for over an hour and a half while repairs were made. It caused consternation at Mansfield and the concert manager was not worried only about the possible delay in starting the concert but what sort of temper Pachmann would be in on his arrival.

When the car did pull up outside the hotel the concert manager ran forward, and with anxiety stamped all over his face asked, "What happened, sir, are you all right?" The big fellow smiled benignly and said: "I have enjoyed myself. We had to wait, but it was a beautiful repose and a very beautiful day." The contented sigh of the manager could be heard all over Mansfield!

Yes, Pachmann was unpredictable. The best indication of the man's remarkable mind and his hypersensitivity is this story:

As a young man Pachmann suffered a certain amount of adverse criticism. Taking this to heart, he became a recluse, but not through pique at his treatment by the critics. On the contrary, he displayed a resolute tenacity of purpose. He studied for *twenty years*—principally Chopin. The result of this astonishingly lengthy period of study gave the world a genius of the piano. The world's critics raved about his brilliance. So much so, it is not surprising that Pachmann changed completely from the sensitive neophyte to the dogmatic prodigy.

On the question which pianist is the *maestro* of all *maestros*, I must answer, "I do not think that any critic can state unequivocably that 'So-and-So' is or was the greatest of all."

It would be rather like asking cricketing enthusiasts who was the finest batsman, bowler or wicket-keeper that ever played.

Some would name Grace, Barnes and Lilley; others Bradman, Spofforth and Oldfield. Yet others would argue, and with reason, Hobbs, Verity and Ames. And so on, *ad infinitum*!

Here is a list of the pianists I have had the pleasure of meeting, and hearing play: Wilhelm Backhaus, Harriet Cohen,

Arthur de Greef, Vladimir de Pachmann, Mark Hambourg, Myra Hess, Frederic Lamond, Benno Moséiwitsch, Moriz Rosenthal, Irene Scharrer and Eileen Joyce.

The first of these great artistes I had the good fortune to meet was Wilhelm Backhaus. It was about eighteen months after I had arrived in England and twelve months after beginning my studies with Sir Charles Santley. The leading impresario of those days was Hugo Gorlitz, of Bond Street, London. He gave what he called 'a presentation performance of artistes' to an audience of musical agents. I was in my twenties, and was much overawed when I arrived at the St. James's Restaurant, in Regent Street, and found that I was being presented to the agents in company with Wilhelm Backhaus, Jean Gerady and John Harrison.

I was not only overawed by being in such company, but by Backhaus, who wore an enormous head of hair which reminded me then—and I can still see it—of a lion's mane. Never before, or since, have I seen such a display of hair on a human being.

And now, although I never met him, I should like to tell you a story I heard about Artur Schnabel. Here was the man who persistently refused to have his name associated with gramophone work. He would go off into a violent temper every time he was approached to make a record. He considered it beneath his dignity. The brothers Gaisberg finally offered him an open cheque if he would consent to make records! However, it was not until other famous artistes had recorded their voice or instrumental performance that Schnabel (quite reluctantly) consented to perform. But having succumbed, he became extraordinarily enthusiastic and made many titles. I believe the first record he made was Bach's "Toccata and Fugue in C Minor" on two double-sided records, or four single-sided records, I am not sure. He afterwards played through a big repertoire, and included duets with Karl U. Schnabel. I was told of his delight when he heard their record of Mozart's "Concerto in E Major" for two pianos. They were accompanied by the London Symphony Orchestra. "To think that I was stupid enough not to appreciate this wonderful invention earlier. It helps my reputation, it helps my finances, and it helps my technique." The last remark applies, of course, to the fact that a record is played over to an artiste during a recording session, and in this way the artiste can correct or alter any particular phrasing or revise any part of the work.

I received quite a shock when I first met Frederic Lamond to learn that he was a Scot. Apparently he had lived many years in Germany and become teutonized. Moriz Rosenthal lingers in my memory as a man with the most powerful arms I have ever seen in my life, and that includes those great fellows who toss the caber at the Scottish Games. Despite the huge power in those arms he was as gentle on the keyboard as a fairy.

Of Eileen Joyce I have nothing but the highest praise. She is possessed of a colossal technique. She is also an indefatigable worker. Practice, practice, and more practice. . . .

Just before her last tour of Australia she explained why she prefers to fly to any long-distance engagements. "I can fly to America in a day, South Africa in three, and Australia in five. In that way I lose a minimum of the practice that I find absolutely essential to keep in touch with my work."

This insistence on practice applies to another modern pianist, Horowitz, Toscanini's son-in-law. I have not yet had the pleasure of meeting him, but I have heard him play. And what a cascade of melody came from his piano! (*Apropos* of practice, naturally all the finest pianists are constantly rehearsing, but the two I have mentioned are exceptionally assiduous.) An unforgettable hour in my memory is when I heard Horowitz record Rachmaninoff's "Concerto No. 3 in D. Minor", with the London Symphony Orchestra conducted by Albert Coates.

This recalls an incident at the recording studio when Toscanini came to conduct the orchestra in the overture from *William Tell*. It is common knowledge that the great Italian *maestro* is temperamental. One might go further and say that this brilliant conductor surpasses Pachmann in his unpredictable temperamental nuances. On this occasion Toscanini took up his position on the conductor's stand, and after a few preliminary remarks started the overture. Almost immediately he tapped furiously on his music-stand and stopped the orchestra. "The 'cellos. You are not in tune. Please." The 'cellos proceeded to tune. Let me interpolate here that the 'cellists were all well-known and brilliant musicians. The rest of the orchestra tactfully took the opportunity of again tuning up. A fresh start was made, but once more he stopped the orchestra. This time he asked the 'cellists to tune in to the oboe. For the third time he ascended the rostrum, and for the third time a fresh start was made. But after less than a minute he stopped the orchestra, shrugged his shoulders, descended from the rostrum and slowly walked out of the studio.

The orchestra waited for the next move. The recording engineers waited for his return, the recording manager after a few minutes followed Toscanini out of the studio. The members of the orchestra discussed the tuning incidents, were satisfied that they were in tune, and continued to wait for the *maestro's* return. Instead of Toscanini returning, the recording manager came in and announced to the orchestra that Mr. Toscanini had left the building and had to the best of his (the manager's) knowledge returned to the Langham Hotel. Later it was confirmed that the tempestuous Toscanini had walked straight out of the studio, hailed a taxi and returned to his hotel.

That demonstration of mood recalls that fine Anglo-Australian actor Oscar Asche to my mind. Oscar, like myself, had a great affection for his native Australia. Chatting in the Green Room Club in London, he mentioned with regret that I was not singing any Australian songs and deprecated the fact that no composers had set to music the fine poetry of the Australian poet Lindsay Gordon.

I explained to Oscar the trouble was that the poems were all too long. "But surely," Oscar replied, "something could be done about it? There must be a few good lyricists about capable of condensing the poems to song length without emasculating the poetry?"

Oscar spoke so eloquently on the matter that he had me 'hopping enthusiastic'! Almost immediately I took a volume of Lindsay Gordon's poems to William James, a brilliant composer, to discuss with him the best lyricist in London to undertake the job. We agreed that Edward Lockton (better known to many as Edward Teschmacher) was the best choice. Without delay I visited Lockton and put the proposal to him. To my great delight Lockton knew the Lindsay Gordon poems, and expressed his sincere admiration for them. He was particularly delighted to be given the opportunity of writing song-length lyrics. In a couple of days—long days—he had completed the lyrics for six songs, and had done a magnificent job. It is a most difficult task to reduce a long poem to song length. It is also a thankless task, for lovers of the poet resent any interference with the poet's lines, and however cleverly the transposing is carried out some of the beauty of the poetry must go. We knew it was a delicate, onerous and intricate task for Lockton, but the results were worthy of his labour. At six o'clock on the second day after talking to Oscar Asche, I was at William James' home with Lockton's lyrics. We discussed the settings for the six songs, and I left him to tackle the business of setting them to music.

Ten o'clock the following morning a weary-eyed but happy William James called on me with the six songs set to music! A most incredibly clever achievement. We immediately tried them over. They were remarkably good. Without hesitation I took William along to Ricordi's, in Regent Street. There I showed the songs to Mr. Ross, who played them over. I waited expectantly to receive his verdict, for he was probably the finest judge of a song in London at that time.

To my delight he, too, was most enthusiastic, and signified his intention to publish them without delay.

Now, as happy as a schoolboy with a pocket full of money, I rushed along to the Green Room Club to find Oscar Asche. Fortunately he was there, and in a few minutes we were speeding back to Ricordi's where he would be shown and hear the songs he had so eloquently advocated. I always remember what a job I had in getting Oscar into the taxi, for at that time he was an enormous man, weighing over twenty stone. Once in the music-studio he was given a copy of the lyrics, which he read as I started to sing the first song. I had not reached the end of the first page when I was interrupted by hearing Oscar shouting at the top of his great voice. I stopped, turned, and found Oscar standing up, with his fist raised, and shouting, "How dare this man parody our great poet?" He looked for all the world like some huge angry gorilla. And he trumpeted again, "I say, where is this man who dares do this to our great poet?" And before any of we poor astonished creatures could vouchsafe a reply, Oscar stamped out of the studio, violently angry, and shouting: "Better not let me meet him! If I do, I'll——" and he disappeared out of the studio, out of the building and out of Bond Street.

After we had recovered from this devastating and totally unexpected outburst we discussed the big fellow's criticism. Other executives of Ricordi's were asked their opinion of the lyrics, and we heard nothing but praise for the work Lockton had done. Of course, Ricordi's went right ahead with the publication and I sang them at my next concert. They were an instantaneous success.

They have been sung all over the world, have been translated into several languages and were hailed with enthusiasm in Australia.

Although Oscar Asche knew of their success and immense popularity, he remained contemptuous of what he called 'Lockton's desecration of Lindsay Gordon's poems'. So we had the paradoxical circumstance that the man who inspired the writing of songs about Australia through the eyes of her greatest poet is probably the only man who loathed what he had helped to create!

In London at this time was another popular artiste who weighed over twenty stone. This was Herbert Grover, the tenor. When he heard the songs he was as laudatory as Oscar had been contemptuous.

Herbert Grover must have been the heaviest man that ever risked his weight on some of the rickety concert platforms to be found in Britain in those days. Most of Herbert's weight appeared to be carried in front of him. He accentuated this by wearing an outsize gold Albert spread across his colossal stomach.

On this chain, in the centre, hung a huge gold medallion. I do not know what it was or how he won it, but I do know that on Herbert it had the effect of making him very conspicuous—almost as though he were carrying a searchlight on his tummy. And it was the combination of this gold chain (with medallion) and the Australian songs that caused a sensation on the terrace of the House of Commons. Herbert and I had been invited and we sat down to tea with four others. During tea, Herbert was explaining the wide difference between reading a Lindsay Gordon poem, while sitting in a chair, and acclaiming or singing Lockton's lyric from the concert platform. To emphasize his point he stood up. Unfortunately, the medallion and/or chain caught the edge of the table, which was overturned. The teacups and everything on the table went flying with a fearful crash. The noise not only embarrassed those who were sitting at the table, but caused a few moments' apprehension, for it was the time when a few Irish terrorists were letting off 'annoyance' bombs. To my amazement, Herbert did what I afterwards called an 'Oscar'. He disappeared!

He vanished from the terrace, and it was four weeks before I saw him again.

How strange that these Australian songs had affected two men in a somewhat similar manner! One had walked out of a studio in disgust and the other had fled the terrace of the House of Commons in disgust at having accidentally created a scene over the same songs.

Yet another hefty fellow whose memory will never leave me is Charles Saunders, the tenor. He was a contemporary of both Grover and Asche. He scaled about twenty-four stone and was a huge man. Charles was, and looked, such a big man on the concert platform that he insisted on changing the lyric in that lovely song "Lend Me your Aid". When he first sang that song in London he was astonished to notice quite a number of the audience tittering, which upset him very much. Stamping off the platform in a towering rage, he asked his accompanist, "What the hell happened?" He could get no explanation from the pianist. It was not until the concert was over that the manager was able to 'suggest', tactfully, that perhaps the line '*How frail and weak a thing is man*' coming from a powerful giant such as himself had tickled the humour of some of the public. After that Charles altered the line whenever he sang the song. Just how, I do not know. And to see and hear Charles Saunders sing that stirring song "Sound an Alarm" from *Judas Maccabæus* was a sheer delight.

My reason for never forgetting Charles Saunders was not on account of his singing, but because of what happened during an interval when we were appearing on the same programme at the Queen's Hall, in London. He had very kindly congratulated me on my first numbers, which to a young artiste like myself was a big compliment.

When he had finished his own part in the first part of the programme, he put his arm round my shoulder and said, "Come along, young fellow-me-lad, we'll just slip along to Paganini's and have a little refreshment." I was very flattered, for it's very pleasant to be 'accepted' by a star artiste—I was only twenty-five and on the threshold of my career. Arriving at the restaurant, he called for something, and two glasses filled with an amber liquid were given to us. With the remark, "This'll do you good," he emptied his glass. I did likewise, but it burnt my throat and made me gasp. "What was that, Mr. Saunders?" I asked. "Lager beer or something?" "What! Do you mean to tell me that you can't tell the difference between good Scotch whisky and lager beer? We must have another." And he ordered two more. This time I did not gasp, but was not very impressed, probably because I had decided to fill my glass with the soda water from the siphon which the waiter kindly left on the table.

On my return to the Queen's Hall I felt quite well, but a little light-headed. But when I walked on to the platform I was uneasy. The audience appeared a wee bit blurred, and I seemed to be suffering with astigmatism. Nevertheless I must have sung well, for I received a very warm reception. It was the first time I sang "Hey! For the Town's Factotum", and I recall singing it with gusto. For my encore I have no recollection what I sang, but it was again successful.

What I shall never forget, however, is that on my return to the artistes' room I felt very ill. I had never tasted alcohol before!

I remember getting out of the Hall, hailing a cab and driving to my rooms. I went to bed immediately and was shortly very sick. And I was ill in bed for three days! A pretty grim experience.

Since that incident I have never taken an alcoholic drink before or during a concert. You can guess why I shall always remember that giant Charles Saunders. That is the advice I give to any young singer. Avoid alcohol before you sing, and during the performance, whether you regard the concert seriously or otherwise.

In my long career I have seen too many fine singers fall by the wayside on the road of their career through an over-indulgence in strong liquor.

From the physically big men I should like to return to the musically big men, and the first name that comes to mind is that prolific writer of music, Granville Bantock. Known affectionately to his friends as 'Granny', he is one of the few that can be called a musical genius. I once saw him sitting at a table scoring an orchestral work, while a few yards away a singer (myself) was trying over a song with an accompanist. G. B. was oblivious to all contra melodies and wrote as fluently as if he were alone in his own study.

On the other hand, he was immediately put out of action if someone commenced whistling! In this kink in his otherwise unflurried mind we are alike, for whistling disturbs me just as strongly. I often take a rest during the early evening before a concert, and I have inured myself against extraneous noises of all kinds; but if someone starts whistling my rest is shattered, and until it stops have no hope of resting.

Granville Bantock also possessed the most remarkable faculty of being able to memorize whole scores of music. I recall that on one of his overseas tours he forgot to take the score of his brilliant work "The Five Ghazels", those beautiful, if somewhat sensuous, lines of Sir Edward Arnold from the Persian that he had set to music.

Most men would have thrown a fit of temperament, but not 'Granny'. He decided almost without hesitation to make another score from memory! A truly wonderful achievement! He told me, a year or so later, that on his return home he compared his 'memory' score with the original and they were almost facsimiles. Probably the only other man capable of such a scoring feat was Mendelssohn.

Bantock's works are legion. He was a glutton for work. He told me that he was never really completely happy, or his mind wholly content, when he was *not* writing music.

Yet despite his overwhelming concentration on music he was a delightful friend, had a dry wit and was good company. It was he who introduced me to that 'succulent' dish *goulash*. He had invited myself and our mutual friend Bowker Andrews to lunch at his favourite Soho restaurant. Well, the succulent dish duly arrived. I have no desire to put others off this dish, but I thought it the most awful concoction I had ever tasted. I managed to consume it, but it recalled to my memory most forcibly the brimstone-and-treacle effort I had to make in my boyhood days. There was only one other dish which caused me worse suffering and that was my first introduction to artichokes. Not having the slightest idea how to start eating this peculiar vegetable, and glancing—rather too surreptitiously—at my fellow guests, I proceeded to pluck the small leaves off and devour them whole. Having consumed a half dozen or so, I was very relieved to discover that all one had to do was to suck off the fruity portion at the end of the leaf and throw the rest aside. But that was not nearly as embarrassing as what happened to a young accompanist I met in the north of England. He was given a portion of melon while the others in the party had *hors-d'œuvres*. Not having previously met up with this fruit he decided to be bold, and attacked the slice of luscious melon by cutting a portion off through the rind and consuming it, including the rind. It was not until he had battled his way through three parts of the slice that I decided to rescue him. "I wouldn't eat the peel of that, old man. It will give you the most awful indigestion. I know a man in Australia who preferred the peel to the fruit, but he darned nearly died of dyspepsia."

Speaking of luncheons, I am reminded of my first meeting with the great little Don Bradman. It was at a cheery family party at the home of my old friend W. A. (Bert) Oldfield, probably Australia's finest wicket-keeper, and of course a really good batsman. Mr. and Mrs. Oldfield, Mr. and Mrs. Bradman and myself with Nanny. It was what we Australians call a 'real dinkum' lunch. Afterwards we reminisced and I remember how both Don Bradman and Bert Oldfield expressed their love of the old country, England. Don was particularly eloquent in his praise of the great and unbiased sportsmanship of the crowds. "You know, Peter, that when I was piling up a lot of runs, they encouraged me with their applause. I didn't understand it at first, but I soon found out that it was genuine all right. Although I was scoring a lot of runs against their team they didn't hold back their applause for any good scoring strokes I made. That put me

in a good mood with English crowds, and I have ever since felt
very happy whenever and wherever I play in the old country.
It's a great help to a player to know that he is playing in front of
a crowd who are friendlily disposed towards him. I can honestly
say that I feel as nearly at ease before English crowds as I do at
home. Nobody could wish for anything better than that!" Bert
Oldfield agreed, and added: "They certainly love cricket. And
they know all the points of the game. Naturally I was a bit anxious
about my play in my first matches over there, but I didn't have
to worry long. They started to applaud some of my leg-side work,
and that made me feel good. Then the cricket writers said some
very kind things about my work behind the wicket and about
my batting, and that made me pretty happy. They're fine people;
and no crowds know their cricket better than the English
crowds."

Don is a reliable and trusty fellow. Like most celebrities, he
suffers from being too well known and too popular. On his
appearance anywhere there is scarcely a minute without someone
trying to 'have a word' with him. I am not merely referring to the
inevitable autograph hunters, but friends, acquaintances, business
contacts, representatives of business houses hoping to interest
him in some commercial proposition, sports reporters, book
publishers, photographers, advertising agents, charity organizers,
Press agents; and in the cricket pavilions, cricketing friends or
acquaintances introducing their friends to the famous Don
Bradman. I was therefore fortunate in meeting him in the privacy
of Bert Oldfield's home, and I learnt a lot about the 'Don'. He is
a fluent speaker, tells a good story and is perfectly natural and
modest. He is fond of music. Incidentally, I have not yet met a
sportsman who wasn't fond of music in one form or another.
Don Bradman likes playing the piano—by ear. His taste is not
classical. He really enjoys playing the latest popular songs, and he
plays them exceedingly well. He is gifted with good acumen for
business. When he finally retired from Test cricket he was sadly
missed, for he was not only Australia's greatest ever batsman, but
he possesses that indefinable quality of 'personality' which made
him so genuinely popular wherever he played. I really had very
little leisure from my work, because if I wasn't touring I had a
lot of practice and revising to do, and trying new publications
and composing my own settings to good lyrics that I had found,
or which had been sent to me. I also had recording sessions and
broadcast dates needing rehearsals. It left little spare time.

I did like to see a good fight, and any opportunity I was able to snatch for that purpose I certainly took. My interest in boxing is well known in Australia, and at one time I actually put up some money. That was some years ago, when that wonderful two-fisted fighter Les Darcy was hailed as the greatest fighter of the century.

I saw Les Darcy beat Eddie McGorty to his knees, and McGorty was one of the world's greatest. But the fight I 'supported' was between Les Darcy and Fred Dyer. Dyer was known as the 'singing boxer'.

After every fight, it didn't matter how gruelling, Fred Dyer would oblige with a song. He had quite a nice voice, but he was a better fighter. He was one of my greatest admirers, and one day he came to me and asked whether I thought he would do better if he trained as a vocalist. This was just before his fight with Les Darcy. I told him that I would give him a good try-out after the fight.

The fight duly took place. Fred put up a grand show, for he was a good boxer and fighter. But up against a man like Darcy there was not much hope. Fred went in fighting and gave Darcy one of the toughest two rounds he had so far experienced; but after that the skill and terrific punching of Darcy began to tell. Despite some gallant work by Fred, Darcy proved too good and too strong, and in the sixth round it was all over. By this time Fred Dyer's right eye was closed, his left a mere slit and his lips were badly swollen and cut. He was in bad shape, but he had fought the fight of his life. I moved to his corner immediately after the fight was over, and patted him on the arm, congratulating him on his fine show. With a brave attempt to show a smile on his battered face, he whispered out of the corner of his mouth, "How did it look?" I assured him he had made himself a hero. With another attempt at a smile he said: "Peter, do you think I'd make more money as a singer?" Fred is settled in London, where he has his own physical-training establishment. Darcy died a few years after this fight with Dyer. He left for America during the First World War to carry out fight engagements. The American Press, with its customary 'good sportsmanship' to a foreigner who looked like taking a championship from them, went out of their way to attack him.

Why wasn't he fighting for his country? That was the general trend. And when once that campaign started, the insults became more vulgar and insulting. They did not trouble to find out the real reason for his American trip, they just 'gave him the works'.

Darcy became ill with a poisoned eye-tooth; blood poisoning set in and the young man who would most certainly have become one of the greatest boxing champions of all time came to an untimely and sad end. His best friends said he died broken-hearted.

It was that fine boxing writer Norman Hurst who told me about Darcy's death. What can I say about Norman? Of all the men I have met in my travels, he is the most remarkable of them all.

To listen to Norman recounting some of the incidents in his life is like reading a thrilling story. Even back in 1930 a well-known journalist told me that he would pay £1,000 down for the option on Norman's life-story. His experiences include everything that can be read in a dozen of the world's greatest thrillers, but they are all *true-life stories*, not fiction! Make a note of the name, and if he ever decides to write his autobiography, make sure you read it.

His life covers three countries: Britain, the United States and France.

I will tell one story which will illustrate his 'inside' knowledge of boxing. It is some years ago, but the fight is fresh in most of our memories. The Carpentier-Battling Siki fight.

Norman was present at the signing of the contract. He was also behind the scenes. Back in London, just before returning to see the fight, he called on his friend Tom Noble, managing art editor of the Kemsley newspapers in London, and whispered, "It will be worth your while sending your own man from London to cover the fight, and it will be worth while taking a chance to send an aeroplane to bring the pictures back." Knowing Norman, Tom did not worry about asking any questions, but proceeded to arrange for his best photographer to cover the fight. He also arranged with Alan Cobham, who was then an air taxi pilot, to fly to France and be prepared for a possible take off in the dusk.

We all know what happened. Carpentier, to the surprise of the whole world, was knocked out. The picture, showing Carpentier 'on the floor' with an excited Siki standing over him, was rushed to the aerodrome where Cobham was waiting anxiously, because it was nearly dark. And in those days, before wireless, it was a hazardous trip in darkness.

Cobham made a successful flight and the picture duly appeared as one great picture on the front page of the *Daily Sketch*. That was a terrific scoop. No other paper had a picture.

How did Norman know that there might be a surprise result? I must leave that for him to tell.

Talking of Carpentier reminds me how age plays its part in the whirligig of life. His fine career as a boxer ended before he was thirty-five. Don Bradman retired from Test cricket in 1948. He was born in August 1908.

Contrast that with singers and musicians.

Ben Davies could sing delightfully after he had reached the age of eighty—not weakly, but with resonance and clarity of tone. I first met this grand old man when he was approaching his seventieth birthday. I listened to him singing at the Queen's Hall, and was spellbound by his technique. His voice was not powerful, but its quality was superb.

Such was his technique that I made it my business to go and listen to him on any and every opportunity. That is my advice to all young singers: listen to the men who have reached the top of their profession. You have no need to follow their particular technique to the letter, and become mere copyists; no, but by studying their renderings you will learn a wonderful lot that is beyond the teaching of any singing master. Ben Davies was not only a grand vocalist, but an actor. I learnt a great deal from his manner of standing during his singing. I have passed this sort of advice on to youngsters in another chapter. After I had known Ben for some time, and we had become good friends, I approached him after a concert at the Queen's Hall and asked whether he could recommend me to a club; I felt I ought to become a member of some club or other. After considering my request for a few moments he asked, "You are married, aren't you, Peter?" "Yes, of course," I replied. Then after a few more moments' reflection he said with quiet sincerity, "Are you in love with your wife?" to which I answered with alacrity, "Why, certainly." Another reflective pause, and he asked me a third question: "Are you happy at home? I mean, are you enjoying your home life?" I assured him that I was happy at home and loved home life. Then he delivered this homily with a serious face: "Well, in that case, Peter, I will give you my serious opinion about your request. You do not want to join any club. The best club I can recommend is your own home. To a man like yourself on the threshold of your career—a career that will carry you to all parts of the world—believe me, your own home is the best club that I can or shall ever recommend."

Needless to say, the great tenor was right. Some years later I did become a member of the Savage Club in London. I enjoyed meeting some very cheery fellows, and we had a number of memorable musical evenings. Quite frankly, for a singer, it is better not to make a habit of his club, for with all the good will in the world the smoke-laden air of the average club 'room' is not good atmosphere for over-indulgence in the case of singers.

It is quite a different piece of cake for artistes who do not depend on their voice for a living. My visits to the club were accordingly rare, but always most enjoyable. I must tell you of a story I heard at the club from Robert Radford. Charles Saunders and Bob were engaged for a concert which included free hospitality. Both Saunders and Radford enjoyed a drink. On arrival at the town in which they were to sing, they were met by two men. These were to be their hosts during their stay. One was a parson and the other a bluff, cheery, sporting individual. The artistes had to go straight to the concert hall for a rehearsal. In a corner of the concert platform, Charles and Bob decided who was to stay with the parson and who with the sportsman. Robert Radford lost the toss and of course, you will have guessed, had to stay as guest with the parson. Charles was very happy about this and commiserated with Bob on his 'luck'. The following day the two singers met. Bobbie Radford was wearing a look of supreme content, whereas Charles was grim, truculent and tired.

It appears that when Radford arrived at the home of the parson, after the concert, a wonderful meal was served. Before the meal the parson opened a large cupboard and said: "You will find all kinds of drink in here. I should be very happy if you would please help yourself to any of them. I only take sherry myself, but please do make yourself at home. I expect you can do with a good meal and some refreshment now that the concert is over. And I should like to thank you for giving me a most delightful evening. I enjoyed your singing. And also the singing of Mr. Saunders." "I looked in the cupboard," said Robert Radford, "and there I found white and red wines—claret and Burgundy—some German hock, various bottles to make myself an *apéritif*, gin, whisky, brandy and a special shelf for port!"

The parson added: "I can recommend the brandy and the port after the meal. And I will join you as this is a special occasion." Sure enough, he had a sumptuous feast. "After the meal," continued Bob, "the parson and I had a most interesting talk as we sat sipping some grand old brandy while we reclined in a couple of huge easy armchairs. I went to bed, let me say reluctantly, at one o'clock, after one of the most enjoyable nights of my life."

Charles, on the other hand, had quite a different experience. He had a very good meal, but just before sitting down the host said: "I haven't much to offer you in the way of refreshment, but I don't suppose you mind that. Singers are usually teetotal; are you?" To which devastating assumption Charles could only stammer: "No, sir; I am not a teetotaller. Do not distress yourself about that." The host then went on to explain that at one time he was a very heavy drinker, but following a stroke he was forbidden to touch alcohol in any shape or form, and that no alcohol was allowed in the house.

So Charles had to choose between tea and coffee! He was in bed at ten forty-five, and did not sleep more than an hour because he had drunk too much coffee!

Ever after that experience Charles was suspicious of all men with the appearance of being the bluff, hearty, sporting type.

From those cheery fellows I pass to that remarkable baritone Wilfred Douthitt. Wilfred was blessed with extraordinary power for sustaining notes an incredible length of time. I recall that he held a middle 'G' for sixty seconds! This ability was not appreciated when overdone. And that grand old man of music, Sir Edward Elgar, when conducting a rehearsal of "The Apostles" in which I took part, had occasion to make the following rebuke to the baritone: "Mr. Douthitt, I should be glad if you would please stop that rather vulgar style of singing. Remember, you are singing the part of the Saviour. Please modify the phrasing. I am quite sure that the Saviour was not gifted with such breath control." Nevertheless Wilfred had a fine voice, and could sing almost anything. Soon after this he disappeared from the concert world in Britain, and is believed to have gone to the States. There was a story that he had decided to change his name and adopt a foreign one like so many others were doing at this time. A friend tells me that he met someone he swears was Douthitt in New York, but when he greeted the man with, "Hullo, Wilfred old man, what a surprise!" he received the icy reply: "You must have made a mistake. I am not Douthitt. My name is 'So-and-So'." Anyhow, Wilfred Douthitt was a loss to Britain. His breath control was phenomenal, and people used to pay to hear him sing because they knew that in at least a couple of songs he would demonstrate his gift and sustain a last note for a minute!

Let me say at once that Sir Edward Elgar did not mean his remark in any derogatory sense; Sir Edward was too much the English gentleman to hurt anyone's feelings. He had to restrain the singer firmly from bad phrasing. Elgar brings my mind to another musical genius, Sir Walford Davies. I was brought into contact with that exquisite teacher through his admiration for my diction. He wrote and invited me to take part in a music festival he was promoting in connection with the Great Western Railway, which included singing competitions. "I should like you to sing so that these young singing aspirants can learn, far better than I can teach them, what I mean by clear diction." I accepted, not for the reason I was asked but because I wanted an opportunity of meeting the man who had enthralled me, as he must have thousands of others, with his fascinating 'Soldiers on Parade' series for the B.B.C.

What a musical brain he had! There has never been anyone like him; possessing not only musical genius, but a charm that he was able to waft over the air. So brilliantly did he demonstrate that even people who possessed no musical knowledge were intrigued by his charm of manner and his delightful musical examples on the piano.

Of course, his lectures were crowded with sound advice. Yes, Sir Walford Davies deserved the honour he was given as "The Master of the King's Music".

It was after my last meeting with Sir Walford that I first met another brilliant musician. He had just arrived from Germany with his wife and boy; the year was 1938. We met at the Gramophone Company's recording-studio. It was Walter Goehr. I watched him conduct the orchestra and it was obvious to me that here was a master musician.

I have met him many times since, and my opinion is strengthened. He is really the indefatigable worker. I met him once on the top of a bus; he was busily writing. When I looked over to see what he was doing, he was orchestrating! I did not meet him again until 1947, and that was on my reappearance for the B.B.C. with the B.B.C Theatre Orchestra. It was a very pleasant surprise to learn on my arrival for the rehearsal that my old friend Walter Goehr was its conductor. When he heard me rehearse "*Waiata Poi*" ("Tiny ball on end of string") he was very excited and insisted on making his own orchestral arrangement. Many of you will have heard what a truly fine job he did. I know he will forgive me for telling a story about his English soon after his arrival here. Walter was conducting the orchestra in the record we were making with a large crowd of children of "Nursery Rhymes". The children, as usual, were getting a little difficult after they had weathered their first few minutes' nervousness at the beginning of the session. Walter, who is a most kind-hearted man and a lover of children, called them together and in a serious voice said, "Children, I want you to sing 'A Fwog 'e vood a-vooin' gwo'." Kids, being kids, just could not help yelling their heads off. Poor Walter was crestfallen. But he is a kindly man, and enjoyed the joke as much as any of us.

Today his English is impeccable. His success in the music world has made the same rapid progress.

Speaking of progress reminds me that Sir Edward Elgar in his early days composed a piece which he called *Salut d'Amour*. At the time he was not well known. He sold the rights to the music publishers for £5—in those days a satisfactory fee for that sort of piece from a man who had yet to make his mark as a musical composer of the highest international degree.

Some time later the publishers, although they were not obliged to, sent Sir Edward a cheque in appreciation of the success the number had achieved.

Instead of accepting it, Elgar sent it back. I have heard two reasons for this. One was that the cheque was not large enough for the success that *Salut d'Amour* had achieved. The other reason (and one which is generally believed by those who were close to Sir Edward) is that he regretted the work as something beneath his dignity, and resented its success.

Which recalls a somewhat similar story of how an early work, written by a composer who later made his fame world famous, was brought to the composer's notice in a most embarrassing manner.

Granville Bantock in his early days was in the habit of 'obliging' his friends in the musical world by setting their lyrics. He would do this while sipping tea in a tea-shop. One day he was asked to set a song called "Who'll give a Penny to the Monkey?" Bantock did not worry about the title. Or if he did, he probably never thought that the doggerel would be published, but it *was*!

Some years later, when Granville Bantock arrived at Harvard University in America to give lectures on music, he was met by two rows of students who sang in harmony "Who'll give a Penny to the Monkey?"

'Granny' Bantock says it was the most embarrassing moment in his life. He had forgotten all about the wretched thing, and here he was being greeted with it *as a compliment*!

I don't know whether it is the fact that I was born in Australia, but I certainly pick up a cold far too easily in Britain. I cannot make up my mind whether it is the changing rapidity of the temperatures, or the atrocious draughts one cannot escape or the rains.

I remember travelling to Chesterfield, and slowly growing

painfully aware that I had a bad attack of influenza. I was in pretty poor shape at the concert, and it was obvious to the audience that my announcement that I had a bad cold was not exaggerated.

During the interval, a charming man was shown into my dressing-room. The attendant said, "The Duke of Portland would like to have a word with you about your cold, Mr. Dawson." The Duke said to me: "Forgive me worrying you, Mr. Dawson, but I regard myself as an old friend of yours. I have a large supply of your records, and I hear you sing as often as I can." I felt very flattered. The Duke went on to explain that he had come round because he thought he might help me get rid of my cold. He had been a martyr to colds, but he had recently been recommended a formula that had served him well. Today he rarely suffered for more than a day, thanks to this prescription. For any that may be interested in the formula, here it is:

Mixed Anti-Coryza and Anti-Influenza Vaccine, Detoxicated. One course consists of three injections with the interval of a week between each.

In a note to me, sent from Welbeck Abbey, the Duke cautioned me to have the injections only after I had received the sanction of my own doctor.

I am referring to the father of the present Duke of Portland.

CHAPTER XVII

WORLD WAR II

ONCE again I was in Australia when the news came through that Britain had been compelled to declare war on Germany a second time.

Fortunately it was during the last week of the ten weeks' tour I had undertaken for the Greater Union Theatres.

As in 1914, everything stopped! The concert world had been knocked out for the duration. What could I do? I was too old for active service. After some consideration I agreed to join my brother's firm of Messrs. T. Dawson and Sons, Proprietory Ltd., as 'No. 1 Handshake'.

The job? I was to pay 'courtesy' calls on prospective customers, and on certain government officials who would be interested in contracts for the manufacture of tin containers for foodstuffs, tins for oil-drums, etc., which the firm made in a very large way. They turned out millions of these things every year.

Let me say right away I brought in lots of orders. True, the firm was famous for its work, but I certainly did a great deal.

After a while I got so many orders the company could not cope with them. So things went on till 1942, when the New Zealand Government invited me to fly to New Zealand for a four-weeks' tour to help in their effort to raise a £15,000,000 War Loan. I sang and talked to thousands of people all over the Dominion. I spoke from the town halls, in the streets, at sports grounds; everywhere a concourse of people assembled.

The money was raised in a fortnight, and I received a number of congratulatory messages on my help. On my return to Australia I went back to my £12 per week job as 'No. 1 Handshake'.

But from then on I was putting in a lot of time helping to raise money for Australian War Loans, 'Comfort Funds' and 'Food for Britain' parcels.

I was singing my "V for Victory" song up and down the country. I have already told how thrilled I was to hear the military bands play it on the march. Here are the words of the chorus:

> Say it, sing it, play it, swing it,
> "V" for Vic-to-ry.
> Write it, talk it, on walls chalk it,
> "V" for Vic-to-ry.

Tho' we've taken hard blows on the chin, chin, chin,
In the end we are bound to win, win, win;
So say it, play it, swing it,
"V" for Vic-to-ry.

It was about this time that Russia was calling for help in every way from the Allies. She needed more 'planes, tanks, ammunition and more military offensives against the Germans. In Australia recruiting was lagging. The Government decided on a big campaign and I was one of those chosen to help in the effort.

The A.B.C. invited me to make a broadcast appeal and I gladly accepted. It occurred to me that Australia's most popular Army figure, General H. W. Lloyd, would be the ideal man to make a speech to introduce me. I had a chat with 'Bertie', for we were good friends, and he replied: "I shall be delighted to do it, Peter. What do you want me to do?" It was arranged that we should be at the broadcasting studio about half an hour before the broadcast and talk things over.

In the meantime the A.B.C. asked what I thought of calling the appeal, which was to be made at the inaugural session of the Government's recruiting campaign.

With Russia's urgent call in my mind, I decided on calling the appeal I was to make 'Now or Never'. Australia is a vast continent, and thousands of men were quite unaware of the serious need for manpower, and they were ignorant of the seriousness of the situation in the world war. They had no bombing, heard no guns, saw no wounded, they had too much of everything and too few to eat it!

When General Lloyd arrived at the studio I showed him what I had prepared, with the remark: "Please read it, Bertie, and help me revise it. But remember, we shall be talking to men who would not appreciate fine language. It must be 'straight-from-the-shoulder' stuff." The General read it carefully, and then said, "Peter, leave it as it is, it's marvellous for the job."

The General made some very kind and flattering remarks about me in his introduction, and then I made my appeal to the eligible men of Australia in a nation-wide broadcast. It is crude to read, but it served its purpose in rallying great numbers to the recruiting offices throughout the country. Here it is:

"NOW OR NEVER?

In this war, which we are ultimately going to win, much depends on the young men of this great country, who are at present, for some reason or other, standing aloof and with deaf ears to the urgent call of King and Country.

The stoic heroism displayed by the British Expeditionary Force in its fight against overwhelming odds in Belgium and France is surely sufficient inspiration to every eligible person in the Commonwealth to rush headlong to the colours.

The response by the flower of the manhood of this country up to now has been magnificent, but not enough. This hanging back by the eligible men, this 'watching the other fellow do it' is a fatal mistake.

It has been said that Great Britain has always won the last battle. It has also been said that in the event of a Nazi victory, America would protect Australia. *Don't you believe it*. Should such a calamity as a Nazi victory overtake us, it would be the end of us, and of everything worth living for.

Are you content to stand by complacently, and with the thought that everything will come right in the end? No, I think not!

You are made of better stuff than that!

Nazi domination would be the end of the Christian era, and the cruel extermination of the British race. We are of the British race, and it is up to all of us to defend ourselves. The Nazis are out for world domination, just as Bismarck and Kaiser Bill were. Remember, there's only one good German, and he hasn't reached the ground from his burning bomber!

Unity is wanted here. Cut out party politics, and install a system of 'all for all'. How often have you joined together in singing:

'Rule, Britannia. Britannia, rule the waves,
Britons never, never never shall be slaves.'

See to it, my countrymen. Would you care to see the Nazis come to our beautiful shores, to practise their well-known system of extermination by murder, and the rape of our womenfolk? Yes. Yes. It *is* as serious as that.

And it's now or never. It is up to you to join the mighty throng to liberate us all from the Nazi menace.

So, Johnny . . . get your gun. . . . It's Now or Never!"

For some stupid reason I completely forgot to wait for the switch-off before I turned to General Lloyd and said, "How was that, Bert?" Ever after that General Lloyd was called 'Bert' by all and sundry! For every listener knew to whom I was speaking.

One important politician, Arty Fadden, was not impressed with my personal appeal to the public, and to my suggestion that I would sing on behalf of any campaign his Government launched, he replied: "I don't think so, Peter. We can get as many records of yours as we need. Another thing, we can use them when we want and they are always in good voice!" That got my goat, and I retaliated: "All right, Arty. All you need to do is make a small seven-inch record, and you can get all you ever have to say on that." I didn't meet him again until just before he died. He hadn't forgotten my taunt, but we had a good laugh together.

John Curtin was a very different kind of man, big-hearted, liked and respected. My first meeting with John was at a Governor-General's party at Government House, Canberra. After the party, Lady Gowrie entertained a number of guests to dinner and kindly included me. During the coffee and liqueurs, John Curtin, who was then Prime Minister, came up to me and said: "I've been wanting to meet you for years. I have so many of your gramophone records you may say that you have occupied first place as our favourite 'in the bosom of the family'." We had a long chat, and I was astonished at the great number of my records he possessed and his reasons for liking some more than others.

He paid me a very great compliment when I paid my first visit to Parliament. I was sitting in the visitors' seats, and had just settled down, when I saw the Prime Minister get up from his seat and make his way across the floor of the House to where I was sitting. With extended hand he said: "I am very glad to welcome you to this House, Mr. Dawson. I extend the welcome on behalf of my colleagues as well. I should like to thank you for all the good work you are doing on behalf of your country. Thank you. And a hearty welcome to this Chamber."

I had the pleasure of meeting him again at a Red Cross Rally where he made a speech and at which I sang. I chose a couple of numbers that he had mentioned in our first meeting at Lord and Lady Gowrie's dinner party. A few months later he died. A great loss. A good Labour man, but not a 'red'. A dynamic speaker. A sincere and good man.

The Gowries were very popular in Australia—not an easy

achievement in our 'young' country. They were cultured folk capable of mixing with all sorts and conditions of Australians, with sincerity and without even a suspicion of patronizing. A rare gift, but one which I have found among the real aristocrats of Britain. Some of the 'made' peers are very poor fish in comparison and are dreadful snobs.

But of course we have plenty of good 'rough diamonds' of our own in Australia. One is Mr. W. McKell, the present Governor-General. I have known him for many years. He is Bill and I am Peter. There was a lot of nonsensical outcry on his appointment, but only from those who did not know his sterling character. Certainly he had been a hard-working man: he came of a family of boxers. But he has experienced more variety of life than a thousand other notabilities in the Commonwealth. Today, by working the hard way, he has made himself a rich man. There need be no qualms about Bill McKell's ability, his decorum, or his forthrightness and his loyalty to the Throne.

My pleasantest recollection of the new Governor-General was when the Lord Mayor of Sydney rang me up and asked: "What are you doing tomorrow night? I am giving a small party to the Governor-General, and we should like you to join us." I went along, not forgetting to put a few songs in my pocket, for I knew that Bill McKell, like all good fellows, enjoys a song or two. My first surprise on arriving in my grubby-looking Ford Ten was to find the front of the place 'reserved for Senators' cars only'. There were large luxurious cars, including quite a few of the 'mobile soda-fountain' type of American cars. But every policeman knew my car, and thanks to their good fellowship I was given much license in where I parked it. These kindly privileges I received in return for the work I have done on behalf of various police charities. I have even played cricket for the police. It was in a match against the 'speedway' riders, a private affair. I know that I scored twenty-two runs. But I was out five times, and each time I was out, caught or bowled, the umpire yelled, "No ball!" So occasionally when I infringed a traffic regulation the policeman concerned would look at the number plate, LX—— and say, "Hands off that, it's Peter's."

But the police here were different. However, after telling them that an artiste was above an alderman, they finally let me park my car. But it took nearly ten minutes before they consented to let my dirty little car nestle alongside the Senators'!

The dinner went on till nearly eleven o'clock, when someone suggested playing "God save the King" to break the party up. But the Hon. R. Semple whispered to me, "Don't go yet, we are going to the Mayor's parlour for a chat and a drink."

We did. I sang a few songs, and it was not until 1.30 a.m. that the party broke up. It was here I met Bracegirdle, the A.D.C. to the Governor-General. A grand chap, and an admirer of McKell's, which is a good augury for the success of the Governor-General.

I spent a great deal of time during the war in travelling all over the country, giving my services on behalf of all sorts of war funds and loan rallies. I was happy to be able to do something to help. The news of the dreadful bombing that Britain was suffering wrung our hearts. When I returned in 1947 and saw the pitiful sight of the City of London, with its devastated churches and acres of bombed space, I nearly wept with grief. A sad and terrible sight.

You are probably wondering about my job at the factory. That went on as usual, for remember that I was the 'No. 1 Handshake', and that even when I travelled about I was still meeting important people who might be interested in getting containers made.

I had an exciting time when the American service men arrived in Australia. I gave dozens of concerts for them, and I am glad to say they seemed to appreciate my singing. Their great favourite was "Waltzing Matilda". It became their favourite song. So much so that the Gramophone Company sent thousands of copies to the States.

We had many anxious months in Australia when the Japs were overrunning the Philippines, Malaya, New Guinea and approaching near to Australia, so the arrival of the American troops was a great comfort.

We knew that the old country had her hands too full to be able to help us with troops, and the U.S. troops acted as a tonic on nerves that were wrought with apprehension as to what would happen should the yellow men invade us. A most disturbing thought, as you will agree.

But we were also sustained by the example of Britain, and the initial panic was quickly dispelled by the reiteration of Britain's example: the Battle of Britain, the bombing, Greece, Crete, and the triumphs in North Africa. To say that we were proud of Britain would be an understatement. By this time we were overwhelmed with deep and sincere admiration, and glad that we, too, were of the British race.

Like everyone else in the world we were deliriously happy

when the war ended. There had been times when I wondered
how it would end and whether I should ever see any of our
friends and relations in Britain again, for when the war ended I
was in my sixty-third year. Fortunately I felt like a man of
thirty. My voice was in fine fettle. In 1946 I decided to 'resign'
from the family firm and continue with my career. I accepted an
engagement in New Zealand, and was anxious to get the verdict
of the critics. I knew that I was ready to sing for another twenty
years if my health held, but I wanted the views of the experts. If
their criticisms were favourable I should certainly return to
Britain. Nan, too, was naturally anxious to get home again after
an absence of nearly ten years.

A few extracts from the reviews of the critics will give the
clue to my arrival in London in August 1947:

"The veteran Australian singer, Peter Dawson, commenced his sixth tour of New Zealand last night, receiving
the warmest of welcomes from an audience that filled every
seat in the Town Hall. The popular baritone's tonal resonance, robust homeliness of approach, and interpretative
artistry are still virtues that hold the public, as witness the
enthusiasm with which his songs were received last night . . ."

and so on for a whole column.

Here is the programme which the critic dealt with too praise-
worthily for me to worry you with: Recitative and air (of Poly-
phemus) from Handel's cantata, "Acis and Galatea", "I rage, I
melt, I burn" and "O ruddier than the Cherry", "The Clock"
(Loewe), "The Erl King" (Schubert), "I heard a Forest praying",
"If Music be the Food of Love", "The Kerry Dance", "Shall I
compare You to a Summer Day", Sanderson's "The Glory of
the Sea", and by request "Simon the Cellarer" and "The Floral
Dance".

In the second half of the programme I sang these songs:
Song *scena* on "Mandalay", each of the verses being by different
composers—Oley Speakes, Willeby, Hedgcock and Cobb;
Keats' "The Roads beside the Sea", "Money O", "The Farmer's
Pride", "The changing of the Guard", "The Drum Major",
"Waltzing Matilda" and "*Waiata Poi*" ("Tiny ball on end of
string").

Other snippets from other towns:

"The ability of Mr. Dawson to sing a good song well has
not diminished with the passing of years, as the big audience

at the Opera House last night discovered. After 48 years of active singing, Mr. Dawson's voice still has the rich over-tones which have always been characteristic of it, and his faultless diction made the printed words on the programme supererogatory. This admirable quality and the verve with which he sang every number made the concert highly enjoy-able and the audience obviously desired more than he so generously gave."

And finally:

"The quality that makes a champion in any profession or calling has seldom been more convincingly demonstrated than by Peter Dawson, world celebrity of the concert stage who, last night sang to a capacity audience. For decades he has stood in the first flight of concert singers, delighting his hearers everywhere, and defying the passage of the years. Durability is one of his great assets, but personality ranks next to his voice among the qualities which have made Peter Dawson a headliner on stage, screen, radio and gramophone discs throughout the world. Above all he has the gift of winning appreciation for songs above the common standard of the day. . . ."

These very gracious notices determined my future for the next few years. For it is one thing to *know* that you are in good voice, but it is another to be told by others that you are.

So I set my plans to return to dear old London for another tour, and for further broadcasts with that wonderful crowd of people at the B.B.C. And let me end on this note: don't make any mistake, the B.B.C. is the finest organization of its kind in the world today. It caters for all tastes, and variety is the spice of life.

APPENDIX I

West Maitland. Sept. 30th.
Brisbane. Oct. 2nd, 4th, 5th.
Gympie. Oct. 6th.
Bundaberg. Oct. 8th.
Rockhampton. Oct. 9th, 11th.
Mt. Morgan. Oct. 12th.
Brisbane. Oct. 14th.
Toowoomba. Oct. 15th.
Warwick. Oct. 16th.
Inverell. Oct. 18th.
Moree. Oct. 19th.
Narribri. Oct. 20th.
Tamworth. Oct. 22nd.
Newcastle. Oct. 23rd.
Forbes. Oct. 25th.
Dubbo. Oct. 27th.
Orange. Oct. 28th.
Bathurst. Oct. 29th.
Sydney. Oct. 30th.
Goldburn. Nov. 1st.
Cootamundra. Nov. 2nd.
Melbourne. Nov. 4th, 6th.
Leongatha. Nov. 5th.
Bairnsdale. Nov. 8th.
Sale. Nov. 9th.
Tarralgon. Nov. 10th.
Warragul. Nov. 11th.
Benalla. Nov. 11th.
Albury. Nov. 15th.
Corowa. Nov. 16th.
Shepparton. Nov. 17th.
Wangaratta. Nov. 18th.
Kyabran. Nov. 19th.
Echuca. Nov. 20th.
Charlton. Nov. 22nd.
Maryborough. Nov. 25th.

St. Arnaud. Nov. 28th.
Castlemaine. Nov. 29th.
Bendigo. Nov. 30th.
Ballarat. Dec. 3rd.
Geelong. Dec. 5th.
Colae. Dec. 7th.
Camperdown. Dec. 8th.
Warrnambool. Dec. 9th.
Casterton. Dec. 11th.
Mt. Gambier. Dec. 13th.
Adelaide. Dec. 17th.
Adelaide. Dec. 19th.
Adelaide. Dec. 21st.
Balaklava. Dec. 23rd.
Launceston. Dec. 31st.
Hobart. Jan. 1st.
Hobart. Jan. 2nd.
Melbourne. Jan. 8th.
Inglewood. Jan. 10th.
Euroa. Jan. 12th, 14th.
Beechworth. Jan. 15th.
Seymour. Jan. 17th.
Yarrawonga. Jan. 18th.
Tatura. Jan. 20th.
Bendigo. Jan. 23rd.
Swanhill. Jan. 24th.
Kerang. Jan. 25th.
Melbourne. Jan. 26th.
Stawell. Jan. 27th.
Horsham. Jan. 28th.
Warricknabeal. Jan. 30th.
Dimboola. Feb. 1st.
Nhill. Feb. 2nd.
Perth(W.A.). Feb. 8th to Feb. 12th.
Koolgardie. Feb. 14th, 15th.
Boulder City. Feb. 16th.

END OF TOUR

APPENDIX II

List of songs sung by Peter Dawson in the series of twelve concerts in the B.B.C. programme "Our Pleasure to Present".

1st programme:
> "Sincerity" (Emilie Clarke). Herbert Dawson at the organ.
> "The Star" (J. H. Rogers). Hubert Greenslade at the piano.
> "O Star of Eve" (Wagner). Herbert Dawson at the organ.
> "Jerusalem" (Sir Hubert Parry).

The final song in each programme was a famous song of a sacred nature.

2nd programme:
> "Coronach" (E. Barratt). A lament for the death of Cuthullin, a great Skye chieftain. Herbert Dawson.
> "Who is Sylvia?" (Schubert). Hubert Greenslade.
> "Sylvia" (Oley Speakes). Herbert Dawson.
> "There is a green Hill" (Gounod). Herbert Dawson.

3rd programme:
> "Loveliest of Trees" (Set by Arthur Somervell of part of A. E. Housman's poem, "A Shropshire Lad"). Herbert Dawson.
> "Don Juan's Serenade" (Tchaikowsky). Hubert Greenslade.
> "None but the lonely Heart" (Tchaikowsky). Herbert Dawson.
> "Little Prayer I love" (A. Rizzi). Herbert Dawson.

4th programme:
> "The Arrow and the Song" (Balfe). Herbert Dawson.
> "Silent Worship" (Handel, arr. A. Somervell). Hubert Greenslade.
> "Honour and Arms" (Handel). Herbert Dawson.
> "The Knight of Bethlehem" (Maughan-Thomson). Herbert Dawson.

5th programme:
> "I Heard a Forest Praying" (P. de Rose). Herbert Dawson.
> "Sherwood" (James R. Dear). Hubert Greenslade.
> "Silver" (Armstrong Gibbs). Herbert Dawson.
> "The Lost Chord" (Sir A. Sullivan). Herbert Dawson.

6th programme:
> "The Dreamer" (J. P. McCall, Peter Dawson). Herbert Dawson.

"The Lute Player" (Frances Allitsen). Hubert Greenslade.
"Orpheus with his Lute" (Vaughan Williams). Herbert Dawson.
"Love Triumphant" (A. Wheeler). Herbert Dawson.

7th programme:

"Myself when young" (Liza Lehmann). Herbert Dawson.
"Edward" (Setting by Loewe of the ballad "Edward"). Hubert Greenslade.
"Turn ye to Me" (trad. Scots air, arr. M. Lawson). Herbert Dawson.
"Bless this House" (May Brahe). Herbert Dawson.

8th programme:

"She is far from the Land" (F. Lambert). Herbert Dawson.
"Isobel" (Frank Bridge). Hubert Greenslade.
"Eleanore" (Coleridge Taylor). Herbert Dawson.
"The blind Ploughman" (R. Coningsby-Clarke). Herbert Dawson.

9th programme:

"Think on Me" (Lady John Scott). Herbert Dawson.
Scena: "Mandalay", arr. Peter Dawson.
(*a*) Music by Oley Speakes. ⎱ With Herbert Dawson, organ;
(*b*) Music by Charles Willeby. ⎰ Hubert Greenslade, piano.
(*c*) Music by Walter Hedgcock.
(*d*) Music by Gerard Cobb.
    A song *scena* which I arranged, based on the four best-known settings of a famous Rudyard Kipling poem.
"The Birds" (Peter Warlock's setting of Hilaire Belloc's poem, "The Birds"). Herbert Dawson.

10th programme:

"If Music be the Food of Love" (F. Allitsen's setting of Shakespeare's lines). Herbert Dawson.
"The Erl King" (Schubert). Hubert Greenslade.
"*Ave Maria*" (Schubert). Herbert Dawson.
"There is no death" (O'Hara). Herbert Dawson.

11th programme:

"Lovely kind and kindly loving" (Gustav Holst). Herbert Dawson.
"On the idle Hill of Summer" (R. Ainsworth). Hubert Greenslade. (A Shropshire Lad)
"Is My Team Ploughing?" (George Butterworth). Herbert Dawson. (A Shropshire Lad)
"Nazareth" (Gounod). Herbert Dawson.

12th programme:

"O could I but express in Song" (Malashkin). Herbert Dawson.

"The Song of the Flea" (Moussorgsky). Hubert Greenslade.

"Even bravest Heart" (Gounod). Herbert Dawson.

And the final song of the series, chosen by Doris Arnold, a musical setting of a prayer we all know so well:

"The Lord's Prayer" (A. H. Malotte). Herbert Dawson.

APPENDIX III

"Auld Lang Syne."
"Ah, shall this great day of Wrath" (from Bach's *Watchet Betet*).
"All Souls' Day." Mrs. M. Lawson. Eduard Lassen.
"An old garden." Hope Temple.
"Australia" (home of the brave and free). Henry Baxter. Peter Dawson.
"Air Pilot." M. M. Webster. T. Garrat.
"A Christmas Card." John Masefield. M. Davidson.
"Admiral's Yarn." Paul Reubens.
"Admiral's Broom, The." Bevan.
"Anchored." Watson.
"Annie Laurie." Anonymous.
"Arrow and the Song." Balfe.
"Ave Maria." Schubert.
"At Evening Prayer." Bach. (St. Matthew Passion.)

"Boots." Rudyard Kipling. J. P. McCall.
"Banjo Song." Sidney Homer.
"Brothers of the Empire." Pat Thayer.
"Border Ballad." Cowen.
"Blow! blow! Thou winter wind."
"Bonnie wee thing." Burns.
"Blind Ploughman." R. Coningsby Clarke.
"Beyond the Sunset." Frank E. Tours.
"Bonnie Earl of Moray." Malcolm Lawson.
"Bushrangers." Peter Dawson.
"Bow Bells." Charles Wilbye.
"Bandolero, The." Leslie Stuart.
"Blue Dragoons." Kennedy Russell.
"Bless this house." May Brahe.
"Birds, The." Peter Warlock.
"But who may abide." (*The Messiah.*)
"Bellringer."
"Barber of Turin." K. Russell.

"Chanson de la Touraine." Massenet. (French.)
"Credo" (*Othello*).
"Clock, The." Loewe.
"Cargoes." Shaw.
"Cowboy Ballads." Liza Lehmann.
"Christ is Risen." Rachmaninoff.

"Captains Three." Geoffrey Cavendish.
"Call of the Pipes." Alan Murray.
"Chip of the old Block." W. H. Squire.
"Curtain Falls." Guy d'Hardelot.
"Come away, Death." Dr. Arne.
"Christmas Carol." Malcolm Davidson.
"Captain Harry Morgan." Granville Bantock.
"Cells." Rudyard Kipling. J. P. McCall.
"Changing of the Guard." Flotsam and Jetsam.
"Crabbed Age and Youth." Hubert Parry.
"Coronach." Edgar Barratt.
"Cobbler's Song" from *Chu Chin Chow*.
"Crown of the Year." Easthope Martin.

"Dawn Song." Eric Fogg.
"Don Juan's Serenade." Tschaikowsky.
"Drink to me only with thine Eyes." Johnson.
"Drake goes West." Sanderson.
"Drake's Drum." Stanford.
"Devon, O Devon." Stanford.
"Down by the Sally Gardens." H. Hughes.
"Donkey, The." Maurice Besly.
"Droop not, young Lover." Handel.
"Deep Sea Mariner." J. P. McCall.
"Dreamer, The." J. P. McCall.
"Diapheia." Harold Samuel.
"Dinder Courtship." Eric Coates.
"Dandy Deever."
"Down among the dead Men." (XVIIth century.)
"Dreaming of England." J. P. McCall.
"Devil-may-care." Valerie May.
"Drum Major, The." Ernest Newton.

"Edward." Loewe.
"Erl King, The." Schubert.
"Eleanore." S. Coleridge Taylor.
"Eternal Father, strong to save."
"Empire is Marching, The." Dudley Glass.
"England all the Way." Longstaff.
"Even bravest heart. (*Faust*.)
"El Abanico" (March song).
Elizabethan lyrics set to music by Roger Quilter:
        "Weep you no more."
        "My life's delight."
        "Damask Roses."
        "The faithless Shepherdess."

"Fairy Lough." C. V. Stanford.
"Fishermen of England."
"Follow me 'ome." Ward Hicks.
"Fairy Town." Parry.
"Father O'Flynn." C. V. Stanford.
"Fiddler of Dooney." T. E. Dunhill.
"Floral Dance, The." Katie Moss.
"Fret Foot." J. P. McCall.
"Farmer's Pride." K. Russell.
"Four jolly Sailormen." Edward German.
"Farewell." (Songs of the Fleet.) Stanford.
"Fair Rosalind." Orlande Morgan.

"Glorious Devon." Edward German.
"Garden of Allah." Charles Marshall.
"Green hills of Somerset." Eric Coates.
"Give me the spice of Life." Michael North.
"Gate of the Year." P. Spencer Palmer.
"Gipsy River." K. Russell.
"Gesu Bambino." Pietro A. Yon.
"Green grow the rushes O." Burns.
"Glory of the Sea." Sanderson.
"Gallants of England."
"Gae bring tae Me." Burns.
"Gay Highway, The."

"Honour and Arms." Handel (*Samson*).
"Hybreas the Cretan."
"Hear me, ye winds and Waves." Handel.
"Hinton and Dinton and Mere." J. C. Holliday.
"Hope the Hermit." (XVIIth century.)
"Heart of the Romany Rye." J. P. McCall.
"How's my Boy?" S. Homer.
"Hills of Devon." Jalowicz.
"Hail immortal Bacchus." Dr. Arne.
"Here is my Song."
"Holy City, The." Adams.

"I travel the Road." Pat Thayer.
"I'll walk beside you." Alan Murray.
"In memory of you." J. P. McCall.
"Isobel." Frank Bridge.
"It was a song you sang Me." Hermann Lohr.
"I heard a forest praying." Peter de Rose.
"Invictus." Bruno Huhn.
"I see a Tree." Michael Hodges.
"Is my team Ploughing." George Butterworth.

"Internos." MacFadden.

"I'll go with You." Alan Murray.

"If music be the food of Love." A. Travers. (*Twelfth Night.*)

"In a monastery garden." Ketelbey.

"I Fear no Foe." Pinsuti.

"I am a Roamer." Mendelssohn.

"In Prison." J. Harrison.

"In a Persian Market." Ketelbey.

"In an old-fashioned Town." W. H. Squire.

"If I were King." Eyton.

The Indian Love Lyrics. Amy Woodforde Finden:

        "Temple Bells."

        "Less than the dust."

        "Kashmiri Love Song."

        "Till I awake."

"Jerusalem." Sir H. Parry.

"Journey's End."

"Jolly Roger." J. P. McCall.

"Jack Overdue." Martin Shaw.

"John Grumlie." (Scots.)

"John Anderson, my Jo."

"Joggin' along the Highway." Samuel.

"Just for today." Seaver.

"Kerry Dance, The." J. Molloy.

"Kangaroo and Dingo." Edward German.

"Knight of Bethlehem." D. C. Thomson.

"Kingfisher Blue." Finden.

"Le Manoir de Rosamonde." Duparc. (French.)

"Lute Player, The." Allitsen.

"Low-backed Car." S. Lover.

"Lake Isle of Innisfree." Muriel Herbert.

"Life and Death." Coleridge Taylor.

"Little prayer I Love." A. Rizzi.

"Lord is King, The." J. P. McCall.

"Lord's Prayer, The." A. H. Malotte.

"La Caravane." H. Ribaud. (French.)

"Last Revel, The." J. Harrison.

"Little Admiral." C. V. Stanford.

"Lowland Sea." Branscombe.

"Love could I only tell thee." J. M. Capel.

"Largo al Factotum." Rossini.

"Loch Lomond."

"Lorraine, Lorraine, Lorree." J. M. Capel.

"Love's Appeal." M. Hope Lumley.

"Le Rêve passé."
"Lasseter's last Ride." J. P. McCall.
"Legion of the Lost." Pat Thayer.
"Lights Out." Ivor Gurney.
"Laird O' Cockpen." Lady Nairne.
"Lovely kind and kindly Loving." Gustav Holst.
"Lord Rendel." Arranged: Cecil J. Sharp.
"Lament of Shah Jehan, The." Landon Ronald.
"Land of Mine." J. P. McCall.
"Loveliest of Tress." A. Somerville.
"Love Triumphant." A. Wheeler.
"Lost Chord, The." Sullivan.
"Lead, Kindly Light." Dykes.
"Lover in Damascus."

"Must I go Bound." H. Hughes.
"Money O." Michael Head.
"Marins d'Islande." Foudrain. (French.)
"My Old Shako." Trotere.
"Man who brings the Sunshine." E. Cooper.
"McPherson's Farewell." J. P. McCall.
"Mandalay Scena." Arranged: Peter Dawson.
          Hedgcock. Speakes. Cobb.
"Mountains o' Mourne." Percy French.
"My love is like a red, red Rose." Burns.
"Myself when Young." (*The Persian Garden.*) L. Lehmann.
"Marna." Oliver.
"Molly O'Donegal."
"Menin Gate." Bowen.

"Now your days of philandering are over." (*Marriage of Figaro.*)
"New Moon." M. Hope Lumley.
"Nearer, my God, to Thee." Dykes.
"Nazareth." Gounod.
"Non frin Andrai." Mozart.
"None but the lonely Heart." Tschaikowsky.

"Oh! My Warriors." Elgar. (*Caractacus.*)
"On the road to Mandalay." O. Speakes.
"Old Soldier." Hely Hutchinson.
"Outward Bound." Stanford.
"Old Superb, The." Stanford.
"Oh Shady Trees." M. Hope Lumley.
"O Mistress Mine." (*Twelfth Night.*)
"O Star of Eve." Wagner. (*Tannhaüser.*)
"Onaway! Awake Beloved." Coleridge Taylor.
"Orpheus with his Lute." R. V. Williams.

"Old Father Thames." R. Wallace.
"O ruddier than the cherry." Handel. (*Acis and Galatea*.)
"Oh that it were so." Frank Bridge.
"Once I loved a maiden Fair." McFadden.
"Old Kettledrum." J. P. McCall.
"Old Kite." K. Russell.
"Our Star." J. P. McCall.
"On the idle hill of Summer." R. Ainsworth.
"Old Brigade, The." Weatherley.
"Oh. Could I but express in Song." L. Malishkin.

"Prologue to Pagliacci." Leoncavallo.
"Pari Siano." Verdi.
"Phil the Fluter's Ball." Percy French.
"Phyllis has such charming Graces." Arranged: H. Lane Wilson.
"Pauper's Drive." S. Homer.
"Pibroch." C. V. Stanford.
"Phantom Fleets." Alan Murray.
"Pride of Tipperary." A. Lochead.
"People that walk in Darkness." (*The Messiah*.)
"Poor man's Garden." Russell.
"Parted." Tosti.
"Pirate goes West."
"Passing By." Purcell.
" 'Prentice lads o' Cheap." J. P. McCall.
"Punjaub March 'Song'."

"Rann of Exile." Padraic Colum. Arnold Bax.
"Rolling down to Rio." Edward German.
"Richmond Hill." Purcell.
"Red Road." Edward Black.
"Route Marchin'." Rudyard Kipling. J. P. McCall.
"Reminiscence." R. Noel Cripps. Vera Buck.
"Red Devon by the Sea." Clark.
"Rose of my Heart." Hermann Lohr.
"Rock of Ages." Redhead.
"Roads beside the Sea." H. Keats.
"Rip Van Winkle."
"Recruit, The." Ainsworth.
"Roses of Picardy." Wood.

"Sincerity." Emilie Clarke.
"Silent Worship." Handel.
"Spirit of England." J. P. McCall.
"Snow Bird, The." Pat Thayer.
"Simon the Cellarer." Hatton.
"Spirit Flower." C. Tipton.

"Shipmates o' Mine." Sanderson.
"Sea Winds." Paul Askew.
"She alone charmeth my Sadness." Gounod.
"Surely the Time." J. H. Rogers.
"Swinging Along." H. Cohan.
"Song of the Flea." Moussorgsky.
"Sink, red Sun." Teresa del Riego.
"Strong go on, The." Bruce Sevier.
"Seminarian, The." Moussorgsky.
"Speak, Music." ("The Professor.") A. C. Benson. Elgar.
"Santa Barbara." Russell.
"Scots wha Hae." Burns.
"Song of the Drum." J. P. McCall.
"Sea Gipsy." R. Hovey.
"Sonnet XVIII." Aitken.
"Sunday." Brahms.
"Sylvia." Oley Speakes.
"Sands o' Dee." Frederick Clay.
"Ships of Yule." Martin Shaw.
"Smuggler's Song, The." Rudyard Kipling. Arranged: C. G. Mortimer.
"Silver." C. Armstrong Gibbs.
"Summertime on Bredon." A. Somerville.
"Sons of the sea." S. Coleridge Taylor.
"Sherwood." James R. Dear.
"Star, The." J. H. Rogers.
"She is far from the land." Frank Lambert.
"Sanctuary of the Heart." Ketelbey.
"Song of Australia."
"Six Australian bush Songs."
"Song of the Toreador." Bizet.
"Song of the Highway." May.
"Sons of the Brave." Bidgood.
"Somewhere a voice is calling."
"Sacred Hour." Ketelbey.
"Shall I compare thee to a summer Day." Aitken.
"Spice of Life, The."
"Shipwright."
"Sirs, your Toast." (*Carmen.*)

"Thus saith the Lord." (*The Messiah.*)
"Thou most blest all quickening Day." Bach.
"There is a flower that Bloometh." V. Wallace.
"Tam I' th' Kirk." M. Barclay.
"Three Souls." J. P. McCall.
"Turn ye to me." M. Lawson.
"Travellers all." Balfe. Dawson.
" 'Tis I." Pinsuti.

"Take O Take." (*Measure for Measure*.) Parry.
"Traveller, The." B. Godard.
"Three fine Ships." T. E. Dunhill.
"Travelling down Castlereagh." Louis Lavater.
"Think on Me." Lady Joan Scott.
"There is a Green Hill." Ch., Gounod.
"To Anthea." Hatton.
"To the Forest." Tschaikowsky.
"Time for making Songs." MacFadyen.
"Tramping through the Countryside." Peter Alison.
"Thou art passing Hence." Sullivan.
"There is no death." Geoffrey O'Hara.
"Trumpeter, The." Dix.
"Two Grenadiers, The." Schumann.
"To Chloe." Sterndale Bennett.
"Trees." Rasbach.
"The West's Asleep."

"Under the greenwood Tree." M. N. Tedesco.
"Unless." Caracciolo.
"Up from Somerset." Sanderson.

"Volunteer Organist, The." Lamb.
"Vagabond." Vaughan Williams.
" 'V' for Victory." Peter Dawson.
"Vulcan's Song." Gounod.
"Village Blacksmith, The." P. Dawson's version. (W. H. Weiss.)
"Veteran's Song." Adams.

"When icicles hang by the Wall." F. Keel.
"Wood Magic." Martin Shaw.
"Winter." (From *Love's Labour's Lost*.)
"We shall Prevail." D. Gerity.
"Westward Ho!" J. P. McCall.
"When the Swallows." M. V. White.
"Wanderthirst." Jean Fordell.
"Who is Sylvia?" Schubert.
"Where'er you Walk." Handel.
"When valiant Ammon." J. Battishill.
"Woo thou thy Snowflake." A. Sullivan.
"Walk down the Road." Pat Thayer.
"Whalin' up the Lachlan." J. P. McCall.
"Wandering Player." Alan Murray.
"Wandering the King's Highway." L. Coward.
"Waltzing Matilda." B. Paterson.
"Will you go with Me?" Alan Murray.
"Waratah and the Wattle." Henry Lawson. Peter Dawson.

"Winding Road, The." David Arale. Paul Andrew.
"Waiting for the good Times." Alba Rizzi.
"With my shillelagh under my arm." R. Wallace.
"We are Seven." Pain. Ros.
"White in the Moon." A. Somervell.
"When I come back Home."
"Within these hallowed Walls." Mozart.
"Will o' the Wisp." Cherry.
"With a Song." May.
"When the guards go marching by." Barker.
"With Sword and Lance."
"When the Sergeant-Major's on Parade." Longstaff.
"Watchman, what of the Night?"
"Waiata Poi." Alfred Hill.
"We saw the Sea."
"Why do the Nations." Handel. (*The Messiah.*)

"Yeomen of England." Edward German.
"Young Tom o' Devon." K. Russell.
"Yon assassin is my Equal." M. Head.
"Ye twice ten hundred Deities." Purcell.
"Yeomen of the Guard." Gilbert and Sullivan.

INDEX

T

Tait, John, 50
Tato, Signor, 92
Tauber, Richard, 137
Teschmacher, Edward, 198
Tetrazzini, Luisa, 21, 92
Thayer, Pat, 158
Thornton, Edna, 94, 126
Thring, Charles, 91
Tibbett, Lawrence, 137
Tivoli, London, 45
Toscanini, Arturo, 181, 197, 198
Tree, Beerbohm, 22
——, Charles, 72, 181
Tucker, Sophie, 175
Turner, Eva, 137
——, John, 133

U

Uren, Tommy, 89

V

Van Leer, Mr., 41, 169
Verne, Adele, 25

W

Wales, Prince of, 144, 189
Walker, Nellie, 126, 132
Warren, Betty, 93
Weatherley, Fred, 168, 173
Weekes (Publishers), 157, 161
Whelan, Albert, 137
Wigmore Hall, 51, 52, 95, 191
Wilde, Harold, 126, 137
Williams, Billy, 33
Wolf, Johannes, 25
Wood, Haydn, 65–7
——, Sir Henry, 39, 67–70, 155
Woodman, Flora, 93
Wright, Lawrence, 93

Y

York, Duke and Duchess of, 189, 190
Young, Leonard, 20, 21

Z

Zeigler, Anne, 136
Zonophone Company, 42, 139